About the book

Imbalances between functional responsibilities and financial resources at different layers of the government are an inherent part of a federal polity. This is so because revenue-raising capacities and revenue needs of various federating units are different. The mismatch between functions and financial powers occurs partly because of changing responsibilities of different tiers of government and partly due to the dominant position of the national government in regard to taxation powers. Therefore, vertical imbalances in resources and expenditure responsibilities emerge between different levels of the government, calling for transfer of resources from the centre to the states.

In federal finance, the use of quantitative techniques is very important. In fact, policy formulation is very much influenced by the quantitative results pertaining to extent and degree of vertical fiscal imbalances, trends in centralization and decentralization, extent of horizontal fiscal imbalances, inter-state disparities in taxable capacity, tax efforts, and fiscal needs of federating states. Another area where quantitative methods are used is the forecast of revenue and expenditure. These are some of the major issues dealt with in this book for appropriate policy formulation.

Author's profile

Dr. (Mrs.) Hemlata Rao received her Ph.D. degree from the Delhi School of Economics, University of Delhi. She has 37 years of research experience in the areas of public finance, regional development and regional planning. She has published a number of research papers on these subjects in reputed national and international journals. Besides, she has 14 books to her credit. Dr. Rao was the recipient of Shastri Indo-Canadian Fellowship for the year 1990-91 which enabled her to visit and lecture at various universities in Canada. She was a Visiting Professor, University of Fort Hare, South Africa during February-March 2000. She was awarded Visiting Research Fellowship by the Institute of Developing Economies, Japan for the year 1997-98. In July 1996, she lectured at IMF, Washington DC. She has been a member of Sales Tax Advisory Committee, Government of Karnataka since 1996. Presently, she is Professor and Head, Economics Unit, Institute for Social and Economic Change (ISEC), Bangalore.

Fiscal Federalism

Issues and Policies

Hemlata Rao
Professor and Head, Economics Unit
Institute for Social and Economic Change (ISEC)
Bangalore

New Century Publications
New Delhi, India

New Century Publications
4800/24, Bharat Ram Road,
Ansari Road, Daryaganj,
New Delhi-110 002
Tel.: 23247798, 55396605
Telefax: 011-51017798
E-mail: indiatax@vsnl.com
www.newcenturypublications.com

Editorial office:
34, Gujranwala Town, Part-2,
Delhi - 110 009
Tel.: 27247805, 27464774

First Published 2006

ISBN: 81-7708-102-0

Published by New Century Publications and printed at Singhal Print Media, Delhi -110 007

PRINTED IN INDIA

PREFACE

Finance is the life blood of a government. Arrangements for finance are more tedious in a federal set up than in a unitary form of government. A federal set up creates a dual political system based on divided governmental functions and powers. Fiscal federalism deals with financial arrangements and their working in a federal polity.

Imbalances between functional responsibilities and financial resources at different layers of the government are an inherent part of a federal polity. This is so because revenue-raising capacities and revenue needs of various federating units are different. This is a characteristic feature of all federations, particularly of those whose economies are more dynamic. The mismatch between functions and financial powers occurs partly because of changing responsibilities of different tiers of government and partly due to the dominant position of the national government in regard to taxation powers, which is often by design. Therefore, vertical imbalance of resources and expenditure responsibilities emerges between different levels of the government, calling for transfer of resources from the centre to the states.

In federal finance, the use of quantitative techniques is very important. In fact, policy formulation is very much influenced by the quantitative results pertaining to extent and degree of vertical fiscal imbalances, trends in centralization and decentralization, extent of horizontal fiscal imbalances, inter-state disparities in taxable capacity, tax efforts, and fiscal needs of federating states. Another area where quantitative methods are used is the forecast of revenue and expenditure. These are some of the major areas dealt with in this book.

I take this opportunity to thank my numerous colleagues, research assistants and research students for their help and constructive comments on earlier drafts of this work. In particular, I would like to record my gratitude to the following persons for their help and cooperation: Professor G. Thimmaiah, Professor T.

Krishna Kumar, Professor N.S. Iyengar, Mr. K.N. Amarnath, Dr. S. Madheswaran, Dr. Madheswaran, Ms. B.P. Vani, Mr. Badrinarayan Rath, Mr. Subir Sen and Mr. B.H. Chandrashekara.

October 2005 Hemlata Rao
Bangalore

CONTENTS

1

INTRODUCTION

1.1 Major Issues in Federal Finance

Federal Finance is an important branch of Public Finance. It deals with the fiscal systems prevailing at different layers of government. Issues pertaining to distribution of responsibilities, and resources between the federal, states and local governments and issues relating to federal fiscal transfers to states and local bodies and such transfers from states to local bodies assume lot of importance in a federal system. This is the subject matter of fiscal federalism. As a sub field of public finance, fiscal federalism addresses the vertical structure of the public sector. It explores, both in normative and positive terms, the roles of the different levels of government and the ways in which they relate to one another through such instruments as intergovernmental grants.

1.1.1 Concept of Federalism [1]: There are different types of government in the world. The two extreme forms of government, which one could visualize, are:

1. Highly centralized, and
2. Highly decentralized form.

In between there exist various other forms of government with a combination of centralization and decentralization in varied degrees. This can be put under one group named Federal form of government. Federalism represents in one sense a compromise between unitary form and extreme decentralization. Thus, the word federation connotes the union of two or more states. In a federation, there is one federal government, which forms the upper layer of government and there are states or provinces, which form the lower layers of government. It should be remembered that in a federation no federating state is a sovereign state. Thus, federation is the union of states in which there is a dual state authority. [2]

Both the layers of government make decisions concerning the provision of certain public services in their respective geographical jurisdiction. Thus, each level of government, rather than performing all the functions of the public sector, does what it can do the best.

1.1.2 Genesis of Federalism: In this section an outline is drawn about the genesis of Federalism. We do not intend to discuss various models of federalism. However, intended readers may refer to some of the books mentioned below. [3] The idea of federation originally emerged out of the political need to stand united against "political insecurity". [4] The federating units also desired to be independent of foreign powers. It was realized that only through union independence could be secured and sustained.

Apart from the need for common defence, another strong motivation to form federation was to achieve rapid economic development and free access to national market. In a federal state freedom of inter-state trade and commerce is guaranteed. It was realized that free flow of goods and services across the states and absence of tariff barriers not only help expansion of market but also leads to economies of scale. Their desire for a single unified customs area is often one of the motives for forming a federation.

Federal formation was also motivated by the objective of pooling of scarce resources for rapid economic development.

A federation also aims at achieving 'equality of all citizens', i.e. no discrimination is made between different people. All citizens, irrespective of their state of residence are expected to make sacrifice by way of taxation uniformly and receive the benefits from public goods equally. However, all the federating states are not equal in terms of economic development, social development, natural resource endowments, and fiscal capacity and so on. Because of these and several other factors, there exists a serious problem of regional disparity. Some states are backward, while some are developed. One of the objectives of federal government is to reduce such disparities by helping the backward states in a special way.

These motivating factors for the formation of a federation may be conflicting in nature in the short run. However, in the long run they are inter-dependent. The extent to which these objectives can be realized depends upon the federal fiscal system of the country, where the allocation of powers and functions assume lot of importance.

1.1.3 Allocation of Powers and Functions [5]: Federal fiscal system of a country is invariably associated with the formation of federations. Initial assignments and reassignments of powers and functions determine the strength of the central government and of the states.

Most of the federations have come to exist either through a process of aggregation of pre-existing units or by the desegregation of an existing unit i.e., by the process of devolution and decentralization. According to Richard Bird [6], "only the former sort of federation is likely to correspond to the conventional picture of a federal government in the strict sense of a system. The central and sub-national governments are each" "within a sphere, coordinate and independent." [7] However, a broader view considers all multilevel systems – "by which are meant systems in which there is some degree of autonomous decision making at different government levels – to be federal system." [8]

Thus, there are two approaches to analyse inter-governmental relations. One is the "aggregation model" and the other is the "devolution model." [9] When a federation is an out come of the 'devolution model' the Centre happens to be more dominating, than when a federation emerges out of 'aggregation'. According to Bird, with regard to inter-governmental grants, for example, the devolutionist will in all likelihood tend to stress the inducement (substitution effect), because his real interest is in imposing central preferences on local governments, while the aggregationist will stress the additional resources (income effect) received by the locality, because his interest is in realizing local aspirations. The former is therefore, prone to recommend conditional grants and the latter unconditional grant." [10] This implies that 'aggregation model' makes the federating units strong while 'devolution model' makes central government strong. Thus the distribution of powers and functions depends upon the centripetal and centrifugal forces prevailing at the time of formation of a federation.

There are basically three problems, which are commonly found in all the federations. The first pertains to; "Vertical Fiscal Imbalances"(VFI), the second pertains to "Horizontal Fiscal Imbalances"(HFI) and the third to "Fiscal Adjustments (FA).

The central government accepts primary responsibility for stabilization and fair distribution of income and supply of such public goods, which maximize the welfare of the entire county. Complementing these, states supply those goods and services, which are of primary interest only to the residents of their jurisdiction.

In all the federations, it is the federal government, which is endowed with 'expansive resources', and this layer enjoys surplus, while the federating units have to perform 'expensive' functions and have resources emerging from the local base, which do not commensurate with their expenditure requirements. The states invariably experience huge revenue gap or 'non-correspondence'. The very fact that the federal government commands resources, while states have to look for federal fiscal transfers gives rise to the problem of VFI. These imbalances are in-built.

The second i.e. the Horizontal Fiscal Imbalances arise due to the differences in the resource raising capacity and fiscal need of various similarly situated states. Horizontal fiscal imbalance is also inevitable mainly because of diversity in natural resources and disparities in economic structure and socio-economic levels of development of federating units. This determines on the one hand the varying degree of fiscal capacity and on the other hand the fiscal need of the states. HFI coupled with the VFI, increases the need for federal fiscal transfers to the states in any federation. [11] In the literature on federal finances, more than the issues of 'Vertical Fiscal Imbalances', it is the issue relating to HFI, which has attracted lot of attention of the scholars and the policy-makers.

In order to correct the vertical fiscal imbalances, federal fiscal transfers in the form of shared taxes /duties, grants etc. are effected.

While transferring resources to the federating units care is taken to bring down the problems of HFI.

Like the division of functions, even the tax and non-tax resources are divided between the two layers of government. The resources, which have an inter-state base, are usually assigned to the federal government. Even resources generated out of foreign trade, foreign exchange, also are with the upper layer of government. Resources, which have local base, are assigned to the states.

Some sources of revenue and a few functions also fall within the purview of both the layers of government and these are included under the concurrent list. Besides these demarcated powers and functions, there exists interdependency between different federating units and the federal government.

1.1.4 Use of Quantitative Measures in Fiscal Federalism: There is strong desire among economists and federal finance experts to quantify all important policy variables. As discussed above the three important issues often discussed in any federation are the problems of vertical fiscal imbalance, the horizontal fiscal imbalance and the methods of fiscal adjustments to bring down the vertical and the horizontal fiscal imbalances. In fact it is here that the need for the adoption of clear principles and criteria arise.

The two important bases of fiscal transfers are the principles of equity and efficiency. The criterion of equity demands a measure of the relative levels of development, tax efforts and fiscal capacity of the states and local bodies. The measure of inequality also assumes importance in the process of eliminating horizontal fiscal imbalances. The principle of efficiency requires a measure of tax effort and economy in expenditure by the federating units.

When the federal government draws a plan of assistance many times it becomes necessary to forecast the resources and expenditure need of the lower level as well as of the federal government. Thus, quantitative techniques for assessing the relative levels of development, extent of poverty, taxable capacity and tax effort, tax elasticity/buoyancy, fiscal need and forecasting of the need and resources, becomes important in the field of federal fiscal studies.

In the literature on fiscal federalism, various quantitative techniques inclusive of such simple measures as averages, growth rates, coefficients of variation, and coefficients of concentration are used along with sophisticated and rigorous econometric tools like Multiple Regression Models, Principal Component Analysis, Factor analysis, Discriminant analysis and so on.

The literature is thus, full of quantitative techniques. However, these techniques are not applied or illustrated in any one book. We only come across the application of specific methods in specific studies. This book is an attempt to facilitate accessibility to various quantitative techniques used by different scholars and different policy making bodies in the field of federal finance. In this study an attempt is made to explain various quantitative techniques, their application and their theoretical relevance, and their application in policy formulation. The quantitative techniques and their uses are illustrated with the help of data and the results are analysed. However, it should be borne in mind that the use of data is purely for illustration purpose and not for any empirical analysis or for drawing any policy conclusions.

End Notes and References

1. K.C. Wheare, (1963), *Federal Government*, Oxford University Press, London, Part II, Chapter II, p. 37.
2. Sobie, Mogi (1970), 'The Problem of Federalism', quoted in 'R.K. Sinha, (1970), "Finance Commission in India", Economic Affair, March, p.59.
3. For detailed analysis of initial assignments and re-assignment of powers and functions reader may refer Breton. A and Anthony Scott(1978), *The Economic Constitution of Federal States*, UOT Press, Canada, Also see G. Tullock, "Federalism: Problems of Scale", *Public Choice*, VI. Spring 1969. Wallace Oates (1972), "Fiscal Federalism", New York
4. K.C. Wheare, op. cit.
5. Excellent exposition of Five Classes of functions, namely, (a) regulatory, (b) supply, (c) revenue, (d) redistribution and (e) stabilisation functions are available in Breton. A and Anthony Scott (1978), op. cit.

6. Bird, R.M. (1979), 'Central-Local Fiscal Relations and the Provision of Urban Public Services', Centre for Research on Federal Financial Relations, the ANU, Research Monograph No.32, p. 12.

7. Wheare K.C., op. cit.

8. Bird, R.M. op cit., p.12.

9. Bird R.M., op cit., p.13.

10. Bird R.M., op cit., p.14.

11. G. Thimmaiah and Hemlata Rao, (1986), *Finance Commission and Centre-State Relations*, Ashish Publications, New Delhi, 1986, p .2.

2

ISSUES IN VERTICAL FISCAL IMBALANCES

2.1 Vertical Fiscal Imbalances

"Fiscal Imbalance" is a phrase that comes up almost as frequently in discussions on federal finance as centralisation. Vertical Fiscal Imbalances are the result of initial assignment of powers and functions between the two layers of governments. Which layer of government possesses more power depends upon the centripetal or centrifugal forces prevailing at the time of formation of the federation. In fact the distribution of functions and power depends upon the genesis of the federation. If the federation is an out come of aggregation of federating units the federating units tend to be more powerful than the federating units of a federation which has emerged out of a process of devolution. In the latter type the centre tends to be more powerful.

The strength of a particular level under goes changes due to reassignment of power and functions in the succeeding years and this process not only influence the level of VFI but also the degree of Centralization.

2.2 Principles of Allocation of Functions

The traditional theory of fiscal federalism lays out a general normative framework for the assignment of functions to different levels of government and the appropriate fiscal instruments for carrying out these functions (Richard Musgrave 1959; Oates 1972). This theory contends that the central government should have the basic responsibility for the macroeconomic stabilisation function and for income redistribution in the form of assistance to the poor.

In both cases, the basic argument stems from some fundamental constraints on lower level governments. In the absence of monetary and exchange-rate prerogatives and with highly open economies that cannot contain much of the expansionary impact of fiscal stimuli, provincial or state, and local governments simply have very limited means for traditional macroeconomic control of their economies. Similarly, the mobility of economic units can seriously constrain attempts to redistribute income. An aggressive local program for the support of low-income households, for example, is likely to induce an influx of the poor and encourage an exodus of those with higher income who must bear the tax burden. In addition to these functions, the central government must provide certain "national" public goods (like national defence) that provide services to the entire population of the country.

It is common to allocate functions of international character to the federal government; matters pertaining to foreign relations, foreign trade, tariffs on exports-imports etc. come under the purview of the federal government. Even those functions, which extend beyond the boundaries of individual state, are also assigned to federal government for achieving efficiency. Those functions of a state, which, affect the affairs of other states, are also assigned to the federal government. Functions such as defence, currency and coinage, administration of justice at the highest level (Supreme Court), civil rights, immigration policies, foreign exchange, posts, telegraph, broadcasts etc., also come under the Centre's domain. In most of the federation especially in the developing ones, redistribution is also an important function of the federal government. Thus reductions of regional disparities, removing inequality among citizens are the federal responsibilities.

Lower levels of government have their raison d'etre in the provision of goods and services whose consumption is limited to their own jurisdictions. By tailoring outputs of such goods and services to the particular preferences and circumstances of their constituencies, decentralized provision increases economic welfare above that which results from the more uniform levels of such services that are likely under national provision. The basic point here is simply that the efficient level of output of a "local" public good (i.e. for which the sum of residents' marginal benefits equals marginal cost) is likely to vary across jurisdictions as a result of both differences in preferences and cost differentials.

The preferences of different groups of citizens in a federation vary from place to place. Consequently one national government cannot supply certain essential public services to suit such variety of tastes and preferences. Efficient supply of these services requires lower Level government like the State Government to render these services. As a result, decentralisation of these functions becomes a necessary condition for achieving efficiency in rendering these services. The states are assigned functions, which influence the local people directly.

2.3 Allocation of Taxing Powers

Generally, there is a constitutional division of functions and powers between the two layers of government. Almost in all the federations, federal government is endowed with vast powers. The need for a virtually unlimited federal taxing power is obvious. It is the federal government, which is in a position to meet any emergency that may arise. Tax imposed by federal government is not meant only to raise resources but is also meant for the promotion of anti-cyclical and other economic policies. Finally, federal government is the only competent government to redress the economic imbalance among the provinces. The poorer states cannot be left dependent on the largesse of the wealthier ones.

Invariably in all the federations it is the central government that has larger resources at its command in relation to the responsibilities. Further, the resources are more elastic in nature owing to the national base available to the centre. Efficiency in tax administration for certain revenues requires central administration. It may be reasonably presumed that some kind of comparative cost advantage principle is used for allotting sources of revenue, which, have a national base, and whose cost of collection would enjoy economies of scale would automatically go to the federal government. Therefore, guided by this principle most of the elastic sources of revenue would be justified and tend to be allotted to the federal government.

On the contrary, the lower level governments have power to tax only the local tax base. The states are expected to tax the persons and all types of transactions falling only within their jurisdiction. Hence, the resources available to the states are narrow and less elastic than the federal taxes. However their expenditure responsibilities are large.

The method of allocating taxing power in a federation may vary between two polar extremes. As Forest (1981) puts, "One may calculate the foreseeable revenue requirements of each level of government and allocate sources of taxation in accordance with these needs." [1] This has been done to a marked extent, for example, under the Basic Law of the Federal Republic of Germany. At the opposite extreme one may give both levels of government ample and overlapping powers of taxation, leaving the actual distribution to be made in accordance with changing political reality. In any event modifications are made to take into account the economic effects of vesting a particular tax in one government or the other.

Thus, customs duties may be placed within the ambit of one level of government as much for economic as for revenue purposes. This is referred to "tax-assignment problem" (Charles McLure 1983). And the basic issue here is the normative question: Which taxes are best suited for use at the different levels of government? The question is typically posed in a setting in which there exists a nation state with a central government, where there is little or no mobility across national borders; at decentralized levels, in contrast, economic agents, goods, and resources have significant mobility across jurisdictional boundaries with the extent of this mobility increasing at successively lower levels of government. "Local" government, for analytical purposes, may sometimes be characterized as operating in a setting in which economic units can move costless among jurisdictions.

The difference in the mobility of taxed units at the central and lower levels has important implications for the design of the vertical structure of taxation. Taxes can be the source of distortions in resource allocation, as buyers shift their purchases away from taxed goods. Or sellers may try to sell their products in states where the tax rates are lower. In a spatial setting, such distortions take the form of locational inefficiencies, as taxed units (or owners of taxed items) seek out jurisdictions where they can obtain relatively favourable tax treatment. High taxes in one jurisdiction, for example, may lead purchasers to bear unproductive travel costs in order to purchase the taxed items in jurisdictions with lower tax rates.

Such examples can suggest the conclusion that the lower level government should avoid the taxation of highly mobile economic units (be they households, capital, or final goods). But this in itself is not correct. The real implication is that the states/provinces should avoid *no benefit* taxes on mobile units. Or, more accurately, the analysis shows that on efficiency grounds states *should* tax mobile economic units with benefit levies (Oates and Robert Schwab 1991). Such economic units, in short, should pay for the benefits that they receive from the public services that local governments provide to them.

Thus the division of functions and resources between the federal and the federating units is not guided by the ability of the federal or federating units to discharge their functions according to their resource raising capacity. The federating units (states/provinces) are assigned the responsible functions of socio-economic development and welfare, and internal law and order on the basis of efficiency of administering these functions and meeting the local needs effectively. On the contrary, the productive and expanding sources of revenue with national resource base are assigned to the federal (Central/Union) government. This is so because the states have greater ability to assess properly the local needs, ability to prioritise the needs, and administer these functions effectively and efficiently. The federal government has the administrative superiority in collecting resources from the national base and foreign sources.

The allocation of functions and powers is done generally on the basis of conflicting principles. The revenue sources that have been allocated (or are likely to be allocated) to state and local governments are inadequate to finance their expenditures. This inadequacy, moreover, tends to grow over time, owing to the relatively lower elasticity of these own-source of revenues compared to expenditures. The initial assignment may reflect history – perhaps the intentions of the designers of the original constitution, or it may reflect the great efficiency of central collection of revenues owing to their greater 'span' of control. [2] It may even reflect the desire to restrain regional political independence and potential secessionist movements. [3]

This invariably leaves more and highly elastic sources of revenue with the federal government and more expanding items of expenditures with the State Governments. Unlike the federal government, which is endowed with large resources having wide national base, the states are endowed with less lucrative resources of local origin and invariably these resources fall short of their expenditure responsibilities. This gives rise to the problem of 'non-correspondence' of revenue and expenditure or in other words the problem of Vertical Fiscal Imbalances.

The gap between the sources of revenue and expenditure of States is required to be filled by the federal government under certain obligatory and discretionary conditions by transferring a portion of its revenue to the State Governments. [4]

2.4 Methods to Reduce Vertical Fiscal Imbalances

A common argument in federal finance writings is that in principle "...both general and regional governments must each have under its own independent control financial resources sufficient to perform its exclusive functions." [5] In this deal "own-source" of revenues of each level of government should suffice to finance the expenditures for which it is responsible without recourse to intergovernmental fiscal transfers. Only thus can the desired position of both local autonomy of action and local responsibility for those actions are attained. [6]

Fiscal balance in this sense would seem to require the assignment to each order of government of separate and independent revenue sources sufficient to finance the expenditures assigned to that jurisdictional level. [7] Such tax separation ensures local autonomy and accountability and the related improved transparency of the tax system.

A clear cut separation of resource raising power to enable all the levels of government to meet their expenditure requirement may not be feasible in a federation where, the federal government is deliberately given large powers for purposes of maintaining economic stability, inter state distribution of resources to reduce disparities for purposes of defence and other crucial functions. These functions require the federal government to have control and command over large resources. Any time, any emergency may emerge which has to be tackled by the federal government. Hence to some extent vertical fiscal imbalances are inevitable in any federation.

There are several ways of bringing down vertical fiscal imbalances. In principle, the gap could be closed in the following ways:

1. Expenditure functions could be moved up to the higher level of government, the one with more money.
2. Taxes could be moved down to the lower level, the one with more need for money.

The first solution has of course occurred to some extent in most countries, but by no means uniformly or exclusively. The second has also occurred occasionally – indeed, perhaps more so in Canada than elsewhere – but has understandably not been very popular either with the central authorities, who have to give up the power their "excess" revenue gives them, or with the state authorities, who have to accept the responsibility for levying their new taxes with no offsetting political bonus points from being able to expand expenditures.

Some other methods to bring down the surpluses of the federal government or to reduce the non- correspondence problem of the federating units are:

2.4.1 Bringing Down Resource Surplus of the Federal Government: As described above, the federal government commands, more resources than its expenditure need. If the federal government opts for any of the following actions that would reduces the surpluses available with the federal government.

- Not to raise more resources through rational tax and non-tax policies;
- Increases its expenditure by expanding the scope of its functions or due to inefficiency in spending such as: resorting to heavy implicit subsidies, expansion of administrative strength and spending more on salaries and wages, subsidies, interest payments, defence and so on. Such a phenomenon exists in federations like India
- Resorting to both (a) and (b), so that the surplus of resources shrinks drastically and narrows down the vertical fiscal gap.

The above methods of reducing imbalance are not conducive for healthy federal state fiscal relations. This would only promote distrust among the federal and the federating states and the very foundation of a federal government is threatened. These measures lead to inefficient use of scarce resources and development gets retarded. Thus the very purpose of forming a federation gets defeated.

2.4.2 Raising Tax Revenue and Lowering Expenditure of States: This is another method of reducing state's 'non correspondence'. The states may try to mobilise more resources. And the states may resort to non-performance of functions relating to socio-economic development, welfare, internal law and order, etc. Until balance is restored, at both levels, (abstracting, of course, from the stabilisation aspects of such policies) Governments can always rectify any fiscal imbalance by taxing more and spending less.

There are practical problems in adopting this method. States cannot raise resources beyond a point. Citizens may not accept any reduction in essential functions. Hence, even this is not a healthy way of reducing vertical fiscal imbalances.

2.4.3 Reallocation of Functions: According to Bhargava, it is desirable when reallocation of functions is "not contrary to the principle of efficiency" The federal government which has larger resources may be assigned some state functions which it can perform efficiently. This would reduce the burden on state budgets. [8]

All does not accept this method. States may consider this as 'inroads' made by the Centre into the state subjects. Further, this method cannot completely solve the divergence between functions and resources that exist under the federal system. In India, through various amendments some of the state functions were also brought within the ambit of the federal government.

2.4.4 Federal Fiscal Adjustments: There is constitutional provision in various federations to bring down vertical fiscal imbalances by way of transferring resources from the federal to the federating units. This is the most common method for closing the gap.

The federal government has the constitutional power to transfer resources to federating units. These transfers can be effected in several ways, some of the tools of fiscal adjustments prevailing in most of the federations are explained and their economic rationale are examined in the following.

2.5 Different Forms of Fiscal Adjustments [9]

The various means adopted in different countries to reduce vertical fiscal imbalances depend upon the circumstances, which led to the formation of the federation. In most cases federations are unions of pre-existing governments and hence each union has its own special heritage. Its constitution has its own special provisions, conventions and practice. The various tools adopted for effecting federal fiscal adjustments are: Tax-sharing; Tax-credit or Tax-abatement, Revenue sharing in general or in relation to specified tax proceeds and grants and grants-in- aid of various types. A brief description of these measures is given below:

2.5.1 Tax Sharing and Tax Assignments: This is used as a tool to reduce vertical fiscal imbalance. Usually the surplus revenue raised by the central government is shared with the states. "The term revenue sharing is used and applied to such a variety of actual and or potential programs that it's meaning is quite nebulous, says Anwar Shah. [10] It is common to find that revenue sharing is used to mean different things. It is also not uncommon to find some conditions being associated with shareable fund. Generally speaking, revenue sharing is meant to describe the situation in which one level of government has the right to a specified share for its unconditional use of certain revenues raised by another government. However, this is seen as a source of providing states a share in the expanding and elastic revenue may be from specified taxes or all taxes rose by the federal government. The idea of divisible taxes consisting of all major federal taxes is to help reduce the dependency of the states on conditional transfers. This problem of non-correspondence was sought to be corrected by the centre by transferring resources to states, a large chunk of the increment to federal revenues in the form of a sort of unconditional grants-in-aid on which the federating units have a right.

2.5.2 Supplementary Levies [11]: This is another method of achieving fiscal adjustment. In order to augment the state resources, sometimes the states are authorised to levy supplementary taxes on federal tax. Such levies are to be collected by the federal government and the proceeds are assigned to the states. However, this is not a very popular method.

2.5.3 Tax-base Sharing: Tax sharing or more precisely tax base sharing is a popular method of fiscal adjustments in some of the federations like the US and Canada. Under this method the federal government retains the current arrangements for tax administration. But, it vacates tax room for the states, by reducing its own rates for various types of taxes. The states are left free to tap the remaining tax base by applying their own tax rates. The tax base is defined and the centre, of course, decides the scope in consultation with the states. In this method, both the centre and the states are free to tax the same base.

2.5.4 Tax Rental Arrangements: In this method the federating units give away their right to tax a base to centre on consideration of economy, administrative convenience, etc. and in return they get back revenue in different ways from the centre. In some federations, on consideration of maintaining uniformity of base and rates, administrative convenience and considering the fact that the tax base may out flow one state's jurisdiction, certain taxes are levied and collected by the centre and the entire net proceeds are assigned to the states e.g. Under Article 269 of the Constitution of India.

2.5.5 Tax Credits: A modified version of tax credit is the tax abatement. Under this system a deduction is allowed from the federal tax up to a maximum limit for a corresponding provincial tax. If no provincial tax is imposed no credit is allowed. In Canada, this was prevalent.

Another variation of the tax credit/abatement is the provision of tax room. In this method federal government no longer rested provincial taxes in return for compensation, but undertakes to allow rooms against its own taxes up to specified rates for taxes to be levied by the province.

Thus, tax sharing, tax-rental arrangements and their variations are various means of fiscal adjustments prevailing in different federations.

Whether a country opts for revenue sharing from one or two specific taxes or all taxes would depend upon the forces, which led to the constitutional arrangements in that federation. However, one thing common with revenue sharing is that it is unconditional transfers of resources to states and states have a right to get a share in the revenue from pooled federal taxes.

2.5.6 Grants and Grants-in-Aid: In fact, grants occupy a coveted place in the federal fiscal literature, as they form an important means of federal fiscal adjustments. These grants are the tools for achieving the basic objectives of federation namely equity, equalisation, efficiency or any other objective. Grants are given in various forms like conditional, unconditional, specific, general, block grant, matching grant, open ended and closed ended and so on. Grants are used for reducing horizontal Fiscal imbalances.

These are discussed in the chapter dealing with the issues in Horizontal Fiscal Imbalances.

The above fiscal tools of adjustment are extensively used both for reducing Vertical Fiscal Imbalances and for reducing Horizontal Fiscal Imbalances (HFI). While grants are mainly used for reduction in horizontal fiscal imbalances, other tools are used to reduce vertical fiscal imbalances. However, other tools also help reducing horizontal fiscal imbalances if the criteria for the distribution of resources among the states are based on the principle of equalisation or fiscal need, and similarly grants also bring down vertical fiscal imbalances.

The above mentioned tools of federal transfers can bring down VFI and HFI effectively only when these concepts are understood properly and the extent and magnitude of such imbalances are measured in a rational manner. These issues are discussed in the succeeding Chapters.

End Notes and References

1. G.V. La Forest, 'The Allocation of Taxing Power under the Canadian Constitution, Second Edition,' Canadian Tax Paper, No.65, May 1981, Chapter 9, pp. 195-204.

2. This useful term is adopted from Albert Breton and Anthony Scott, 'The Economic Constitution of Federal States', Toronto, University of Toronto Press, 1978, p. 15.

3. This last point is particularly important in such developing federations as Nigeria. See, for example, Richard M. Bird, 'Central-Local Fiscal Relations and the Provision of Urban Pubic Services', Canberra, Australian National University, Centre for Research on Federal Financial Relations, 1979, p. 21.

4. Tax Separation (Richard M. Bird, Federal Finance in Comparative Perspective, Canadian Tax Foundation, Toronto, 1986, p.231-239 (Section on Fiscal Imbalance).

5. K.C. Wheare, 'Federal Government', 4th ed., Oxford University Press, London, 1963, p. 93.

6. "In a federation the states must be able to act independently within their own sphere of competence; and they must be responsible for their actions", J.S.H. Hunter, 'Federalism and Fiscal Balance' (Canberra:

Australian National University, Centre for Research on Federal Financial Relations, 1977), p. 21.

7. This is precisely the position taken in the 1954 Tremblay report in Quebec. See David Kwavnick, ed., 'The Tremblay Report', Toronto, McClelland and Stewart, 1973, p. 215.

8. R.N. Bhargava, *The Theory and Working of Union Finance in India,* 3rd edition, Chaitanya Publishing House, Allahabad, 1971, Chapter 8, p. 109.

9. Hemlata Rao, (1994) *Principles of Federal Fiscal Transfers* chapter 3, Ashish Publication, New Delhi

10. Anwar Shah, Inter-governmental Fiscal Relations in Sri Lanka, mimeographed, August 1990.

11. For details, see R.N. Bhargava, op cit., p. 111.

3

VERTICAL FISCAL IMBALANCES: CENTRALISATION AND DECENTRALISATION

In the previous chapter the term Vertical Fiscal Imbalances (VFI) was explained. One can simply say VFI indicates the distribution of power to raise resources and the distribution of expenditure responsibilities between the federal and the federating states where the former is invariably endowed with surplus of resources while the latter experience huge resource gap. Quite often the term VFI is interpreted to mean centralization or vice a versa. If centre is mobilising more resources or more funds are transferred from the centre to the states, many times it is considered as growing centralization. However there is a subtle difference between centralization and VFI. If more resources are under the exclusive control of the centre and the states have no right to claim a share or a role in formulating the federal fiscal transfer schemes the central power goes up and leads to centralization. Under the centralization centre makes conditional, specific or discretionary transfers of resources to states and states are not given autonomy to utilize the funds in the manner they want or they are not sure of what they are going to get from the centre.

Thus, centre only takes unilateral decisions regarding the federal fiscal transfers. When we talk of VFI, though more resources are with the centre, the fiscal adjustment is such that it empowers the states with fiscal autonomy regarding the use of the funds received from the centre as a part of the fiscal adjustment scheme.. One can say whether centralization is on an increase or the VFI is on an increase depending upon the nature of fiscal adjustment schemes and the fiscal autonomy of the states. Hence the measures of these closely resembling concepts differ. The term decentralization is almost the reverse side of the coin centralization. The measures, the concepts and issues relating to these closely related terms are examined in the following sections.

Section 1

3.1 Vertical Fiscal Imbalances (VFI)

3.1.1 Introduction: As discussed earlier, the concept of VFI is easy to understand, however, one encounters lot of practical problems while actually measuring the extent of vertical fiscal imbalances in a federation. One does not know whether the VFI that is present in a federation is entirely due to the initial allocation of resources and assignment of duties or due to fiscal policies pursued by different layers of government. A sub optimal level of resource mobilisation and inefficient expenditure policies can yield wider VFI. While measuring the extent of VFI, it is important to know whether the two layers of government are putting enough efforts to mobilise the constitutionally allotted resources and their expenditure policy is judicious. In case the resource mobilisation efforts of the federal government is not to its fullest capacity and at the same time if federal government spends on items, which are best suited to be within the state's sphere or if there is no rational expenditure policy pursued by the government the resource balance of the federal government will fall. Just by looking at the budgetary figures therefore, one may jump to the conclusion that VFI is not very wide.

Similarly states may also be lacking in tax mobilization efforts and may be spending on non-productive items; in that case also the estimation of VFI can get biased. If central government is mobilising good amount of revenue and is not spending on non-essential and unproductive items, the federal government will have huge surplus and if the states are not pursuing a prudent fiscal policy the non correspondence in the state budgets will widen thus causing the VFI to widen. This prompts one to measure VFI in an objective manner. *However, in practice it is difficult to set what is an optimum level of resource mobilisation or expenditure*. When all the states are put together vis-à-vis the federal government, a few states' bad performance can alter the extent of VFI. Therefore, it is difficult to have a precise measure of VFI and one can only have some indicative measure.

In order to know the direction of vertical Fiscal imbalance and to measure the extent of such imbalances, it is very important to define the resources accruing to different layer of governments meticulously and to examine the expenditure requirements of these governments rationally. This apart a few other important questions crop up in this context, which need to be properly looked at. For example:

- Should vertical fiscal imbalances be measured after the devolution of taxes and after making adjustments for grants in aid and grants and loans given to the states?
- Or should VFI be measured after excluding only conditional grants and loans by the Centre to the States?
- Or VFI measure should include shared taxes in the resources of the States and excludes the States share from the initial revenue of the Centre?
- Should we take out only that part of the resources, which are constitutionally assured such as states own tax and non tax revenues, own capital receipts and market borrowings and exclude the proceeds of shareable taxes in the central resources and exclude grants from Centre's expenditure. In other words should resource and liabilities of both the layers be assessed before any kind of central transfer of resources made to the states?

Vertical Fiscal imbalance by it is not bad. However, if the vertical imbalance increases over a period of time and the federal fiscal transfers neglect the various criteria of transfers (as explained in the earlier section), it is not good for a healthy federation. In fact the worrisome feature of this is that in a number of federations 'vertical fiscal imbalances' are widening and 'centralisation' is becoming stronger. This necessitates an understanding of the phenomenon and calls for a rational measure of vertical fiscal imbalances and of centralisation.

The Issues pertaining to Vertical Fiscal Imbalances are different from the issues pertaining to state's fiscal autonomy or issues relating to centralisation. Vertical Fiscal Imbalances refer mismatch of resources with expenditure arising due to initial allocation of resources and functions between the two layers (sometimes three layers) of governments, and subsequently due to reassignments. Keeping this in mind various measures of VFI are examined below:

3.1.2 Measures of VFI: There are several studies attempting to measure vertical fiscal imbalance in terms of a simple comparable number. Some of the measures are explained below:

I) Hunter's pioneering comparative study, for example, calculated what was called a "coefficient of vertical balance" for the four federal countries he studied. [1] He calculated three such coefficients for four federations. These coefficients were defined as follows:

$$V1 = 1 - \frac{G_c + B}{E}$$

$$V2 = 1 - \frac{G_u + G_c + B}{E}$$

$$V3 = 1 - \frac{G_u + G_c + B + T_s}{E}$$

Where

G_u = unconditional federal grants to states

G_c = conditional federal grants to states

B = net borrowing by states

E = state expenditure (including transfers to local governments)

T_s = shared taxes.

The above measures show, if all state expenditures were entirely centrally controlled, the coefficient thus calculated would be zero, and if none were controlled, it would be one. In other words, the higher the coefficient, the more "balanced" are the federal finances in the sense of being closer to "...a situation in which governments at each level can command the financial resources necessary for them to carry out their expenditure responsibilities and to be held accountable for both spending and taxing decisions." [2] He holds that if the states fiscal autonomy is more; lesser will be the VFI i.e. Vertical Fiscal Imbalances.

If we look at the measure carefully, it may be seen that what Hunter was trying to measure was the extent of centralisation rather than measuring VFI. As Bird has rightly expressed, "These calculations are intended to separate out that part of the financing side of state budgets that is considered to be determined by the federal government". Hunter is talking about state autonomy. He is concerned with the question what types of transfers reduce state's decision taking power. These are further elaborated in the section on the measures of centralisation.

Thimmaiah in his study has attempted to measure Vertical Fiscal Imbalances. [3] The same was reproduced in his subsequent study also. [4] He holds, "any attempt to measure these fiscal imbalances should cover both revenue and capital accounts of the State Budgets." [5]

For measuring VFI, he defines the variables required in the following manner: [6]

T_o = States own tax revenues exclusively mobilized from their constitutionally allotted sources over which, States have the power to levy, collect and appropriate the yield.

R_o = States own non-loan non-tax revenues raised from their constitutionally allotted sources which includes receipts from fees, fines coming from Public Enterprises, interest earnings etc.

T_s = States share in the revenue raised by the Federal Government either from a Constitutionally defined concurrent source or a source Constitutionally allotted to States but rented out to the Federal Governments by the States or a discretionary revenue share from the yield from an exclusively federal source of revenue.

G_o = Unconditional grants

G_r = Conditional grants for current budgetary purpose

E_r = Current expenditure of the entire constituent States.

The Capital receipts of the States include:

B_m = State's own market borrowings including borrowings

from the Financial Institutions or allocations from a unified voluntary/statutory borrowings pool.

B_f = State's borrowings from the Federal Governments

O = All other receipts of revenue other than Bm and Bf such as receipts from repayments of loans etc.

G_c = Conditional grants for the States capital budgets.

E_c = States capital expenditure:

Thus

$$E = E_r + E_c \qquad \text{......... 1}$$

$$E_r = T_o + R_o + T_s + G_o + G_r \qquad \text{......... 2}$$

$$E_c = B_m + B_f + O + G_c \qquad \text{......... 3}$$

$$E = T_o + R_o + T_s + G_o + G_r + B_m + B_f + O + G_c \qquad \text{......... 4}$$

The balancing federal fiscal transfers from the Federal Government to the States on current budgets are: T_s, G_o and G_r such that

$$E_r - (T_o - R_o) = T_s + G_o + G_r \qquad \text{......... 5}$$

Further, Thimmaiah explains; it is quite possible that Ts may be Constitutionally binding on the part of the Federal Governments to give to the States, in which case:

$$E_r - (T_o + R_o + T_s) = G_o + G_r \qquad \text{......... 6}$$

If a part of Go is a substitute for Ts then:

$$E_r - (T_o + R_o + G_o') = G_r + G_o'' \qquad \text{......... 7}$$

Where:

$$G_o = G_o' + G_o''; \; G_o' = T_s \quad and \quad G_o - T_s = G_o'' \qquad \text{......... 8}$$

Thus V'f on current budget is equivalent to

$$V'f = 1 - \frac{T_o + R_o}{E_r} = 1 - \frac{T_o + R_o + T_s}{E_r} = 1 - \frac{T_o + T_s + R_o + G_o}{E_r}$$

$$= 1 - \frac{T_o + R_o + G_o'}{E_r} \qquad \text{......... 9}$$

$$= \frac{T_s + G_o + G_r}{E_r} = \frac{G_o + G_r}{E_r} = \frac{G_o'' + G_r}{E_r} \qquad \text{......... 10}$$

As the case may be.

On the capital budget of the States, the balancing federal fiscal transfers are G_c and B_f such that

$$E_c - (B_m + 0) = G_c + B_f \qquad \text{......... 11}$$

Therefore, $V''f$ on the Capital budget is equivalent to

$$V''f = 1 - \frac{(B_m - O)}{E_c} \qquad \text{......... 12}$$

Combining Vf on current and capital budgets, that is $V'f$ and $V''f$ we get

$$Vf = \frac{E_r V'f + E_c V''f}{E_r + E_c} \qquad \text{......... 13}$$

From 13, we derive the aggregate Vf as

$$Vf = 1 - \frac{T_o + R_o + T_s + B_m + o}{E} \qquad \text{...... 14}$$

$$= \frac{G_o + G_r + G_c + B_f}{E} \qquad \text{......... 15}$$

Where 'E' is always positive.

When $Vf = 0$, there is a total absence of vertical federal fiscal imbalance.

When $Vf = 1$, there is an absolute vertical federal fiscal imbalance. However, in reality Vf is generally greater than zero and less than one depending upon several factors influencing it.

In the above exercise, Thimmaiah [7] names 'Vf' as Vertical Fiscal Imbalance. Though the residual, after subtracting the states above the line items from 1 shows the financing items, it cannot be considered as vertical fiscal imbalance. These calculations actually show only the mismatch between receipts, (revenue and capital receipts and aggregate receipts) and expenditure (revenue expenditure, capital expenditure and aggregate expenditure) of States only. The above equations given by Thimmaiah reflect upon the federal fiscal transfers used for closing the gap in the revenue accounts, capital accounts and aggregate budgetary account of the states. The tools used are shared taxes grants of various kinds and borrowings from the Federal Governments.

3.1.3 Alternative Measures of VFI: When one considers VFI, it is necessary to compare the budgetary surplus non-correspondence of the federal government with the budgetary deficit non-correspondence of the states. This is not attempted either by Thimmaiah or by Hunter. In the absence of such comparison we only get to know the states dependency on the centre or the extent of federal government transfers to states or the position of own resources of the states vis-à-vis their expenditure responsibilities. The equation does not measure VFI which should reflect the relative position of State's fiscal balances with that of the Centre's.

Vertical fiscal imbalances may be reviewed from the angle of revenue account or capital account or both. In fact, a correct measure of vertical fiscal imbalances should cover both the revenue and the capital accounts. Vertical fiscal imbalances need to be assessed both in terms of resources and in terms of expenditure. In order to assess the resources and the expenditure liabilities of both the Centre and the States, it is important to identify the items, which should be included/excluded while calculating vertical fiscal imbalances. There could be more than two options to assess the resources/liabilities of the different layers of governments. Different options are given below:

Option 1:

Central Revenue Resources before devolution:

$TR_c = GR_c + CR_c$

GR_C = Gross Revenue receipts of the Centre

$GR_C = GDT_c + GIT_c + NTR_c$

TR_c = Total Receipts of the Centre

GDT_c = Gross Direct Taxes (inclusive of State's share)

GIT_c = Gross Indirect Taxes (inclusive of State's share)

NTR_c = Non-Tax Revenue of the Centre

CR_c = Central Government Capital Receipts

Central expenditure before grants given to the states

$CE = (RE_x - G_r) + (CE_x - OG_r)$

RE_x = Revenue Expenditure (Dev + Non-Dev)

G_r = Revenue Grants

CE_e = Capital Expenditure (Dev + Non-Dev)

OG_r = Other Grants (Dev + Non-Dev)

In the above model, vertical fiscal imbalances are measured before any type of Central transfers to States in the form of devolution of taxes, grants-in-aid and grants are made.

Devolution of taxes and various types of taxes are the 'fiscal adjustment tools' to bring down vertical fiscal imbalances and hence they should be excluded while calculating VFI.

Option 2:

Often it is argued that States have a right to a share in the divisible pool of taxes collected by the Central Government hence while working out Central resources, States' share in taxes should be excluded. In this model:

$NR_c = NDT_c + NIT_c + NTR_c + CC_r$

NR_c = Net Revenue of the Centre

NDTc, NITc = Net Direct and Net Indirect Taxes excluding States tax share

NTR_c = Non-Tax Revenue of the Centre

CR_c = Central Government Capital Receipts

In this study, we have opted for Model 1 to measure vertical fiscal imbalances because any kind of central transfer is considered as a fiscal adjustment tool to reduce VFI. Model 2 actually shows the fiscal adjustment only.

In order to measure Vertical Fiscal imbalance, it is very important to examine revenue receipts, capital receipts, aggregate receipts, revenue expenditure, capital expenditure and aggregate expenditure of the Federal Government as well as of the states. [8] These should be divided by a common denominator like aggregate receipts (revenue receipts of all the States and of the Federal Government, capital receipts of all the States and that of the Federal Governments). Similarly, expenditure should also be divided by the aggregate expenditure. Once we know the relative proportion of the federal government in the aggregate receipts and expenditure, we can work out the proportion of the states in the aggregates:

State per cent share =100-Centres' per cent share

(St % share = 100 – C%)

This exercise requires following information for the Federal Governments:

CT_r = Exclusively Central tax resources'

CNT_r = Centre's non-tax resources

CG_r= Grants received from other Countries and International Agencies on revenue accounts

CR_c = Capital Receipts of the centre

R_{Ex} = Expenditure of the Centre on revenue accounts, similarly

CC_{Ex} = Total capital expenditure of the Centre.

In the case of the Centre total expenditure comprising of total revenue expenditure and capital expenditure before federal transfers are invariably less than the aggregate receipts. One should then workout the following percentages:

- Percentage of revenue resources at the command of the federal government in the total revenue resources(Federal and the states),
- Percentage of revenue expenditure of the federal government in the aggregate revenue expenditure.
- Percentage share of the capital receipts of the federal government in the aggregate capital receipts and
- Percentage share of the federal capital expenditure in the aggregate capital expenditure.

This can be compared with the states percentage shares in the above aggregates. Expressed in a simple way:

Thus,

Vertical fiscal imbalances relating to resources.

$$V_{flr} = \frac{(C_r / A_r)}{(S_r / A_r)}$$ This can be expressed as

$$V_{flr} = \frac{Cr}{Sr}$$

If the V_{flr} is greater than '1' it indicates presence of vertical fiscal imbalances. If it is equal to 1, there is absence of VFI and if it is less than 1 that means resources are more decentralised or the States have more resources at their command then the Centre.

Thus,

$V_{flr} > 1$ if $C_r > S_r$

$V_{flr} = 1$ if $C_r = S_r$

$V_{flr} < 1$ if $C_r < S_r$

Similarly, vertical fiscal imbalances in expenditure liabilities can also be examined.

$$V_{fle} = \frac{(C_e / A_e)}{(S_e / A_e)}$$

or $\dfrac{C_e}{S_e}$

V_{fle} is low if $C_e > S_e$

V_{fle} is equal if $C_e = S_e$

V_{fle} is steeper if $C_e < S_e$

In order to know the overall situation V_{fle} needs to be compared with V_{fle} or

C_r vis-à-vis C_e and

S_r vis-à-vis Se should be compared.

If $C_r > C_e$ and $S_r < S_e$, vertical fiscal imbalance will be very steep.

If the federal government commands disproportionately high resources and shares relatively fewer responsibilities compared to the states vertical Fiscal imbalances will be steeper and to bridge the gap more resources are needed to be transferred from the federal to the states. Usually, larger the fiscal transfers from the federal government to the states, wider are the vertical fiscal imbalances.

It should be remembered that VFI are not always bad. It depends upon the nature of federal fiscal transfers. If the federal fiscal transfers do not reduce states fiscal autonomy or do not force the states to change their expenditure plans and priorities, such transfers do not result in increased vertical fiscal imbalances.

3.2 Vertical Fiscal Imbalances in India (1950-51 to 2000-01)

To illustrate the measure of VFI described in the previous section, we have taken data from Indian Federation for selected years starting from 1950-51. Table 3.1 presents a picture of tax resources at the command of the Centre and States before devolution.

It is evident from the Table that Centre invariably had larger share in direct taxes at its command than all the states put together. In 1950-51, Centre commanded 75.95 per cent and the same increased to 88.29 per cent in 2000-01. Similar trend is visible for the aggregate tax resources. Even in terms of indirect taxes, Centre commanded more resources till 1999-00 than the States. Centre's command over indirect taxes was around 58 per cent in 1950-51 and gradually it fell to the level of 53 per cent by1999-00.

However, after the devolution of taxes, position of states improved. As may be seen from Table 3.2 after devolution, states command over direct taxes improved from 10.97 per cent (Table 3.1.) in 2000-01 to 30.08 per cent (Table 3.2). In all the years there has been significant transfer of tax resources from the Centre to the States which brought down VFI significantly. States which had only 50.64 per cent of the indirect taxes in 2000-01 before devolution commanded 60.19 per cent after devolution.

Vertical fiscal imbalances are steeper in case of Non-Tax Revenue. Table 3.3 shows that not only Centre always commanded more of non-tax resources but its share has gone up significantly from 52.05 per cent in 1950-51 to 73.57 per in 2000-01. States have very little control over non-tax resources. Table 3.4 shows the overall position of the Centre and the States with regard to total revenue receipts (Tax and Non-Tax) before devolution. Here also it is the Centre which gets the maximum resources at its command.

Table 3.1: Tax Receipts of the Centre, States & UT and Combined (Centre and States) in per cent Before Devolution (per cent)

Years	Direct Taxes			Indirect Taxes			Total Taxes Direct + Indirect		
	Combined	Centre	States	Combined	Centre	States	Combined	Centre	States
1950-51	100	75.95	24.00	100	57.89	42.00	100	64.57	35.40
1960-61	100	72.66	28.08	100	63.63	36.37	100	66.32	33.90
1970-71	100	84.34	15.55	100	62.84	37.06	100	67.43	32.55
1980-81	100	91.35	8.65	100	61.41	38.57	100	66.34	33.64
1990-91	100	88.84	10.04	100	61.21	38.32	100	65.07	34.37
1995-96	100	93.65	6.19	100	55.55	44.32	100	63.32	36.54
1999-00	100	98.02	4.79	100	52.75	46.76	100	62.78	37.45
2000-01	100	88.29	10.97	100	46.92	50.64	100	56.64	41.31

Table 3.2: Vertical Fiscal Imbalances on Revenue Account: After Central Transfer of Resources to States (per cent)

Years	After Central Transfers				Total Taxes	
	Direct Taxes		Indirect Taxes			
	Centre	States	Centre	States	Centre	States
1950-51	55.39	44.55	57.89	42.00	56.97	42.94
1960-61	50.19	50.55	55.71	44.29	54.07	46.15
1970-71	48.57	51.32	52.48	47.43	51.70	48.30
1980-81	60.67	39.33	44.67	55.31	47.31	52.68
1990-91	56.35	42.52	47.88	51.64	49.07	50.37
1995-96	62.30	37.54	42.76	57.11	46.75	53.11
1999-00	68.08	34.72	40.63	58.88	46.71	53.52
2000-01	69.19	30.08	37.36	60.19	44.76	53.11

Table 3.3: Non-Tax Revenue: Percentage Share of the Centre and the States (Per cent)

Year	Combined* NTR	Centre#	States
1950-51	100.00	52.05	47.95
1960-61	100.00	55.09	44.91
1970-71	100.00	61.71	38.29
1980-81	100.00	66.24	33.76
1990-91	100.00	68.43	31.57
1995-96	100.00	61.14	38.86
1999-00	100.00	71.24	28.76
2000-01	100.00	73.57	26.43

*This is arrived at by adding Non-Tax resources of the Centre including interest receipts from the States and State's Non-Tax resources excluding grants from the Centre.
Includes interest receipts from the States.

Centre's command over total revenue resources has been very high. In 1950, it was 62.07% and the same went up to 66.33% in 1980-81 and even in 1999-00 it was as high as 64.47. States always commanded less than 39% of total revenue receipts. As against this the states had to shoulder the responsibility of financing revenue expenditure to the tune of more than 52% in all the years as shown in Table 3.5.

The VFI on capital account is steeper than on the revenue account. Table 3.6 clearly shows that the Centre commands higher percentage of capital receipts. It was as high as 80.37 per cent and 96.93 per cent in 1990-91 and 1995-96. In the latter years there had been a fall in the percentage share of the Centre. Nevertheless, it had more capital receipts than the States.

On the contrary, Table 3.7 shows capital expenditure of the Centre hovered between 56 per cent and 43 per cent only while States with meagre capital receipts had to shoulder the major part of capital expenditure.

Table 3.4: VFI on Revenue Receipts Before Devolution (per cent)

Year	Total Taxes Direct + Indirect			Non-Tax Revenue			Overall VFI Revenue Receipts		
	Centre	States	Combined	Combined	Centre	State	Centre	States	Combined
1950-51	64.59	35.41	100	100	52.05	47.95	62.07	37.93	100
1960-61	66.17	33.83	100	100	55.09	44.91	63.55	36.45	100
1970-71	67.45	32.55	100	100	61.71	38.29	66.14	33.86	100
1980-81	66.35	33.65	100	100	66.24	33.76	66.33	33.67	100
1990-91	65.44	34.56	100	100	68.43	31.57	65.94	34.06	100
1995-96	63.41	36.59	100	100	61.14	38.86	62.94	37.06	100
1999-00	62.63	37.37	100	100	71.24	28.76	64.47	35.53	100
2000-01	57.82	42.18	100	100	73.57	26.43	61.02	38.98	100

Table 3.5: Revenue Expenditure of the Centre, States and Combined (per cent)

Year	Central Government	Revenue Expenditure		Aggregate or combined
	Total Rev. Exp. (including grants)	After Transfers Rev. Exp. (excluding grants)		
		Centre	State	
1990-91	56.181	48.17	51.83	100
1995-96	53.045	46.66	53.34	100
1999-00	51.678	47.08	52.92	100
2000-01	53.375	47.78	52.22	100

Table 3.6: Capital Receipts of the Centre, States, Combined Governments (per cent)

Year	Central Capital Receipts	States Capital Receipts	Aggregate
1990-91	80.37	19.63	100
1995-96	96.93	3.07	100
1999-00	66.52	33.48	100
2000-01	58.96	41.04	100

Table 3.1.7: Capital Expenditure of the Centre, States and Combined (per cent)

Year	Centre's Net Cap. Exp.	State Cap. Exp	Aggregate*
1990-91	56.48	43.52	100
1995-96	45.82	54.18	100
1999-00	43.30	56.70	100
2000-01	43.04	56.96	100

*net centre's capital expenditure + states capital expenditure

Source: Indian Public Finance 2002-03, various tables.

The data relating to Indian States and the Federal Government clearly shows the extent of vertical fiscal imbalance prevailing in the country. In order to correct this vertical fiscal imbalances, various fiscal adjustment tools like tax-sharing, grants-in-aid, various types of grants and loans have been used. The various fiscal adjustment tools do help in reducing vertical fiscal imbalances. However, mere reduction in VFI does not ensure fiscal autonomy to the States. The use of various fiscal adjustment tools gives rise to issues pertaining to State's autonomy and centralisation. These issues are discussed in succeeding sections.

Section 2

3.3 Centralisation: Concept, Issues and Measures

3.3.1 Concept: As explained in the previous chapter, Vertical Fiscal Imbalances are present invariably in all the federations and they are the outcome of the initial assignments and subsequent re-assignments of powers and functions between the federal and federating units. There is consensus of federating units for such arrangements. Vertical fiscal imbalances are inevitable and these imbalances are sought to be corrected through various fiscal adjustment tools like sharing revenue from the divisible pool or specific tax proceeds with the states, payment of grants and grants-in-aid, etc

Very close to the concept of vertical Fiscal Imbalance is the concept of Centralisation. Quite often scholars have mixed up the two concepts: Vertical Fiscal Imbalances and Centralisation. It is true that higher centralisation of resources lead to wider Vertical Fiscal Imbalances, but the opposite is not always true. Vertical Fiscal Imbalances may not always lead to centralisation. It is important to understand the difference between the two.

When we talk of 'Centralisation' it is more concerned with the unilateral decision of the Federal Governments influencing the scheme of devolution of resources, grants-in-aid and grants. Viewed from another angle it may hamper State's fiscal autonomy. In a federation with comprehensive socio-economic planning, it is common to find the federal government making inroads into state' domain of functions and resorting to transferring resources through conditional and specific grants. This curtails state's fiscal autonomy and makes them dependent on the federal government. This leads to higher degree of centralisation. Thus, with an increase in centralisation, discretionary federal fiscal transfers increase, they impinge upon States fiscal autonomy, and the principles of fiscal transfers, explained in the earlier section get ignored.

When Vertical Fiscal Transfers are brought down by statutory tools of federal fiscal transfers like tax sharing, revenue sharing or grants-in-aid there is not much scope for increase in centralisation. However, if the Centre ignores the initial agreements with the federating units for sharing of prescribed resources and opts to transfer resources at its own will by adopting arbitrary criteria, even, statutory transfers get influenced by the Centre's decision. Even when an independent body like the Finance Commission is appointed to make fiscal transfers, if the terms and conditions set by the President are favourable to the states, the decisions lead to centralisation and states fiscal autonomy is affected. If more resources are transferred through conditional grants/specific grants, though States get more resources and Vertical Fiscal Imbalances get narrowed down, Centralisation increases.

These differences between centralisation and VFI should be borne in mind while analysing Vertical Fiscal Imbalances and centralisation.

3.3.2 Is Centralisation Desirable? The real controversy pertains to the centralisation process, degree of centralisation and its trend. Richard Bird poses the question: "Are we interested in the degree of centralisation because there is some aesthetic merit in being more or less centralised?" [9] Or is it believed that there is a strong correspondence between the degree of centralisation and, for better or for worse, the "welfare state," as some political scientists have argued? [10] Are federal countries less likely to undertake "fundamental social policy reforms?" [11] Or is there in some sense an inevitable tendency for governments to become more centralised over time – a tendency often referred to in the English literature as the "concentration process" and in the German literature as "Popitz's Law." [12]

While to some scholars higher degree of centralisation is desirable from the point of maximising welfare, bringing down regional disparities, promoting growth and efficient use of scare resources, [13] others vehemently oppose such a trend on the ground that it impinges upon state autonomy, state's performances and priorities are neglected and these are forcibly changed and it goes against the interest of local areas. [14] The most difficult issue has to do with grants to the provinces on condition of their enacting certain programmes like shared-cost programmes. These have often had the effect of altering a state's priorities. It is difficult to refuse money for a programme, particularly if it is politically popular, even when it means abandoning or postponing other programs a state might consider more important. In addition, many of the programmes deal with social security, and involve matters which some federating units may consider as of vital importance to provincial culture. On the other hand, there are important federal interests involved. Social security programmes are an important mechanism for maintaining equality of services among citizens, and marked variations in these programs among the states could seriously affect the mobility of citizens.

Some have argued, for example, that the more centralised government authority is, the larger the public sector will be. Others have argued the opposite. Depending on the bias of the observer, federalism may then be seen as a good thing or a bad thing. Mancur Olson (1983) has gone so far as to suggest that, since federalism probably makes it easier to articulate special interests and hence to slow down economic growth, "the efficiency of an economy may be increased either by making narrow special-interest groups weaker or by making the government stronger in relation to them," that is, by increasing the degree of government centralisation. [15] Olson goes on to note that the more centralised structure, the greater the chance of a totalitarian government, his emphasis is definitely that the greater the decision-making authority at the local level, the more likely are government actions to slow down adjustment processes, and hence to slow down the rate of growth. Olson has also suggested, in a different context, that interest groups hostile to change may find it easy to use state governments as a basis for resistance to change, thus slowing down the move toward the uniform and equal provision of services on which many social reformers place a great deal of emphasis. Conversely, other authors, although accepting the argument that decentralisation retards the growth of the public sector, view this outcome more positively. [16]

It is common to find some amount of centralisation in any federation. However if the degree of centralisation increases and the federating units lose their legitimate autonomy, this increase in centralisation becomes harmful to the very spirit of federation. In order to ensure a healthy federal system there is need to have centralisation within proper limits. In fact this necessitates a proper measure of centralisation.

3.3.3 Degree and Measures of Centralisation: "One of the most important mistakes made in discussions of federation is to assume that the degree of centralisation is a generally or universally simple, practical and useful criterion for classifying and assessing the operations of governments." [17] This is partly right. Nevertheless, scholars have made attempts to define and measure centralisation in some way or the other. Besides, serious efforts are made to evaluate judgements on the basis of such measurements.

There are several methods to examine the degree of centralisation. One can compare the degree of centralisation in a particular country with other federal countries i.e. a cross sectional analysis of indicators of centralisation. Similarly one can measure the degree of centralisation over a period of time within a particular federation by using the method of time series analysis of indicators of centralisation.

Oates Wallace examines, in his study on fiscal federalism, inter country variation in the degree of centralisation by using an econometric tool. [18] In such a cross section study one can examine whether e.g. in India, there is excess centralisation or not. Oates aims at exploring with quantitative techniques differences in the over all extent of fiscal centralisation in the public budgets of a substantial number of federal and non-federal countries.

In the literature on federal finance, centralisation is measured by the ratio of central government expenditure to total expenditure. In some studies expenditure is related to GDP. For example, a recent study by Morris Beck, the degree of centralisation is measured by comparing the real and nominal rates of growth of expenditure in relation to the rate of growth of GDP. He found, although the average annual rate of growth of total expenditure was indeed a bit lower in five federal countries for the period 1950 to 1977 than in the total of thirteen countries included in his study when measured in nominal terms, the opposite was true in real terms. On average, the rate of total government expenditure growth in real terms in relation to Gross Domestic Product (GDP) was actually slightly higher in federal countries than in non-federal countries, although the difference was not significant. [19] Wallace Oates tried to examine the degree of centralisation with the size of government. He found that the extent of fiscal centralisation, whether measured in terms of revenues or expenditures, was not significantly related to the size of government. [20]

Fredrick Pryor measured the degree of centralisation in terms of the percentage of total government consumption expenditure accounted for by central governments. He found that centralisation rose in the United States, Canada and Australia (as well as in what subsequently became the Federal Republic of Germany) in the first half of the twentieth century – and rose similarly in non-federal countries – but that in the 1950s this trend reversed in most developed countries. Pryor also found, however, that federal nations tended persistently to have the lowest centralisation ratio, when measured in this way. [21] Similarly, Wallace Oates, who calculated centralisation ratios on the basis of current government expenditure, found an increase in centralisation over time, with an apparent reversal taking place in the 1950s. [22]

More recent studies have produced broadly similar results. Warren Nutter also used central government expenditures as a percentage of total government expenditure, to trace the trends in centralisation in Australia, Canada, Germany and the Untied States during 1950s and 1960s. [23] On the other hand, David Davies used revenue data. [24] This study reinforced the findings by Pryor of the greater fiscal importance of non-central governments in federal countries. [25]

Using OECD data, Watson's [26] principal conclusion is that the importance of both central government receipts and expenditures as a percentage of total receipts and expenditures which is taken as a measure of centralisation, has declined fairly steadily for the OECD countries as a whole over the last 30 years.

Hunter [27] has constructed an index of vertical imbalances, which actually measures the degree of centralisation or looking at it from a different angle, the degree of state autonomy. Hunter, in this study makes a comparison of Inter-Country financial imbalances, he himself admits that the "concept, however lacks precision, especially since the size of the federal transfers may hinge to an important extent on a state's share of tax receipts which ranks as a near perfect substitute for the transfers".

Hunter has made an attempt to specify "the coefficient of vertical balance". The value of this coefficient depends on the nature and treatment of the various income components including financial transfers from the Central Government. He has classified income items into two groups:

1. those which can be changed on State initiatives and which are linked with State expenditure decisions and
2. "all other items" Which "are therefore in the nature of financing items since they merely close the gap which arises from the differences between State expenditure on the one hand and the "above – the line" income components on the other." [28] The larger the gap to be closed in this way, the

larger the extent of Vertical intergovernmental Financial Imbalances.

Next he tries to use a generalized formula (for the coefficient of vertical balance) as a basis for assessing the degree of vertical imbalances in four federal countries – Australia, Canada, The US and West Germany.

Finally, he suggests a criterion which might be appropriate for purposes of Inter-country comparisons.

3.3.4 Coefficient of Vertical Balance: Hunter's Measure of Vertical Imbalance/Centralisation: As explained earlier, Hunter's measure of Vertical Balance actually measured centralisation. Hence, it is discussed here, Hunter holds, for any period, State income from taxes and other sources, including federal grants and net borrowing, must equal total outlay:-

Thus

$$T_o + T_s + R + G_o + G_c + B = E \qquad \text{......... (i)}$$

Here,

T_σ = States own tax revenue

T_s = States share in the divisible taxes (Centre and State sharing the tax revenue)

R = Non – tax receipts

G_o = Open ended (unconditional) grants received from Federal Governments

G_c = Conditional grants received from the Federal Governments

B = Net borrowing by States

E = Total State outlay

He further states, "when G_o is given to the States essentially as a substitute for T_s (as in Australia) equation or identity – can be rearranged to incorporate the idea of "above – and – below the line" items, the former being items which make up the basic deficit and the latter those which finances that deficit.

Thus,

$$E - T_o - R - G_o = G_c + B \qquad \text{......... (ii)}$$

In this equation G_o is assumed to be equivalent of T_s from the stand point of State fiscal autonomy. In this case, States cannot change the tax rates or even tax base, although they receive what amounts to a share in the growth of taxes. In this case (unlike G_c) the States are free to spend the proceeds in any way they please. Hunter felt that the above expression was not very meaningful because it suggested:

- G_c and B are necessarily financing items,
- T_o, T_s, R and G_o are necessarily autonomous in that they are guided by State initiatives; and
- E is independent of the income component.

Neither (a), (b) nor (c) is realistic. G_c may be partly a response to Federal initiative and partly a response to State initiatives and that a rise in G_c is likely to be accompanied by a rise in E, and possibly also by a rise in T_o and R (Especially if matching conditions apply).

Therefore, he suggested a more general formulation which recognizes that:

1. The size of E is to some extent determined independently of the revenue items but is also partly a function of those items;
2. Each of the revenue or income components should ideally be split into two parts;

- change in revenue resulting from State initiatives and related to E ; and
- Changes in revenue which merely fill the gap between E and the "above-the-line" or autonomous revenue items.

Following (ii) he specified "above-the-line" income items at the State level as:

$T_0' + T_s' + G_0' + G_c' + B'$ and below-the-line income items as

$$T_0'' + T_s'' + G_0'' + G_c'' + B''$$

With regard to (i) above, it is recognized that $(T_o' + \ldots + B')$ and E are independent to some degree. E is partly a function of "above-the-line" or autonomous income and partly a function of force other than State income, which we can denote as X.

Thus,

$$E = f[X, (T_o' + \dots + B')] \qquad \text{.........(iii)}$$

At the State level in the absence of stabilisation and distributional policy, $(T_o' + \dots + B')$ will be wholly guided by the size of E, while $(T_o'' + \dots + B'')$ can be seen as simply the difference between E and $(T_o' + \dots + B')$.

Focussing on the income components and assuming E to be given by the X factor, the coefficient of Vertical balance can be adduced as follows:

$$T_o' + T_s' + G_o' + G_c' + B' = vE$$

Where

v is the coefficient of vertical balance and since $(T_o'' + \dots + B'') = E - (T_o' + \dots + B')$

Then

$(T_o'' + \dots + B'') = E - v$ therefore

$$V = 1 - \frac{T_o'' + T_s'' + G_o'' + G_c'' + B''}{E} \qquad \text{.........(iv)}$$

The use of this expression has the advantage of showing that as E rises (from whatever cause), the degree of vertical imbalance will increase if the financing items rise more than proportionately. The greater the financing items in relation to E (i.e. The lesser the scope for State initiative or State control) the closer v will approach to zero (i.e. the greater the extent of vertical imbalance), and vice versa.

Thus, v can have a range of values from zero to unity. At one extreme, when $(T_o'' + \dots + B'') = E$, v = 0. At the other extreme when $(T_o'' + \dots + B'') > E$ then v = 1.

If v = 0 the States do not have any financial autonomy. This would indicate a total dependence by the States on federally controlled grants-in-aid programmes and/or on residual borrowing to meet expenditure commitments. However, this makes the federation redundant. [29]

On the other hand, as the "above-the-line" revenue items come closer to E, independent decision making on the part of the States and State financial autonomy become more marked and v would then come closer to unity.

In reality, of course, v will be somewhere between these extreme positions. If State expenditure commitments rise, the States find it more difficult to increase their own revenues and are obliged to rely increasingly on categorical grants-in-aid and/or on borrowing from the Central Governments.

Hunter has labelled the index as Vertical imbalance, but in fact this will be more relevant if it is labelled as index of centralisation. Hunter's Index can be taken as a measure of vertical fiscal imbalance if more resources are transferred from the centre to the states in the form of statutory transfers which entitles states to get their share in the federal revenue. Under this type of arrangement even though more resources are with the federal government leading to vertical fiscal imbalances, it does not imply centralisation. However, if the resources transferred from the federal government to the states is of discretionary nature, conditional or specific that reduces state's fiscal auton0my and increases central control resulting in centralisation. Hunter is talking about the impact of federal transfers on state fiscal autonomy and hence the index can rightly be labelled as centralisation index.

3.3.5 Vertical Balance Further Considered [30]: The broad framework can be amended and modified theoretically. One may argue that T_0' is necessarily different from T_s' since T_0' represents revenue from taxes imposed by the States, which are by and large free to vary tax rates. T_s', however, does not mean the same thing in each federal country. There are no shared taxes of any consequence in Australia. While in Germany Ts represents the States share of tax yield where tax rates are uniform throughout the country and are set by federal law.

It would therefore, be clearly inappropriate to include only T_0' (and R) in the "above-the-line" category. Another important question is whether G_0 should be placed "above" or "below-the-line". Should open ended grants be regarded as a source of revenue which the States can influence as easily as they can their share of earmarked taxes (T_s). This will depend on the nature of these revenue sources – especially the degree of State control over total. A sharp distinction between G_o and Ts would seem appropriate where States are in a position to influence the amounts they receive under a tax sharing arrangements (i.e. are not dominated by Federal Policy) and have a guaranteed source of revenue which grows broadly in harmony with GNP.

Where States depend largely on G_o and where their bargaining position (viz a viz the Centre) is relatively weak, there would seem to be a strong case for a differing treatment of G_o and T_s. One might therefore, expect that a large part of G_o should be excluded from the "above-the-line" income components and be regarded as a means of correcting for vertical intergovernmental fiscal imbalances. Such exclusion would of course, increase the basic deficits unless compensatory changes could be made in T and R.

At the same time it would not be sensible to suppose that all taxes are regarded as equally advantageous from the standpoint of State fiscal autonomy. Ideally, each income component should be weighed to reflect the degree of State autonomy or the strength of State bargaining power involved.

Equation (iv) might therefore, be put in a slightly different form viz.:

$$V = 1 - \frac{aT_o + bR + cT_s + dG_o + eG_c + fB}{E} \quad \text{.........(v)}$$

The weight, a to f, could each vary from zero to unity depending on assessments made regarding the extent to which the States are able to influence each revenue component in question. The greater the influence,(matter of judgement), the lower the weight. A zero weight would effectively remove an income components from equations (v) implying that the item is entirely "above-the-line" from the stand point of vertical balance. If a State is free to vary revenue of either type, a, b, c would therefore be close to zero. If State's bargaining power is weak, then, 'd' would be close to unity. Where States possess independent borrowing powers and are not subject to stringent Centre limitations on their ability to borrow, the value of 'f' would be close to zero. If States borrowed only to finance revenue producing assets (and the Central Government did likewise but with some variation in accordance with stabilization objectives) there is no vertical imbalance and the 'B' term would drop out of equation. (v). However, in all the federations, some parts of borrowing will be involuntary in a sense and needed purely to finance revenue deficits. Likewise, if it could be established that a significant proportion of G_c was made in response to State initiatives or after due consultations with the States, then, 'e' would apparently be less than unity.

However, a question arises as to what extent States can influence each of the income components: T_o ... B. A sensible answer is difficult to obtain. One must have a thorough knowledge of the Federal State decision making process in each country. If States cannot influence any of the income components "v" will be zero. On the contrary if all the States can act in unison to bring pressure on the Central Government with respect to various grants (total and composition) the "v" is likely to be close to unity even though, reliance on State taxes is relatively modest.

The analysis so far is built on the underlying assumption that States can determine 'E' (i.e. that they can determine their own expenditures within the allocation branch subject to Constitutional limitations and legal rulings regarding the division of functions between each major tier of Government) but take an extreme case in which E was financed entirely by G_c (the latter being "controlled" from the Centre)

Then,

$$V = 1 - \frac{G_c''}{E} = 0$$

It would not be unreasonable to suppose that a large part of G_c is likely to reflect national priorities which cannot be expected to coincide with those set by the States. If G_o appears as a sort of a "pay off" with little evidence of conscious States control on independent decision making then G_o could also be "below-the-line" as a financing item. If B is a pure residual, it too must also appear as a financing item.

Hunter's index has a few objectionable features. Thimmaiah in his article has brought out some of the shortcomings of Hunters proposition. Hunter provided a theoretical framework of "Vertical Inter-governmental Financial Imbalances." [31] He has maintained that the concept as defined in terms of surplus budgetary non-correspondence of the federal government and the deficit budgetary non-correspondence of all the States taken together in a federation is not precise enough and also less meaningful for the purpose of inter-federation comparison. Therefore he has attempted to adopt a positive approach by taking the example of four older federations (Australia, Canada, the U.S. and Germany) and tried to formulate a precise conceptual framework for the analysis of vf.

Thimmaiah [32] has tried to pinpoint the shortcomings in the paper by Hunter and has attempted to give a more comprehensive framework. Vf is indicated quantitatively by the preposition of all the federating units' budgetary gap (excluding any federal fiscal transfers) to the total expenditure of the states in a federation. Thus, if the entire expenditure of the states s financed exclusively by states own resources or in other words if the ratio of states' own revenue to their total expenditure is one, vf will be equal to zero., (vf=0), if it is zero i.e. if the ratio of revenue to total expenditure is zero, then vf=1. vf=0 indicates absence of vertical imbalances, while vf =1 indicates absolute vertical fiscal imbalances. However, these are the two extremes and reality vf lies in between the two limits 0-1.

If vf is nearer to zero that shows lower degree of vertical fiscal imbalances and vice-versa. In fact vf is influenced by the initial constitutional assignments of powers and functions, judicial interpretation of such divisions and actual extra constitutional federal fiscal arrangements. [33] These factors make the vf to differ from one federation to another.

Hunter has derived his 'v' as a residual factor after allowing for states autonomous revenue receipts. Hunter has classified the states revenue into "above-the line" and "below-the-line" [34] to derive 'v' which is equivalent to:

$$v = 1 - \frac{T'' + \ldots\ldots + B''.}{E}$$

According to him "above –the –line items are those which can be influenced by states' decisions. These items are denoted by $(T_0' + T_s' + G_o' + G_c' + B')$ while the other items $(T_0'' + T_s'' + G_o'' + G_c'' + B'')$ are fiancing items intended at filling the gap. However, in practice we do not come across such counterparts for every item of 'above-the line' items.

Hunter also did not distinguish between the current account and the capital account of the state budgets.

Further, Hunter did not analyze the inter-dependency of E' and vf. Actually, vf depends as much on expenditure as on revenue. "If the total expenditure of all the states is taken as given, no federal government can fill the gap arising from vf. Further, Hunter does not explain how v is influenced by T_o, T_s and R (autonomous items of income depending upon states initiatives).vf depends upon the states' actual efforts to raise revenue in relation to their fiscal capacity and the states own actual autonomous and induced expenditure in relation to the standard levels of these expenditures.

In practice vf is also influenced by horizontal fiscal imbalances (hf), which in turn its dependent upon horizontal economic imbalances (disparities) existing between the states in a federation [35] both on revenue and capital accounts of the state budgets.

It is easy to explain and present a measure of vertical fiscal imbalances theoretically. However, in practice it is very difficult. fi is influenced by each federating states budgetary imbalances. Some states may show deficits due to inefficiency, while some others may end up with deficits owing to limited revenue potential and huge fiscal need. Some other states may even experience surplus budget. vfi is an aggregate index of fiscal performance of the states. Therefore if vfi is to be realistic and meaningful it will have to be derived in terms of some objectively determined norms of revenue and expenditure of the state as well as of the central government, this itself is a very difficult task.

3.3.6 Degree of Centralisation: Breton and Scott Method: [36] Breton and Scott devised an index of the degree of centralisation, which they use as a summary of the particular assignment table that is observable in each period. The aim was to provide a measure that has a higher value if the structure of the public sector corresponds to an intuitive notion of 'centralisation' and a low value if that structure is decentralised.

Breton and Scott proceeded as follows.

First, they assumed that the boundaries of lower-level jurisdictions never cross the boundaries of higher-level jurisdictions, so that it is always possible to say that the former are entirely enclosed within the latter.

Second, because their index of the degree of centralisation (γ) applies only to observable assignment tables, they constructed an index that is a weighted average of all the jurisdictional levels to which functions are actually assigned. The weights chosen were total expenditures at each level, regardless of the functions on which money was spent.

Jurisdictional levels are defined in terms of the population (or territory) of a typical jurisdiction at that level. Hence variation in the value of the index is due to variation in the size of the jurisdictions to which functions have been assigned. [37]

Centralisation is then measured in the following way:

Suppose there are three layers of government: Centre, states, and local, add up expenditure at each level and multiply with the respective population. This should be divided by total expenditure i.e. of centre, states and local governments put together and this multiplied by the national population

If E stands for expenditure, P_δ for the population of a typical unit at jurisdictional level δ, and P for total population, then the index of centralisation is:

$$\gamma^{1} = \left[\sum_{\beta=1}^{r}\sum_{\delta=1}^{q}\left(E_{\beta\delta}^{1} P_{\delta}^{1}\right)\right] \Big/ \left[P^{0}\sum_{\beta=1}^{r}\sum_{\delta=1}^{q} E_{\beta\delta}^{0}\right]$$

Where the superscripts denote time periods or different societies depending on what it is that one wishes to compare.

The index is designed to summarise the structure of a public sector in one period relative to another, so that comparisons of γ's for two or more assignment tables will indicate the direction of change of the weighted average of the levels at which activity is carried out.

3.3.7 Constraints: The econometric study involves at the outright a task of defining an operational measure of degree of fiscal centralisation. There are several practical constraints in doing so.

First, as the concept itself is surrounded by ambiguity, it is rather difficult to clearly say what centralisation is.

A second major problem as pointed out by Oates is the association of budgetary information with the appropriate decision-making units.

Fiscal data are typically available on revenue and on expenditure basis and there exists a fundamental question as to which classification provides the most useful measures of fiscal centralisation. Should funds be attributed to the level of government that collects the revenues or to the one which spends them? This raises the whole issue of whether or not we can hope to develop reliable measures of the degree of centralisation on the basis of budgetary data.

As seen above generally, to measure centralisation, federal receipts are taken as percent of aggregate receipts and federal expenditure are taken as percentage of aggregate expenditure. Based on these figures inter-country or inter temporal comparisons are made. It is difficult to know what to make of these figures. The temptation to focus on such public finance data when measuring centralisation appears to be overwhelming. [38] The reasons given for this emphasis range from a declaration with respect to Switzerland that "the true distribution of power within the layers of government appears accurately in the public spending figures" [39] to the more judicious declaration by Oates that fiscal measures are a reasonably satisfactory proxy for what really needs to be measured, namely, "the amount of independent decision-making power in the provision of pubic services at different levels of government." [40] These reasons are not, however, very convincing. [41]

Bird explains, "It is not clear, for example, that the measures used are, in fact, reasonable proxies of "decision-making power" – for example, with respect to regulation." The difficulty in making meaningful international comparisons over time with the available data is also too easily underplayed by those who have not examined the subject closely. There are problems in the comparability of data over both time and country; inevitably arbitrary decisions are made on the treatment of both transfers and social security revenues and expenditures; and, most importantly, the numbers may be fundamentally misleading in any case.

The difficulty and complexity of measuring the degree of centralisation in part reflects the need to specify carefully the purpose that such a measure is intended to satisfy. Even more, it reflects the inherent problems of measuring the effect of distribution of decision-making powers among the levels of government in a federation in a meaningful way.

There are at least three problems in discussing the degree of centralisation (or decentralisation):

1. how to measure it?
2. how to interpret it once measured? and
3. how to compare such measurements across countries or over time?

International comparisons of any sort are, always treacherous and at best may provide rough guides to possibilities rather than precise instruments of scientific measurement. This dictum seems especially sound when the object of comparison is as nebulous as the degree of centralisation. More importantly, even at best, any conceivable index (or set of indexes) of centralisation can reflect only some aspects of the centralisation (or decentralisation) of power that one is really interested in assessing. No simple quantifiable index can truly measure the degree of effective centralisation of decision-making power, and there is no point in pretending that it can. Moreover, there is no necessary correlation between whatever is measured by those indexes that can be constructed and the "real" degree of centralisation of power in any given country. [42]

There are several practical problems one encounters in measuring centralisation. If centralisation is measured in terms of the share of public revenues collected at such level of government, which of the following revenues should be included: taxes, non-tax revenues, or borrowing? All of the preceding sources or some subset of them should be included? What about the receipts of social security funds? What about those of public enterprises? Are revenues to be counted on an accrual or a cash basis? Are taxes to be credited to the level that administers them, or to that level that makes the decision to levy them? If one state receives the bulk of its revenue from taxes that are in effect exported to consumers in other states or abroad, should this fact affect the calculations? How should constitutional restrictions on taxing power be treated?

Matters are no better with respect to expenditure measures. How should intergovernmental transfers be treated: as expenditures of the donor or by the recipient? Should conditional grants go to the donor and unconditional grants to the recipient? Should additional "credit," so to speak, be given to the donor for recipient expenditures that are required to match donor grants? What about programmes that state or provincial governments in effect administer as agents of the federal government, and for which they are reimbursed? What about the wide variance in the dependence on federal transfers in different parts of the country? There are no simple answers to these or the many other questions that arise in measuring centralisation, particularly if the resulting measure is intended to be treated as a proxy for some more profound sense of decision-making power. Perhaps it was recognition of this last problem that led Breton and Scott to argue a few years ago that the need was to design an index of centralisation that would "provide a measure that has a higher value if the structure of the public sector corresponds to an intuitive notion of 'centralisation' and a low value if that structure is decentralised." [43]

Section 3

3.4 Decentralisation: Issues and Measures

3.4.1 Introduction: In the previous section, we discussed the concept of centralisation. Just opposite to the concept of centralization is the concept of decentralization. In fact, centralization and decentralization are the two sides of the same coin. In the recent years there has been growing emphasis on reducing centralization and increasing decentralization of resources as well as of expenditure. The key question here is whether the evolving fiscal structures will be able to improve public service delivery, both in terms of technical efficiency (i.e. producing more while employing the same amount of resources) and allocative efficiency (in terms of generating the right mix of outputs to achieve national and provincial objectives); promote equity, especially in the light of the gross disparities in access to public services in the past, and in the light of the Constitution which enshrines the progressive realisation of socio-economic rights; encourage economic growth while maintaining internal and external balance in an increasingly integrated world economy; balance nation-building and diversity, provincial autonomy and overarching national objectives; foster good governance, which means not only good substantive outcomes (e.g. rising living standards) but also "good" process (accountability, increased civil society participation).

Clearly these objectives may all too often be conflicting - the question is then to find an "optimal" balance, in terms of political and economic realities. Intergovernmental fiscal arrangements therefore reflect a set of basic political choices, and may alter as societies undergo increasing political integration, or disintegration, as well as changing concepts of citizenship and its associated rights and obligations, changing demands upon government and changing perceptions of community [44] (Leslie,

1988:7). It is believed that decentralization fulfils most of these objectives.

3.4.2 Decentralisation Defined: Decentralisation is not easily defined. [45] Decentralisation can be understood in terms of the assignment of fiscal, political and administrative responsibilities to lower levels of government. It takes many forms and has several dimensions. Indeed, a wide variety of institutional restructurings are encompassed by this label, and several variants may be operating at the same time within a country, and even within a sector.

One widely used distinction is among deconcentration, delegation, and devolution (Rondinelli, 1981 and 1989).

Deconcentration occurs when the central government disperses responsibilities for certain services to its regional branch offices. This does not involve any transfer of authority to lower levels of government and is unlikely to lead to the potential benefits or pitfalls of decentralisation. De-concentration refers to the decentralisation of central government ministries. De-concentration with authority means that regional branches of central government offices are created with some ability to make independent decisions. De-concentration without authority occurs when regional offices are created with no independent capacity for decision-making. All deviations from normal practice must be approved by the centre. The "decentralisation" that has occurred in many unitary countries is actually deconcentration, since independent local governments (which are legally accountable to local constituents) do not exist and local field offices of the central government are simply used to improve the efficiency and effectiveness of service delivery. This is the case in many East Asian countries and, until recently, was the rule in Eastern European countries (Kornai, 1992). Deconcentration can also exist for some functions in federal countries when the central government maintains a strong interest in ensuring delivery of a particular service.

Delegation is intermediate between devolution and de-concentration. Sub-national governments (not branches of the central government) are given responsibility for delivering certain services but are subject to more or less detailed supervision by the central government, which also often provides some or all of the finance for the services in question, usually through some form of fiscal transfer.

Thus, in contrast, the central issue for both delegation and devolution relates to the balancing of central and local interests. Delegation refers to a situation in which the central government transfers responsibility for decision-making and administration of public functions to local governments or semiautonomous organisations that are not wholly controlled by the central government but are ultimately accountable to it. These organisations usually have a great deal discretion in decision-making. This form of decentralisation can be characterised as a principal-agent relationship, with the central government as the principal and the local government as the agent. From this perspective, the main design issue is to ensure that the self-interested agent (the local government or semiautonomous organisation) faces incentives that induce it to act as closely as possible in accordance with the wishes of the principal (the central government).

Finally, devolution, a more extensive form of decentralisation, refers to a situation in which the central government transfers authority for decision-making, finance, and management to quasi-autonomous units of local government. Devolution indicates that the independently established sub-national governments are assigned the responsibility for delivery of a set of public services along with the right to levy taxes and fees to finance the services. Devolved governments have considerable flexibility to select the mix and level of services to provide. Some financial support may be provided by the central government.

Thus, devolution usually transfers responsibilities for services to municipalities that elect their own mayors and councils, raise their own revenues, and have independent authority to make investment decisions. In a devolved system, local governments have clear and legally recognised geographic boundaries over which they exercise authority and within which they perform public functions (Rondinelli, 1998).

The shift in responsibility between tiers of government is underpinned by several fiscal, political and administrative instruments. These define the extent to which intergovernmental relations are deconcentrated, delegated, or devolved.

- Fiscal decentralisation - who sets and collects what taxes, who undertakes which expenditures, and how any "vertical imbalance" is rectified – has been especially prominent in recent discussions in many countries, but as just indicated many of the more fundamental questions relate to political and administrative decentralisation.
- Political decentralisation refers at one level to the extent to which political institutions map the multiplicity of citizen interests onto policy decisions (Inman and Rubinfeld, 1997).
- Administrative decentralisation is concerned with how political institutions, once determined, turn policy decisions into allocative (and distributive) outcomes through fiscal and regulatory actions. The political decision to devolve powers from central government, for example, can only be translated into actual powers being shifted if sub-national governments have the fiscal, political, and administrative capacity to manage this responsibility.

3.4.3 Need for Decentralization: Many rationales for decentralisation may be discerned in the literature and in practice. Not all will be relevant in any one country, nor are they necessarily consistent or equally important to all relevant parties.

The most common theoretical rationale for decentralisation is to attain allocative efficiency in the face of different local preferences for local public goods (Musgrave 1983; Oates, 1972; Tiebout, 1956). Problems may arise with respect to coordination - which is itself costly (Breton and Scott, 1978) – where inter jurisdictional spillovers are important, including stabilisation (Tanzi, 1996; Wildasin, 1997) and distribution (Tresch, 1981). Most World Bank work on decentralisation has focussed on this rationale (World Bank 1988, 1994 and 1997).

Equity and distributional concerns about decentralisation cut both ways. Some analysts argue that in some circumstances local governments achieve such goals more effectively than central governments (Pauly, 1973). Others argue that central redistribution is needed both for effectiveness (Musgrave, 1983) and to overcome biases of local elites (Wilensky, 1974; Inman and Rubinfeld, 1997).

Another view is that, regardless of what local governments may attempt to do in the way of redistribution, their attempts will be frustrated by resource mobility and the openness of the local economy (Buchanan and Wagner, 1971). All these views may be found in different Bank country studies in recent years.

An interesting argument asserts that a primary economic rationale for decentralisation is to improve the "competitiveness" of governments – that is, decentralisation will make local governments try to satisfy the wishes of citizens (Breton, 1996; Salomon, 1987).

Although suggestive, there has been little empirical examination of this idea (Kenyon, 1991; Mueller, 1997). Some Bank work has occasionally recognised "horizontal" competition, particularly with respect to taxation (both at the national and local levels), although it has generally been viewed as a problem rather than a potential benefit. Little attention seems to have been paid to the more troublesome question of "vertical" intergovernmental competition and the nature and enforcement of the rules that may make intergovernmental competition beneficial (Breton, 1996). However, Weingast (1995) proposes that competitive local governments act as checks on the central government to prevent it from confiscating wealth; thus federalism preserves markets.

Another political rationale for decentralisation is that good governments are those closer to the people (Inman and Rubinfeld, 1997; World Bank, 1997). This argument has been closely related to questions of political participation and democracy, but it is still undeveloped in theoretical (Breton, Cassone, Fraschini, 1998) or, especially, empirical terms (Martinez-Vazquez and McNab,1997).

A quite different political rationale for decentralisation is to accommodate pressure for regional autonomy and, hence, perhaps increase the legitimacy and sustainability of heterogeneous national states. In a sense, there may sometimes be a trade off between political and economic stability (Treisman, 1998). The emphasis in many studies on the role of "equalisation" transfers can perhaps be attributed to political stability as well as a more magnanimous desire for inter-jurisdictional equity (Ahmad, 1996).

In principle, devolution tool is supported on the ground that it increases the efficiency of service delivery by allowing citizens to determine more directly the mix and level of services and by providing greater incentives for local resource mobilisation. People are more willing to pay for services closely attuned to their demands, and local officials are, it may be argued, more readily able than central bureaucrats in some distant capital to determine what they are able and willing to pay for. Such efficiency gains from decentralisation benefits may be particularly significant in countries with diverse economies, geography, and tastes for services. [46]

On the other hand, delegation may be efficient when sub-national governments can better administer programmes of national interest (education, health) in ways that better match local economic and social circumstances. The central government determines, in essence, how much should be spent in these areas and perhaps sets minimum or standard levels of provision, but the detailed decisions on exactly what is done are to some extent decided by local governments. The detailed design of intergovernmental fiscal transfers and the degree and nature of central government monitoring may critically determine the balance of central and local influence in such delegated areas of responsibility.

Fiscal decentralisation refers to the degree of discretion devolved to sub-national governments to make decisions on fiscal issues, including overall policy to be pursued, the amount of revenues to be raised and the allocation of available resources.

Fiscal decentralisation exists therefore to the extent that sub-national governments have the power, given to them by the constitution or by particular laws, to raise (some) taxes and carry out spending activities within clearly established legal criteria (Tanzi, 1996:297).

Fiscal decentralisation is concerned with:

- The nature of expenditure responsibilities
- Provincial taxation powers: which taxes have been assigned to sub-national governments and the degree of control sub-national governments have over tax base, tax rates and rate structures and total tax revenue.
- The extent of borrowing powers of provincial governments
- The role and nature of intergovernmental transfers

3.4.4 Implications of Decentralisation: For policy-makers and their advisers, the multidimensional aspects of decentralisation – the dispersion of fiscal, political, and administrative powers – suggests three implications that heavily influence the context for thinking through decentralisation.

First, because decentralisation can change the mobilisation and allocation of public resources, it can affect a wide range of issues from services delivery to poverty reduction to macroeconomic stability. (This is called a "cross-cutting" issue).

Second, the management of decentralisation requires intimate knowledge of local institutions and a nuanced understanding of the process of decentralisation – that is, what is driving decentralisation in a country (and sector) and which stakeholders are involved.

Third, limited empirical evidence exists about what works and what does not.

Together these three factors pose a daunting challenge for those responsible for designing and managing decentralisation.

3.4.5 Approaches to Decentralisation: Bird (1986) points out, that there are broadly two approaches to fiscal decentralisation. The stimulus for fiscal decentralisation in the top-down approach is central government's desire to achieve its allocative goals more efficiently by devolving authority to local levels, or to make shift deficits downwards. The main criterion in this case is how fiscal decentralisation serves national policy goals. The bottom-up approach emphasises political values - local responsiveness and increased participation - as well as allocative efficiency. In this case the criteria for evaluating fiscal decentralisation would be different to the top-down approach (these could include provincial autonomy and diversity in delivery of services such as education.

In the economics literature, the unitary state is invariably employed as the benchmark against which the need for national grants to provincial governments is judged. By this token, a given set of decentralised fiscal arrangements is well designed if it closes any fiscal gaps.

The economic literature has tended to focus on efficiency and equity issues, without incorporating autonomy and diversity. In practice, fiscal institutional arrangements – and their degree of decentralisation – will be the outcome of the interplay between all these factors. Any configuration of fiscal structures along the decentralisation-centralisation continuum will reflect the balance of centrifugal and centripetal forces at that point, and will of course change over time.

Typically, in the fiscal federalism literature, specific institutional arrangements are abstracted from, and the locus of decision-making within the various levels of government is the primary focus of analysis. The rationale is that from an economic/financial perspective, as opposed to a constitutional/administrative perspective, the difference between unitary and more federal models may be reduced to differences in degree of centralisation/decentralisation of decision-making. The argument is that irrespective of whether a state is formally unitary or federal, in any multi-tiered government, an array of fiscal problems of central/local finance will arise. These include which functions should be assigned to each level, how these should be financed and relationships between the various levels. Furthermore, these fiscal problems essentially differ in degree rather than kind in unitary states and federations.

This approach ignores the fact that the specific institutional and political features of intergovernmental relations in general may have impact on the functioning and efficacy of fiscal arrangements. They generate incentives and disincentives which may either enhance or detract from the effectiveness of the fiscal framework and overall public sector performance.

Successful performance of any fiscal system depends on how effectively it can integrate political priorities into medium-term planning and appropriate resource allocations to achieve desired outcomes. This is arguably even more crucial in a decentralised system because of its greater inherent complexity. The efficacy of fiscal structures per se cannot be evaluated without considering the related mechanisms they need to support their operation. The study of intergovernmental fiscal relations therefore cannot be pursued in isolation of executive and legislative relations.

However, there is no necessary correlation between the various dimensions of decentralisation described above. Some degree of decentralisation of fiscal decision-making powers does not automatically mean that the administration of those functions will also be decentralised. For instance, some latitude for determining tax policy may be allocated to the provinces. However tax collection and administration may remain at national level due to economies of scale (e.g. in terms of computers and unique taxpayer numbers) as well as lower compliance costs. If the proportion of revenues going to the provinces is large enough, this may reduce national government's incentive to apply great enough tax effort. This in fact happened in countries such as China.

3.4.6 Measures of Decentralisation: The Transfer Mechanism and Provincial Autonomy If the sub national government's own revenues are an insignificant proportion of its expenditure; this might erode sub national government's fiscal autonomy. However, constitutionally guaranteed grants emerging from the revenue sharing process may be regarded as a close substitute for lower tier governments own tax sources. An expanded definition which includes constitutionally guaranteed grants might be more analytically useful under those circumstances.

McLure (1994) points out that in the US, sub national governments have their own tax administrations and substantial revenue capacity and intergovernmental grants are relatively insignificant. The distinction between own revenues and other revenues is therefore clear. But where revenue sharing is of critical importance as in Indian system, a more meaningful definition would extend the conventional concept of own revenues to include grants available with certainty, as a matter of law and on terms known in advance. The crucial distinction under these circumstances is therefore between revenues from taxes raised by or for sub national governments as well as intergovernmental transfers guaranteed by law and predictable since they are formula based; and Un-predictable and ad hoc grants, not guaranteed by law.

Another fundamental concept is the difference between "incremental" and "non-incremental" own revenues. Own incremental funds or revenues are funds that sub national governments raise through actions they take, such as altering the tax base, tax rate or in the case of matching grants, the sub national government may choose its level of expenditure in order to attract matching funds. So tax surcharges would be incremental own revenue since sub national government could choose thc rate at which the surcharge is imposed. However, revenue sharing grants would be non-incremental. Finally, own incremental funds may be derived from taxes administered by sub national government or administered on behalf of it by higher level government (Table 3.8).

The distinction between incremental and non-incremental revenues is important because they create different incentives for politicians and voters. Fiscal discipline is enhanced if any additional spending undertaken by a sub national jurisdiction is also raised by that jurisdiction. Discipline is undermined if expenditures are not funded by the jurisdictions own incremental revenues.

Table 3.8: The Concept of Own Incremental Revenues

Is this an incremental source of revenue? Can the sub national government affect revenues by changing the tax base, rate or administrative effort? Can it affect the amount of grant it receives?	Own revenues? Is this source of revenue from taxes administered by the sub national government? If it is from a higher level of government, is it guaranteed by law and predictable?		
	NO	YES	
NO	1. Not own revenue	3. Own non-incremental revenue	
YES	2. Not own revenue	4. Own incremental revenue	4a. Self-administered
			4b. Centrally administered

Source: McLure, (1994): 31

Thus, a proportion of the transfers that provinces receive (i.e. the basic bloc grant) may very well be considered, to all intents and purposes, as equivalent to "own" revenues. This means that provinces may not be as dependent as a first impression would indicate.

But a further division might be between conditional and unconditional grants. Clearly a constitutionally guaranteed unconditional grant is a better substitute for own tax revenue than earmarked grants, and more conducive to fiscal autonomy. By this token, once conditionality is attached to grants, the fiscal autonomy of provincial governments will be reduced. Provincial priority-setting processes may thus be limited by the introduction of mandated spending or nationally defined minimum standards.

While measuring decentralization, it is important to bear in mind the above concepts.

As discussed earlier fiscal decentralisation is just the opposite of the term centralization. Hence in a very simple manner it can be stated that fiscal decentralisation is:

FdI = 100 - IC

FdI = Index of decentralisation

IC = index of centralisation

However, in a three tier system if one wants to measure fiscal decentralisation one has to measure: fiscal autonomy, revenue dependency, revenue decentralisation, expenditure decentralisation and the ratio of revenue to expenditure at various levels of government i.e. centre, states and Local bodies.

Fiscal Autonomy (F_a) is reflected through share of own revenue (as explained above) of different levels of government in the total income of that government.

F_a = (Ori /tri)x 100,

Ori = tax revenue + non tax revenue + shared and assigned taxes or share in the total revenue of the upper layer government (Revenue sharing)

Tri = total resources of the ith government

Larger the share of own revenue in the total, greater will be the autonomy.

In order to understand overall fiscal autonomy one has to work out the above ratio on revenue account, capital account and aggregate account at the Local/ state level and compare the same with the ratios worked out at the sate/ centre level.

If the lower level governments have large gap in their resources compared to their liabilities they have to depend on the higher level government and hence their autonomy gets restricted.

Revenue Dependency is measured by the percentage share of grants received from upper layers of governments in the total resources of the lower level governments. Higher the percentage of grant higher will be the degree of dependency.

Rev Dep = G/Tri

G = grant

Tri = total resources of the ith government.

This is again a sort of mirror image of the fiscal autonomy. If the grants are of discretionary nature and are meant for specific purpose or tied or conditional the dependency gets accentuated.

Revenue decentralisation can be measured by the percentage share of the different layers of governments in the aggregate resources of the nation i.e. centre+states+Local bodies resources.

R dec = $(Ori / \Sigma Tri) \times 100$

Larger the share of the lower tier greater will be the degree of decentralisation

Expenditure Decentralisation can be measured in the same manner as decentralisation of Revenue by replacing revenue with expenditure

Thus,

ExDec = $(exi / \Sigma Texi) \times 100$

The World Bank (September 27, 2000) in its report, "Overview of Rural Decentralization in India", Volume 1. Calculated four main indicators of fiscal decentralisation and autonomy in revenue and spending. These are:

Fiscal autonomy: share of local revenue from own sources in total local income.

Revenue dependency: share of grants from higher level governments in total local income.

Revenue decentralisation: ratio of local revenue from own sources to total state government revenue.

Expenditure Decentralisation is ratio of total local expenditure to state government expenditure. The studies draw the following conclusions for Indian states:

Fiscal autonomy is very low: Fiscal autonomy measures the extent to which local bodies can raise their revenues independently i.e. on their own account. Fiscal autonomy is calculated by dividing PRIs' (Panchayat Raj Institutions) own revenues (non-tax and tax revenue, including assigned and shared taxes) by their total revenue income. The results for the PRIs show that the degree of fiscal autonomy is very low for PRIs levels in most states, varying between only 6% in Rajasthan to 19% in Madhya Pradesh). Block and Zilla Panchayats which often do not have their own income other than fees, user charges, etc., are heavily dependent on intergovernmental transfers, most of which are tied to very specific requirements or provided as matching grants. GPs (Gram Panchayats) after the constitutional amendment, have the right to raise tax revenues and have a relatively higher fiscal autonomy reaching a level of about half of total revenue in Andhra Pradesh and Madhya Pradesh. The fiscal capacity of the different levels of PRIs varies enormously between different states. To a great extent, this reflects the differences in the functions of these local bodies. The GPs are the dominating level in Kerala, Madhya Pradesh and Uttar Pradesh. The same holds for Maharasthra for which data was insufficient to present an exact number. In Andhra Pradesh, both, the block level and the ZP are relatively strong. Rajasthan is the only state where the block has the highest share in total PRI budget.

Revenue dependency is high: Revenue dependency measures the degree to which local bodies depend on transfers for their incomes. Revenue dependency is almost a mirror image of fiscal autonomy. [47] It measures the share of grants from higher level governments in total local income. Although revenue dependency of PRIs has declined somewhat in a number of states, it is still considerably above 50 % in all states analyzed. In Kerala revenue dependency has increased considerably because state transfers have increased. However, the calculations -as those for fiscal autonomy -are based on actual budgets, i.e. they do not exclude revenue items such as tied grants which are not controlled by PRIs and hence should not be taken into account. [48]

Revenue decentralisation is low: Revenue Decentralization measures the importance of local bodies in total government revenues. These are calculated as the share of local government's own revenue in total (centre, state, local) government own revenues (Table 3.9), these figures have to be interpreted with particular care. Local government includes both PRIs and municipalities. For the latter, no aggregated budgets by state were available and had to be estimated. Per capita own revenue of a 1997/98 sample was used as the basis for estimating income of urban local authorities. The sample includes 250 municipalities, which disaggregated by state leads to outliers and distortions. For example, the sample municipalities in Maharasthra had per capita income of Rs. 1928, while the sample average is only 670 Rs per head and for the other states, the numbers are even lower.. Revenue decentralization is low by international standards. The calculations show a share of local revenue roughly between 1 % and 5 % for most states. These numbers include both rural and urban development funds. On per capita basis, these ratios would be lower because majority of the population is in rural areas, but urban areas account for most of the revenues. For example, in Maharasthra, local bodies account for 17% of government revenues. However, share of PRIs in the share of local revenues is only 5%.

Expenditure decentralisation is increasing only slightly. India has decentralised considerably from the centre to the state level over the last one and a half decades, but fiscal decentralisation to local authorities is lagging. Since the mid nineties, there has only been a slight increase in expenditure decentralisation to the rural areas. Table 3.10 shows, that the share of PRIs in total centre, state and local rural spending increased only from 3.3 % in 1994-95 to 5 % at the end if the nineties, measured as a simple is

Table 3.9: Revenue Decentralisation by Selected States, 1997-98 (per cent)

	Andhra Pradesh	Kerala	Madhya Pradesh	Maharashtra	Rajasthan	Uttar Pradesh	Average*
Centre	41.7	39.3	40.7	35.0	40.9	45.2	41.0
State	56.1	56.2	56.1	48.2	56.4	54.1	54.0
Local	3.2	4.5	3.2	16.8	2.7	0.7	5.0
Total	100	100	100	100	100	100	100
Own revenue of rural as % of total local own revenue	36	40	38	5	9	25	24.0
Rural Population in % of total population	73	55	61	77	77	80	73.0

Note: Averages are weighted by state population.

Source: Bank estimates based on official data from the states/World Bank: Op. cit. September 2000.

Table 3.10: Share of PRIs in Total Government Expenditure for Rural areas by Selected States, Actual Budget Figures, 1994-95 to 1999-2000 (per cent)

	1994-95	1995-96	1996-97	1997-98	1998-99	1999-00
Andhra Pradesh	9.2	8.7	9.3	9.9	10.5	11.0
Kerala	n.a	4.5	7.1	7.8	11.1	11.9
Madhya Pradesh	2.5	3.5	4.5	9.4	6.7	7.0
Maharasthra	6.7	7.6*	8.4	8.5	8.3	8.3
Rajasthan	3.3	4.2	4.6	3.8	4.2	4.6
Uttar Pradesh	1.9	2.0	1.7	2.0	2.1	2.2
Simple average	3.3	3.9	4.1	5.0	4.8	4.9

Note: *not available, but simple average of 1994-95 and 1996-97 figures. Central and State government expenditure for the rural areas in the particular states plus PRI expenditure adds up to 100 %.

Source: World Bank's Own calculations based on official data from State sources. World Bank, Op. cit. September 2000.

considerable, ranging from 11.9 % (Kerala) to only 2.2 % (Uttar Pradesh) in 1999-2000. [49] The level of expenditure decentralisation in India is very low.

Firstly, not all the expenditures accounted for in PRI budgets are actually controlled by the elected authorities. Often, PRI act merely as a channel or at most as a supervisory body for state or central government schemes (sometimes having to match them with own resources). For instance, in Andhra Pradesh, the share of PRI expenditures in total Government spending in rural areas drops from 10.5% to 5.3%, if one deducts those funds that are most clearly not controlled by PRIs.47 It is likely, that there are other non-identified budget items which are not effectively decided upon by the ZP, P8 or GP. Hence, in all probability, in all states analysed but Kerala, the share of local authorities' spending is 5 % or below.

Secondly, when comparing India with other countries one has to take into account the immense size of the country. Most Indian states compare to relatively large countries in terms of their size of population. A district, the highest' local' level in India, often has several million people, and would be comparable in population size to states in other countries (e.g. Brazil). [50] Fiscal decentralisation to the truly local, i.e. GP level, is still extremely low in India, in particular in the rural areas. Data for 1998-99 shows, that with the exception of Kerala, GPs have virtually no fiscal strength. Table 3.11 shows, that even when using the actual budget figure, fiscal decentralization to village authorities ranges only between 0.6 % (Rajasthan) and 3.6 % (Madhya Pradesh) in the states analyzed, Kerala being the exception with 7.6 %. This translates into expenditures by GPs of less than 100 Rs. (US$2) per capita per year in most of the states.

Thirdly, even though most pros have no technical staff, a great share of total expenditure is spent on general administrative services. As shown above, the share of General Administrative Services in Total Expenditures of GPs, PSs, and ZPs amounts to as much as 90 % of a local government's budget. All these aspects confirm the field observations that PRI institutions in most states

Table 3.11: Expenditure of PRI Levels (actual budget) by Selected States in 1998-99 (per cent)

	Andhra Pradesh	Kerala	Madhya Pradesh	Maharashtra	Rajasthan	Uttar Pradesh
Share in total government expenditure in rural areas (%)						
Zilla Panchayat	5.7	1.8	1.9	7.6	0.1	0.4
Panchayat Samitis	3.5	1.7	1.2	0	3.5	0.1
Grama Panchayat	1.3	7.6	3.6	0.7	0.6	1.5
PRI,Total	10.5	11.1	6.7	8.3	4.2	2.1
Expenditure in Rs. Per capita						
Zilla Panchayat	324	117	93	470	3	19
Panchayat Samitis	196	112	59	0	193	6
Grama Panchayat	73	505	177	42	33	70
PRI,Total	593	734	329	512	229	95

Note: Central and State government expenditure for the rural areas in the particular state plus PRI expenditure adds up to 100%.

Source: World Bank's Own calculations based on official data from State sources. World Bank, Op. cit. September 2000.

have virtually no fiscal powers at all. The SFC report for Rajasthan (p.65) puts this very clearly by stating: "For lack of their own resource base to determine d function-related, local need based expenditure pattern, these institutions [PRIs] have merely been reduced to executing arm at the field level, of the external funding agencies."

Overall, there is only minimal fiscal decentralisation even after a decade of the 73rd Amendment and since the SFC recommendations were issued. In all seven states, budgetary resources of pros are very limited, with few taxes and fees and high dependence on transfers. The total shares of revenues and expenditures which accrue to PRIs as a percentage of all in-state revenues and expenditures ranges from about 1% to 4%. This is very low by international standards. Even more disturbingly, a great share of the funds reported in pros' budgets are not under the control of the locally elected authorities. Most of the intergovernmental transfers which are accounted as 'grants' in the PRIs' books, are for CSS with no or very limited discretion of local authorities. They may be administered by 'PRI' staff who, in practice, report to line departments rather than PRIs.

Thus, Fiscal Decentralisation in India can quantitatively be assessed by revenue and expenditure shares of the three levels of the government. Although it is difficult to bring out qualitative aspects of decentralisation from any quantitative measure, the shares of different levels of government in raising revenue and incurring expenditures provide insights into the working of a fiscal federalism in any country. In India for the first time, the report of the Finance Commission (India, 2000) has put together data on revenues and expenditures of local bodies and these estimates are combined with the revenues and expenditures of Union and State governments to get a comprehensive picture of fiscal decentralization in Indian federalism.

Govinda Rao [51] in his paper brings out certain important features of decentralisation in India. The relative roles of Centre, State and local governments in urban and rural areas in raising revenues and incurring expenditures show there is asymmetry between expenditure and revenue decentralisation (Table 3.12). Fiscal federalism in India brings out that decentralization is mainly in incurring expenditures and not in raising revenues. Thus, the Central government could exercise control over one-third of the revenues, but its share in raising revenues is two-thirds. In contrast, State and local governments raised only about one-third of revenues but the revenue accrual to them was about two-thirds. Each of the three levels incurred about one-third of the expenditures. At local level, urban local bodies incurred 28 per cent of total expenditures and the share of rural local bodies was less than 4 per cent. Even within the urban local bodies, the expenditures were mainly in Andhra Pradesh and Maharasthra. Like in all federal systems, the States have significant revenue raising powers. The States raise 35 per cent of total revenues, which finances 51 per cent of their expenditures. The expenditure share of the State governments after giving grants to local governments is 35 per cent. In social services, particularly in education and health sectors, the expenditure share of the States is more than 80 per cent and in economic services, it is about 50 per cent. Of course, the States still have to depend on central transfers to finance a significant portion of their expenditures. Almost 37 per cent of States' revenues accrue from transfers.

The asymmetry in revenue and expenditure decentralization is particularly glaring at local government level. As mentioned above, total revenue raised by local bodies was just about 0.6 per cent of GDP or 2 per cent of total revenues. In fact, Panchayats raised a negligible amount of 0.05 per cent of GDP. They received 1.3 per cent of GDP as transfers. Their share in total expenditures was less than 4 per cent. Thus, over quarter million local governments in rural India incur less than 4 per cent of total expenditures and this includes expenditures on core as well as discretionary services. The expenditures incurred by them also include expenditures on various centrally sponsored schemes such as poverty alleviation and social development programs implemented through the local governments.

Table 3.12: Revenue and Expenditure Decentralisation in India: 1997-98 (per cent)

	Revenue Collection	Revenue Accrual	Expenditure on Core Services	Other Expenditure	Total Expenditure	Own Revenue/ Expenditure
I. Per cent of GSDP						
Center	11.40	6.80			11.20	
States	6.30	10.90			12.30	
Local Bodies	0.60	2.10	6.80	4.58	11.40	
Urban Local Bodies	0.50	0.80	6.70	3.30	10.00	
Rural Local Bodies	0.04	1.30	0.10	1.28	1.38	
District Panchayats	n	0.60	0.06	0.57	0.62	
Taluk Panchayats	n	0.30	0.01	0.40	0.41	
Village Panchayats	0.04	0.40	0.04	0.32	0.35	
Total	18.30	19.80			34.80	
II. Per Cent of Total Expenditures						
Center	62.45	34.43			32.12	102.05
States	34.56	55.03			35.26	51.44
Local Bodies	2.99	10.53	100.00	100.00	32.62	4.81
Urban Local Bodies	2.74	4.07	98.49	72.10	28.65	5.02
Rural Local Bodies	0.24	6.46	1.51	27.90	3.96	3.23

Contd...

District Panchayats	0.03	3.21	0.81	12.33	1.78	0.79
Taluk Panchayats	0.01	1.44	0.14	8.67	1.17	0.55
Village panchayats	0.21	1.82	0.56	6.90	1.02	10.60
Total	**100.00**	**100.00**	**100.00**	**100.00**	**100.00**	**52.49**

Notes: n = negligible.

States' total expenditure has been netted out transfers to local bodies.

Center's expenditure is net of Grants and Loans to States and Union Territories.

Core services are water supply, street lighting, sanitation and roads.

Sources: Rao, M.G, Op cit; Public Finance Statistics 1999-2000, Ministry of Finance, Government of India, 2000; Report of the Eleventh Finance Commission, Ministry of Finance, Government of India. 2000.

Thus, despite constitutional recognition local governments in India do not raise significant revenues and have to depend on higher level governments. As State governments themselves are faced with several resource constraints, the revenue accruals to the local bodies are not adequate to enable them to effectively deliver the required standards of public services. A predominant part of the transfers is for specific purposes, mainly to implement centrally sponsored schemes. Thus the type of decentralisation at local levels seen in India may be characterised as de-concentration rather than decentralisation despite the Constitutional recognition of the local government.

End Notes and References

1. The analytical underpinning of this approach is set out at length in Hunter, supra footnote 14, at Chapter 4, which is basically the same as his "Vertical Intergovernmental Financial Imbalance: A Framework for Evaluation", 32 Finanzarchiv, No.3, 1974, p.481-92. Quoted by Richard Bird in *Federal Finance in Comparative Perspective,* Chapter 8, p. 216.

2. Russel Mathews, 'Revenue Sharing in Federal Systems', Australian National University, Centre for Research on Federal Relations, Canberra, 1980, p. 10.

3. G. Thimmaiah "Vertical Intergovernmental Financial imbalances: A Restatements" (1976, No. 2) 34, Finanzarchive, pp. 497-508.

4. G. Thimmaiah, "A Critique of the Finance Commission", Wheeler Publication, 1981, Allahabad, Ch. 2, pp. 7-10.

5. Op. cit.

6. G. Thimmaiah "Vertical Intergovernmental Financial Imbalances: A Restatements" (1976, No2) 34, Finanzarchive, pp. 497-508.

7. Also See: (a) G. Thimmaiah, "Vertical Intergovernmental Financial Imbalances: A Restatements" (1976, No. 2) 34, Finanzarchive, pp. 497-508. (b) Walter Hettich & Staneley Winer "Vertical Imbalances in the Fiscal systems of Federal States", Working Paper No. 56-82-83, Graduate School of Industrial Administration, Carnegie – Mellon University, Pittsburgh, July 1983.

Note: Also refer to DAL Auld "Optimal Fiscal Balance and provisional – Local Finance"

Occasional paper No.17 (Canberra: Australian National University, Centre for Research on Federal Financial Relations, 1981) and Douglas – G. Hartle, "the impacts of New Tax Policies on National Unity", in the US-Advisory Commission on Inter-governmental Relations, in Search of Balance (Washington).

8. G. Thimmaiah and Hemlata Rao, 'Finance Commission and Centre-State Financial Relations,' Ashish Publishing House, New Delhi, 1986.

9. Richard M bird, Federal finance in Comparative Perspective, Canadian tax Foundation, 1990, p.13.

10. In the words of Harold L. Wilensky, for example, centralisation is good because "political elites who embrace the welfare state in centralised polities can better overcome resistance to the necessary taxes and expenditures than elites in decentralised polities." *The Welfare State and Equality*, University of California Press, Berkeley, 1975, p.52.

11. See Arnold J. Heidenheimer, Hugh Heclo, and Carolyn Teich Adams, 'Comparative Public Policy' ST. Martin's Press, New York, 1975, p.272.

12. On the "concentration process", see Alan T. Peacock and Jack Wiseman, 'The Growth of Public Expenditure in the United Kingdom', 2nd ed., George Allen and Unwin, London, 1967, p.29-30 and Chapter 6. "Popitz' Law" is cited, for example, in Horst Zimmerman, 'Finanz – und Steuerbelastungs – Vergleiche, internationale,' in Handworterbuch der Wirt-schaftswissenschaft (Stuttgart: Gustav Fischer, 1980), 119 and 'Studies in Comparative Federalism: West Germany,' Advisory Commission on Intergovernmental Relations, 1981, p.62 (The original reference is to a 1927 article by J. Popitz). For an earlier discussion of this question with particular reference to Canada, see Bird, supra footnote 12, at Chapter 5 and 'The Growth of Government Spending in Canada', Canadian Tax Foundation, Toronto, 1970, Chapter 9.

13. Mancur Olson, 'The Political Economy of Comparative Growth', in Dennis C. Muller ed. *The Political Economy of Growth,* (New Heaven: Yale University Press), 1983.

14. See, for example, Geoffrey Brennau and James M. Buchanan, *The Power to Tax,* (Cambridge, Massachusetts, Cambridge University Press), 1980, p.184-85.

15. Mancur Oslon, 'The Political Economy of Comparative Growth', in Dennis C. Muller ed. *The Political Economy of Growth,* (New Heaven: Yale University Press), 1983, 7-52, at 23. Olson's views are further developed in his 'The Rise and Decline of Nations', (New Heaven: Yale University Press), 1983, especially Chapter 6, although it should be noted that the nowhere discusses the role of federal institutions, as such, very clearly.

16. See, for example, Geoffrey Brennan and James M. Buchanan, 'The Power to Tax', Cambridge University Press, Massachusetts, Cambridge, 1980, p.184-85.

17. Preston King, *Federalism and federation*, (Baltimore, Johns Hopkins University Press, 1982.

18. Oates, Wallace. *Fiscal Federalism*, The Herrace series, New York 1972.Chapter v, PP 195-213.

19. Calculated from Morris Beck, 'Government Spending,' Praeger, 1981, New York, 60-68.

20. See, Wallace E. Oates, 'Fiscal Federation' Harcourt Brace Jovanovich, 1972, New York, 210 and 'Searching for Leviathan: An Empirical Study,' Working Paper No.83-18, University of Maryland, Department of Economics, College Park, 1983.

21. Frederic, L. Pryor, 'Public Expenditures in Communist and Capitalist Nations,' George Allen and Unwin Ltd., London, 1968.

22. Oates, supra footnote 26, at 230-32.

23. Warren Nutter, 'Growth of Government in the West,' American Enterprise Institute for Public Policy Research, Washington, 1978, 90-94. More or less the same results emerge from a follow-up to the Oates study reported in Werner W. Pommerehne, 'Quantitative Aspects of Federalism: A Study of Six Countries,' in Oates, ed., supra footnote 1, 275-355, at 306.

24. At most, such studies suggest that (1) central government finances tend to constitute a relatively smaller proportion of total public sector activities in federal countries than in unitary countries and that (2) there is no apparent trend toward centralisation in recent years. Indeed, there may even be a slight trend to decentralisation in all developed countries, whether federal or not. Most such studies are properly cautious with regard to their theoretical expectations on both these points, the trustworthiness of the numbers employed, and the weight of interpretation their findings can bear.

25. D.G. Davies, 'International Comparisons of Tax Structures in Federal and Unitary Countries,' Australian National University, Centre for Research on Federal Financial Relations, Canberra, 1976, 37. Davies included the six advanced federations in his sample along with India and Nigeria.

26. William G. Watson, 'Theories of the Growth of Public Expenditures in the Industrialised Countries', (unpublished), 1983, Chapter 2.

27. J.S.H. Hunter, "Vertical Intergovernmental Financial Imbalances: A Framework for Evaluation," Finanzarchive, 1973-74 Vol. 32, 1974, pp. 481- 492.

28. Ibid, (p. 481).

29. In this event, vertical imbalances would be absolute and the States would be unable to vary revenues in response to voter preferences at the State level according to the need

30. Hunter, Op. cit.

31. Hunter, Vertical Inter-governmental Financial Imbalance: A Framework for Evaluation, "Finanzandrive, Vol. 32, no. 3, 1974, pp 481-492

32. G. Thimmaiah, "Vertical Intergovernmental Financial Imbalances: A Restatement"; Finanzarchive, Band 34, 3, 1976 pp. 497-508.

33. Thimmaiah. Op. cit. p. 498.

34. These expressions were used by the British budgetary practice prior to 1965. Hunter does not make any explicit statement in this respect

35. Horizontal federal fiscal imbalances referred to a fiscal situation of the individual federating units when the extent of deficit budgetary non-correspondence between the states' own revenue and expenditure varies from state to state owing to differences in their fiscal capacity, level of economic development etc.

36. Albert Breton and Anthony Scott, 'The Economic Constitution of Federal States', University of Toronto Press, 1978. Chapter 3, p.22-30.

37. The index might also be adapted to give weight to the amount of private expenditure regulated at each level of jurisdiction. That is not attempted here.

38. Richard M. Bird, Federal Finance in Comparative Perspective, Canadian Tax Foundation, Toronto, 1986, p.13-21

39. 'Switzerland: A Survey,' *The Economist*, October 30, 1982, supplement, at 7.

40. Oates, supra footnote 26, at 196.

41. R. Bired, Op. cit ,p18.

42. For yet another discussion of this problem, this time in the context of developing countries, see Richard M. Bird, 'Central-Local Fiscal Relations and the Provision of Urban Public Services,' Research Monograph No.30, Australian National University, Centre for Research on Federal Financial Relations, Canberra, 1989, 5-9, in which the

apparent lack of connection between fiscal and "political power" indexes of centralisation is stressed.

43. Albert Breton and Anthony Scotti, 'The Economic Constitution of Federal States', University of Toronto Press, Toronto, 1978, p.22.

44. Fiscal arrangements are often adapted in order to accommodate the often divergent aims of extending national citizenship rights while preserving or developing distinctive provincial communities

45. Jennie Litvack, Junaid Ahmad, Richard Bird, Rethinking Decentralisation in Developing Countries, Sector Studies Series, The World Bank, Washington D.C., pp. 4-9

46. It is sometimes argued that devolution may provide a better overall framework for the development of private market forces since devolved governments have greater incentives to compete for businesses and residents by selecting an efficient set of revenue sources and service levels, but this point is subject to considerable controversy (see Kenyon and Kincaid 1991) and cannot be discussed further here.

47. In many cases, the figures for fiscal autonomy and revenue dependency add up to 100%. However, additional income sources besides own revenues and grant income such as loans change the picture for some PRIs.

48. As discussed above, the exclusion of certain budget items requires precise knowledge about the various schemes and how they are implemented in practice. While a attempt has been made for other indicators, the picture of fiscal autonomy and revenue dependency presented here is based on actual budgets.

49. The figures computed in Table 12 ensure that (i) total centre government expenditure can be separated between states according to their share in total population, and (ii) total centre and state government expenditure can be separated between 'rural' and 'urban' according to the rural and urban shares in population, the share of total 'rural' expenditure

50. Clearly, focussing entirely on population is a simplifying and crude approach. The size population is not the only criteria based on which to form constituencies and many other factors such as social and cultural aspects, political and economic issues, historical and geographical considerations, population density, etc. should play their role in shaping an 'optimal' area of governance on the various levels within (and between) countries. However, population certainly is one of the most important single criteria when focussing on issues of the degree of accountability or distance between citizens and their government.

51. Rao, Govinda M, *Fiscal Decentralisation in Indian Federalism*, ISEC, Bangalore, 2000

4

ISSUES IN HORIZONTAL FISCAL IMBALANCES

In the literature on Federal Finance, more than Vertical Fiscal Imbalances, it is the Horizontal Fiscal Imbalance (HFI) that has received lot of attention.. At the disaggregate level of different State Governments, though all the State Governments would face vertical federal fiscal imbalance, different State Governments face it in different degrees because of their varying revenue potential and expenditure needs. Horizontal federal imbalance adds to the vertical federal fiscal imbalance and magnifies the fiscal needs of different State Governments. Therefore, the gap between revenues and expenditures of State Governments is required to be filled by the financial transfers form the federal government. It is for this reasons that the issue relating to Horizontal fiscal Imbalances has received a lot of attention in the literature on Fiscal federalism. The meaning of horizontal Fiscal imbalance, the causes of such imbalances, the need to reduce these imbalance and the fiscal tools to reduce theses imbalances are discussed very widely in the literature. These are briefly dealt with in this chapter.

4.1 Meaning of Horizontal Fiscal Imbalance (HFI)

The horizontal fiscal imbalances mean differences in the revenue raising capacity and fiscal need among the similarly situated states i.e. across the states. Horizontal fiscal imbalance is also inevitable mainly because of diversity in natural resources and disparities in economic structure and socio-economic levels of development of federating units. This determines on the one hand the varying degree of fiscal capacity and on the other hand the fiscal need of the states. Horizontal fiscal imbalance coupled with the vertical fiscal imbalance, increases the need for federal fiscal transfers to the states in any federation.

The differences in fiscal capacity could be due to various factors like differences in per capita income, levels of development, sectoral composition of the economy, poverty level, consumption pattern, and so on, Differences in fiscal need arises due to differences in the cost of providing goods and services, need for providing socio-economic infrastructure, due to differences in the tastes and priorities of the local people composition of population, area of the state and so on.

Thus, the horizontal fiscal imbalances arise due to the differences in the fiscal capacity, and due to varied expenditure need.

4.2 Need to Reduce Horizontal Fiscal Imbalances

As explained in chapter 1, there are several motivating factors to form a federation. Apart from having common defence facilities, accessibility to unified common national market and getting best use of the scarce resources of the country, a federation also aims at achieving 'equality of all citizens', i.e., no discrimination is made between different people on the basis of their state of residence. However, all the federating states are not equal in terms of economic development, social development, natural resource endowments, and fiscal capacity and so on. Because of these and several other factors, there exists a serious regional disparity. Some states are backward, while some are developed. One of the objectives of federal government is to reduce such disparities by helping the backward states in a special way. The very objective of forming a federation necessitates reducing horizontal fiscal imbalances. All citizens, irrespective of their state of residence are expected to make sacrifice by way of taxation uniformly and receive the benefits from public goods equally.

It is believed that if the federal fiscal imbalances tend to operate discriminately between States and the expected hopes and aspirations which initiated the formation of a federation fail to materialise, instability sets in. Instability of a federation manifests itself in economic instability of its constituent States and the consequent dissatisfaction or even frustration with the operation of fiscal federalism. If these symptoms of instability are not recognised early and corrective measures are not taken, the federation may eventually break down.

The federal government is, therefore, expected to use federal fiscal transfers to minimise wide inter-State disparities by helping the backward states in a special way for the following reasons:

First, the federal government should use the federal financial transfers to off-set unequal impact of its own taxation as well as expenditure policies on the budgets of the constituent States. Otherwise discriminatory impact of taxation and expenditure policies on the budgets of the poorer States may frustrate them and create the problem of instability of a federation.

Secondly, the federal government should use federal financial transfers to offset adverse impact of inter-State spillovers of expenditure benefits and tax costs of the State Governments. If such spillovers are unequal between States, inter-State fiscal imbalances result and they may give rise to inter-State conflicts and instability of a federation. Such imbalances should be minimised by the federal government through appropriate federal financial transfers.

Thirdly, the federal financial transfers should be used to ensure a minimum level of essential public services to all the citizens all over the federation. Such provision may not be possible in all States because of varying fiscal capacity and fiscal needs of different States. Therefore, federal financial transfer should be linked to the fiscal needs of the State Governments for ensuring minimum level of essential public services.

Finally, with a view to reducing inter-State economic disparities, the federal government will have to use federal financial transfers in such a way as to generate economic activities in poorer States. This, in other words, means the federal government will have to interfere in the process and pattern of development of the constituent States with a view to reducing wide inter-State economic disparities.

4.3 Federal Fiscal Transfers: Principles and Criteria

Federal political organisations involve distribution of powers and responsibilities between the federal government and the federating units. When gaps between needs and resources appear they are sought to be bridged through federal fiscal transfers. But the size of divisible pool and the criteria for devolution has often given rise to a good deal of controversy. Consequently, the basis of federal fiscal transfers has been modified from time to time to suit the needs and objectives of changing complexion of federal polity. The criteria for devolution have also become more refined and sophisticated.

The broad objectives of a federation are:

1. Objective of Equity: This objective envisages that the federal fiscal relations would lead to horizontal fiscal balances. The fiscal system should result in equalization of fiscal pressure on similarly situated persons (This is an individualistic approach to federalism).

2. Objective of Equalisation: The diversity and disparity factors such as distribution of natural resources, climate, soil and so on and also the availability of raw material, infrastructure, etc lead to wide difference in the levels of living, standard of services, levels of income etc among the federating units. One of the objectives of federal finance is to enable the states to attain certain minimum levels of services and hence the federal transfers should strive to equalise the position of each federating units. This is an organismic approach to federalism.

3. Neutrality Objective: Differences in the fiscal pressures exerted by the federal and the state governments, influence the geographical distribution of scarce capital resources and many a times such distribution adversely affect the optimum allocation of resources. Federal finance should strive to neutralise such influences.

4. Objective of Growth: This objective is of great relevance, especially in the context of developing federal countries. This requires a specific direction of federal finance towards the goal of planned economic development.

These objectives are not exclusive but they are closely interlinked. Equity and equalisation are complementary to each other. Similarly, rapid economic growth and equalisation, also supplement each other.

4.4 Approaches to Federal Fiscal Transfers

In the literature on federal finance various approaches have been developed for federal fiscal transfers. These approaches however depend upon the objectives to be achieved by the federation, which vary from country to country.

There are several interpretations of the term Horizontal Fiscal Imbalance. Horizontal Fiscal Imbalance may refer to the equity aspect. In fact in the literature on Public Finance two terms are used to analyse the problem of equity viz. the vertical equity and horizontal equity. Horizontal equity means those who are equals in respect of some relevant circumstances should be treated equally i.e. in a non-discriminating manner. [1] A corresponding concept of "vertical equity" [2] refers to the conflict-ridden issue of equality between unequals which necessitates unequal treatment of unequal.

In the context of a federal system the same principle can be extended and one can say that persons in like circumstances in two parts (states, regions, provinces) of the nation ought to be treated in the same way by their respective governments. While horizontal equity is feasible in a unitary form of country, in a federal set up it may be difficult to achieve. Though persons may bear the same federal tax burden and receive the same federal bundle of goods and services, individuals may be discriminated due to differential state tax burden and differential size of the state bundle of goods and services. Thus, the aggregate burden and benefits will result in inequity.

In the context of a federal system one talks of horizontal fiscal imbalances in terms of equalisation. Equalisation is a scheme for redistributing purchasing power among regional governments. While, equity is concerned with, the relative levels of economic well-being among individuals. Thus Horizontal Fiscal equity in federal design requires persons equally well off before a change be just the same after the change.

The poorer regions are not in a position to provide good quality of goods and services due to limited resources available and at the same time they have to raise resources from the narrow base by applying higher rates. In fact the federal fiscal transfer of resource should result in higher benefits to the poorer states so as to enable them to levy comparable level of taxes and provide comparable level of services. This is more like the concept of vertical equity in Public Finance that is treating unequal unequally.

In the literature on federal finance, it is the equity or equalization, which has received the maximum attention. Hence, a description of these approaches is offered here.

4.4.1 Equity Approach [3]: As explained above equity refers to the distributive aspects of economic activity. Equity approach to federal fiscal transfers generally relates to "horizontal equity". It means that the fiscal burdens and benefits should be so distributed that equally circumstanced individuals are not discriminated against one another.

J.M. Buchanan emphasises equity goal in his well known papers. [4] He argues against a system of fiscal adjustment, which would enable all regional governments in a federation to provide a national average level of public services at average tax rates. He favours, instead, an inter-governmental system of fiscal adjustment that facilitates 'equal treatment of equals'. Thus there are two political foundations on either of which 'Equity' approach can be studied. Buchanan classifies them as "Organismic Theory" and "Individualistic Theory". [5] In the former, the State including all individuals within it is conceived as a single organic entity. In the second, i.e. equalisation approach, the State is represented as the sum of its individual members acting in a collective capacity. "The individual and the state are fundamentally opposing forces in the latter concept, while in the organismic view the state, or general interest, subsumes all individual interests". [6]

Buchanan supports the individualistic approach. While rejecting the organismic theory, Buchanan argues that, the individual has to deal with a plurality of political and fiscal units. Hence he feels that "Organismic Theory" has very little relevance to practice. He did not also agree to limit the application of equity principle to fiscal systems within a federation. He argues that if this were done, individuals similarly situated would be subjected to equal fiscal treatment only if they were citizens of the same subordinate unit of government. Equal treatment of equals would be impossible when different individuals are subjected to different combination of fiscal units. He feels that, in a unitary government, it is easy to observe the principle of horizontal equality. In such a country, the Central fisc has complete power, at least in theory, over the fiscal activities of the subordinate governments. It can therefore, ensure horizontal fiscal equity to all citizens. However, the observance of this principle is more difficult in a federation because the States in a federation have independent fiscal authority which circumscribes the powers of the Central government. The Central government may observe this principle with respect to its own fiscal operations. But this does not guarantee that the equals living in different States are treated equally by the State fiscal.

Thus, net fiscal burden (taxes less benefits) on individuals is likely to be less in States having comparatively higher concentration of higher income population. The reason is that the higher income States can provide a comparable level of services on tax rates lower than those in other States or a higher level of services on tax rates comparable to those in other States. This amounts to discrimination on the basis of geographical location and violates the principle of fiscal equity.

This deviation from horizontal fiscal equity can be corrected if the Central government so adjusts the distribution of its own taxes and benefits, that differentials caused by the activities of the States fiscs are neutralised. This can be done through Central grants to lower income States. The grants by relieving fiscal pressure on State citizens will bring about fiscal equity.

Buchanan thus introduces the concept of "fiscal residuum", which he defines as being equal to an individual's tax-burden minus his benefits from public services. "Only by a comparison of the residuum of individuals", he writes, "Can the total effects of a fiscal system be analyzed and evaluated". [7] Thus satisfaction of the equity criterion will require that the fiscal residuum of similarly placed individuals should be the same regardless of where they live in the federation. At the same time the policy objective, for inter-governmental transfers will become one of providing or - ensuring horizontal equity. Thus, he derives that "the central financial authority must enter the process and treat equals unequally in order to offset the divergences in the income and wealth levels of subordinate units". [8]

Buchanan argues that if the residuum could be equalised, the whole fiscal structure would be as neutral as is geographically possible, and this system of adjustment would neutralise the distorting effects on resource allocation. He holds that higher fiscal pressure in poorer States compared to that in richer states will provide an incentive for migrating to richer areas. The highly skilled technicians, professionals and potential entrepreneurs are more tax conscious. A higher fiscal pressure on them will result in an out migration. On the other hand unskilled labour, which is an abundant resource, remains unaffected except when there is a negative income tax. If Central subsidies are given to the poor regions, it may result in an in-migration of highly skilled labour along with capital and it will also check the out-migration of skilled labour and capital from the poor region. Therefore, when the federal government transfers resources to the poorer regions with a view to equalising fiscal residuum, it does not prevent market mechanism from determining optimal allocation of resources. [9] Thus, he says, in order to meet the objective of horizontal equity, Central fisc should try to equalise fiscal residuum.

4.4.2 Critique of Buchanan's Approach: Buchanan's pioneering work gained much importance in the realm of federal finance. But his proposal has a number of theoretical and operational difficulties. Adebayo Adedji has underlined some of these difficulties. Adebayo's first problem related to provincial or regional autonomy. First, he asks whether in a federation with strong regional autonomy, regions would tolerate a differential federal tax-benefit structure and would such structure be constitutional. According to him the answer to both questions is in the negative. [10] He also expects some administrative difficulties. Due to constitutional reasons, if the federal government cannot impose a differential tax-benefit structure, the only way of achieving horizontal equity would be through unconditional grants, which would vary among regions. Once such grants are received, each region would be free to use them as it pleases, with the result that horizontal equity may not in fact be achieved. [11]

Further, Adebayo observes that, "on theoretical grounds, it is doubtful if the equalising of fiscal residue of similarly situated tax payers would necessarily make their overall fiscal treatment the same." [12] Apart from the net fiscal pressure on a person, the level of public services available to him has a bearing on his welfare. Further, he also agrees with Graham who maintains that:

"But it is the legislators rather than the individual citizens who determine through the legislative processes of appropriations the level of public services for all the residents of the region or federation. It is, therefore, likely that some tax payers will feel that their welfare would be enhanced by more public services and less private goods while others may feel the reverse. Thus, the equalizing of fiscal residuum is, in itself, insufficient to equalize the overall fiscal treatment of similarly situated individuals. It is only when the levels of public services are the same in all the regions that equalising fiscal residuum could achieve the overall fiscal treatment of similarly situated individuals. [13]

Regarding Buchanan's claim that equalisation of fiscal residua would bring about neutrality in a geographical sense, Adebayo holds that, "A fiscal residuum will fit many combinations of taxes and benefits." [14] However, a person with a given income and tastes may be indifferent among many tax-benefit combinations even though the fiscal residuum of each combination differs.

Thus, as Scott says, "to guarantee to a person of given income that he will receive the same fiscal residuum wherever he lives is not to guarantee that he will remain on the same indifference curve. On the contrary, (except by accident) it is almost certain to guarantee that, by moving to an area with the same fiscal residuum but a different tax-benefit combination, he will be made better or worse off, i.e. moved to a higher or lower indifference curve". [15]

Thus, the Buchanan proposal for achieving equity would not necessarily bring about neutrality in a geographical sense between different tax-benefit combinations whose residua are the same.

This approach to equity directly relating the Central fisc to individuals has, however, one serious disadvantage. It is "less federalist and more centralist in spirit." [16] The fiscal impact of the State finance is completely neutralised by the federal fiscal transfers. This neutralization is not confined to equal treatment of equals as between different States but is also extended to any attempt of a State Government to treat the unequals unequally in its own way. In other words, the vertical distribution as between the States also gets uniformed in the process. One finds that it is not possible to isolate and separate the problem of horizontal equity from the much more difficult one of the distribution of fiscal burdens and benefits among unequal, in which an explicit formulation of justice is impossible. Indeed the requirements of horizontal and vertical equity are closely inter-related.

4.4.3 Alternative Approach to Fiscal Equalisation: An alternative approach to fiscal equalisation, which respects the federal spirit, relates the Central fisc to the State fiscs instead of directly relating the former to the individuals. The Central government ensures fiscal equity among different states and leaves the individuals at the fiscal mercy (as it was) of their respective States. In the light of Tiebout [17], Breton [18] formulation of fiscal decentralisation, it can be said that the individuals always have a choice of moving to the jurisdiction of some other States. Out of a given number of States, location decision of the individuals in favour of a particular State will, in fact, reject a rational choice. [19] Thus conceived, this approach has the benefit of being more federalist in spirit and that at the same time it leaves the individual tax payer with a freedom of choice with regard to location in any of the States.

The larger the number of sub national governments, the more the alternatives open to an individual and the nearer the system will reach the most efficient level of output. It logically follows that given the nature of public goods, the best distribution of political authority was the one prevailing in a federation. [20]

In India, the Finance Commission as well as the Planning Commission has explicitly acknowledged their commitment to the principle of equalisation. However, equalisation in terms of States may have several meanings. Buchanan's approach to equity between similarly placed individuals has a definite criterion, the equalisation of fiscal residuum which specifies the principle of horizontal equity. The alternative approach, which seeks to place all the States in a more or less equal fiscal position, does not have a correspondingly well defined and generally accepted criterion. Equalisation here may refer to equal fiscal burdens of the States or to equal fiscal capacities of the States or to the equalisation of performance level of State services or even equalisation of levels of socio-economic development and so on.

The Central assistance is considered to be equalising if its state-wise distribution is such that the poor States receive more than their contribution to the central revenues. For example, if federal revenues are raised through a progressive tax on income, implying thereby that higher income States contribute relatively more than lower income States, even a uniform per capita distribution to States will contain an element of equalisation. More particularly, any federal fiscal transfer which tends to reduce inequalities in state income is said to be equalising. By narrowing down the gaps in the sources of fiscal power, it tends to equate the fiscal position of all the states. If incomes of the States are more or less equal, all states will have at least the same opportunity of providing almost the same level of services at approximately equal levels of fiscal burdens.

The objective of equalisation (however defined) was endorsed by a number of eminent economists like B.P. Adarkar, R N Bhargava, Lady Hicks, Baljit Singh, and many others. Adarkar maintains that the main feature of federal finance is the theory of transferences. He argues that welfare is maximised by real transfers of consumable resources through taxation and public expenditure from the rich to the poor regions. Because more often than not, backwardness breeds backwardness and economic potentialities are not discovered because they are not explored. In such cases it is plainly the duty of the federal government to infuse fresh blood and awaken new life among them. The most important argument in favour of such transfers from richer to poorer regions/states is perhaps the need of establishing certain national minima of social services and other amenities of modern civilization. As Adarkar puts it:

"Here there is a case for supporting the backward parts of the country at the expense of the advanced even though the former did not promise rapid development into industrial or wealthy localities. For if these are not thus protected they might rapidly become nurseries for the bacilli of countless social evils - disease, crime and lawlessness - whose pestilential effects on the advanced areas may cost the latter much more than the federal transference themselves." [21]

R N Bhargava [22] also supports the objective of equalization in a scheme of fiscal transference on the basis of principles of marginal sacrifice and marginal benefit. States as well as the federal governments act, in their own spheres while levying taxes, according to the principle of taxation, i.e. according to the principle of Least Aggregate Sacrifice. The States, however, differ considerably among themselves with respect to levels of development, economic potential and various other factors. Because of this when States as well as the Federal Governments try to follow the principle of taxation, the objective of equal marginal sacrifice at the aggregate level (taking together state and federal taxes) may not be attainable.

In order to bring equalisation at the aggregate level, Bhargava suggests that the States should tax according to the principle of least aggregate sacrifice, whereas the Central government should discriminate in its scheme of taxation in order to make the marginal sacrifice of State plus Central taxation of all citizens equal. The marginal sacrifice in a richer state would be less than that in a poor state. Therefore, the federal government should either impose higher tax burdens on the richer States or keep the tax-burden equal but transfer the excess to the poorer States or operate on both the sides so as to equate marginal sacrifice between the rich and the poor States. Thus he justifies transfer of resources to the poorer states on the basis of the principle of taxation. [23] He also justifies, such transferences on the basis of principle of equi-marginal-social-benefit in expenditure. Both the State and the federal governments may have to act in accordance with this principle of expenditure. The social benefit would be maximised when the marginal social bènefit in all the states is equal. However, the marginal benefit is lower in richer States and comparatively high in poorer States. This inequality will remain uncorrected if the federal government merely confines its attention to equating marginal benefit from expenditure falling within its own sphere of activities. The marginal social benefits vary from State to State.

Therefore, in order to affect the principle of expenditures at the aggregate level (centre and state together), he suggests for a reduction in the public expenditure in the richer States and an increase in public expenditure in poorer states. Because in richer States the marginal social benefit is generally less than that in the poorer States. On this basis he feels that, "benefit from the federal view point will be maximised when more is spent on backward and poor regions". [24] Thus Bhargava makes a case for federal fiscal transference to poorer States on the basis of marginal social cost (sacrifice) and marginal social benefit.

Bhargava's argument for transference to poor regions was questioned by Singer on the basis that the purpose of public expenditure can be two-fold (i.) to increase welfare and (ii.) to increase productivity. He pointed out; Bhargava ignores the latter objective which is more dynamic than the former. He doubts, if productivity can be increased through a federal fiscal transfers to a poor region. [25]

Bhargava in his reply to the above comment brought out the distinction between the terms "productivity" and "benefit" or "welfare". He maintains that in spite of lower productivity in backward areas it is very likely that, up to a limit, development expenditure in these areas will confer greater benefits because of comparatively lower income and expenditure levels and also because of a greater need for an expansion in employment opportunities. With felt differences in needs equal productivity will yield comparatively greater benefit in poorer or backward areas.

Hence in spite of lower productivity, it will be advantageous to incur development expenditure in these areas. Further, he added that redistributive objective and the objective of maximising economic productivity are inter-dependent in the long run. Therefore, redistributive objective becomes as dynamic as economic objective in the long run. [26] The success of national efforts in development is largely conditioned by the ability of the constituent States to discharge their economic responsibilities adequately and efficiently. The inability of some States to adequately provide for certain basic economic and social services must have its adverse effects on the national development. Low level of development in some States must inevitably mean lower productivity of labour. Again under-utilisation of some resources (natural/human) in some States is an obvious loss to overall national development. Thus, in order to help the States to improve their levels of development and increase fiscal potential, federal fiscal transfers are considered desirable. Thus, the objective of equalisation is advocated on economic, social and political grounds.

Paradoxically, these transfers have been criticised in the very name of faster national economic development. The critics argue that if the same resources are invested in higher income states, the returns would be higher than if they are invested in lower income States. Accordingly, the conclusion is drawn that, from the standpoint of economic growth, financial transfers favouring the latter States would be unjustified. As Louis Lefeber puts it:

Barring some special and obvious cases most industrial investment, if located in retarded areas, would have very low current yields, if any, at distant future. Similarly, many government sponsored rural programmes would be of the low yield type. It might be argued that either approach to increase regional balance, that is low-yield type rural programmes or arbitrary location of industrial investment, is more in the nature of a transfer payment to improve income distribution than a contribution to economic development. [27]

Careful examination would show that this criticism is based on certain assumptions regarding the characteristics of backward regions and the exact connotation of the term 'yield'. It seems to have been taken for granted that all lower income regions have *ipso facto* lower development potential or at least give a weaker response to economic stimuli. This may not be realistic assumption particularly for a developing economy. The past development of different areas in these countries may be more the result of various historical and political circumstances, unrelated to their development potential or to growth stimuli. The economic calculus may never have been the guiding force for resource allocations in the past.

A staunch critique of equity/equalisation approach is Anthony Scott. He attacked equalisation objective on the ground of economic efficiency. Criticism of equalisation goal on efficiency ground, according to efficiency approach, in a poor region the returns to various factors of production tend to be lower than the corresponding returns in the richer States. Therefore, national product will be highest when the factors of production move from the poor to the rich regions. However, in a federation, if the federal government intervenes through its fiscal policy and tries to transfer resources from the rich to the poor regions, it retards the rate of growth of national product. This amounts to subsidising inefficiency. Scott is a staunch supporter of this approach.

Scott defines poor regions as those, "provinces located in areas of few resources per capita". [28] By resources, he means the natural endowments like climate, soil, minerals and raw materials, as well as man-made facilities like drainage, transportation, port, etc. These poor provinces cannot levy the same tax per capita as the rich provinces. Therefore, the bundle of services made available to the citizens of poor provinces must be smaller. In the absence of federal intervention the labour will move from poor regions to those where the bundle of services will be more or where the marginal productivity of labour is high. But when a nation tries to augment the services received by the inhabitants of the poor regions through a transfer of resources it results in resource distortion and subsidisation of inefficiency. Scott objects to such transfers on the grounds of inefficiency. His objection is that such transfers provide amenities to poor people in resource poor regions, which is undesirable in the long-run. The maximum income for the whole country and so the highest personal income is to be achieved only by maximising national production. This necessitates that resources and labour ought to be combined in such a way that the marginal product of similar units of labour is the same in all places. An increase will result when the labour is transferred from places where its marginal product is low to those places where it is high. To put it in another way, the intensity of the application of labour to scarce resources should be the same everywhere in order to maximise production.

Such a labour transfer, according to Scott, can come about in two ways: (i) by means of controlled labour allocation, with or without the additional bribes of free transport to new place of work and (ii) by maintaining a differential real wage (amenities) between the two areas in such a way that the worker can better his lot by moving to an area where the amenities received as a right of local citizenship is greater than those available in his former home. It is contended here that transfers of government income from place to place prevent the maximisation of national production by curbing the incentive to labour mobility. [29] Thus, the most efficient allocation is defined as that in which non-labour resources are combined with labour in such a manner that the marginal productivity of similar units of labour is the same in all the stages. This requires labour to be perfectly mobile as between the regions. Any transfer of non-labour resources from the rich to the poor states through Central grants will reduce labour mobility and prevent equalisation of marginal productivity. Scott elucidates this in his other paper on "Federal Grants and Resource Allocation". [30] Here he maintains that transfer of resources to poor states result in higher level of social amenities. When labour in a poor state takes into account the level of wages as well as social services, its incentive to migrate to a richer State will be reduced by a given transfer of resources. Social services financed by such fiscal transfers largely benefit the low paid workers and lead to excessive supply of labour just where productivity is least. Finally, this meets the objective of maximising national product.

In this context question arise as to which factor has low productivity in poor regions and what type of a model of a poor region is being involved. These questions are relevant for determining whether federal fiscal transfers to the poor regions have the effect of blunting the incentive to factor mobility, especially of labour.

In this controversy with Scott, Buchanan maintained that in a poor area, "the returns (in the sense of marginal) to capital and entrepreneurship tend to be higher the return to unskilled labour lower than the corresponding rate of returns in the richer sections. Income differences among regions will tend to be reduced by an out-migration of the relatively abundant resources and an in-migration of relatively scarce resources in all areas". [31]

Buchanan argued that Scott's objection to equalising resource transfers was subject to three errors. [32]

First, attention has been concentrated on the mobility of one of the two basic productive factors; namely, labour. A relative surplus of labour implies a relative shortage of capital resources and the movement of capital is as important as that of labour in attaining long run resources equilibrium. The effect of grants on the inflow of capital to the poor areas has been almost completely overlooked.

Second, homogeneity in the labour force itself has been assumed. This assumption is useful for many problems, but here it leads to some error. Although, the low-income areas are characterised by a relative abundance in the quantitatively important segments of the labour force, many selective types of labour are relatively scarce. Third, the specific way in which the transferred funds are expended has not been considered. If it had been recognised that different means of expending the transferred funds exert different effects this would itself have been sufficient to limit drastically the generality of the argument.

Scott replied to this criticism by specifying the respective assumptions behind their arguments. He assumed that both natural resources and the other factors are scarce and the national product will be highest when the scarce labour, capital and enterprise are attracted to the best soil, ports, mines sites etc. and that the federal transfers will frustrate this attraction, which happens to be, by coincidence, the optimum location of production. Further, he added, that Buchanan's implicit assumptions that natural resources are adequately awaiting only development and that labour in poor areas requires only training and experience for its efficient utilisation lead Buchanan to reject Scott's argument. Thus, according to Scott, a poor region lacks both sufficient natural and non-natural resources, such as capital and entrepreneurs and, therefore, mobility of labour from such areas to rich areas was the only way to maximise production.

Buchanan countered the above arguments by maintaining, "although, natural resources are complementary to mobile capital, they are no more important and probably considerably less important than labour in determining marginal production". [33]

Investment in heavy industry would be ineffective in regions deficient in power potential regardless of the degree of labour surplus, investment in light industry requiring little capital equipment per worker would probably be efficient in regions possessing surplus population no matter how inadequate the natural resource base. [34] Looking at the natural resources in 'Knightian' terms as a subdivision of capital and emphasising its increasing indistinguishability from capital in the wake of technological advance, Buchanan, argues, and even climate to a degree. [35] Thus import of capital in relating to labour and natural resources is the emerging policy prescription from Buchanan's argument. Even if natural resources, following Scott, are made to constitute a crucial point it is largely the growth of heavy industry and not the light industries, which will be uneconomic. Buchanan, finally, brought out an important point that apart from financial productivity, which was the only important consideration for Scott, the social productivity of resources transferred from rich to poor regions was equally important. The importance of social productivity and possibility of increasing aggregate output with balanced regional development in the long-run, have convinced a practical planner to agree that: "There is no conflict between efficiency consideration and regional development in the long run". [36]

It is not necessary that the backward States lack resources. In fact 'poor states' are sometimes rich in natural resources and 'unskilled labour'. The main problem is capital shortage and entrepreneurial skill. The extent of non-utilisation or under-utilisation of resources in these States is not only a measure of their economic backwardness but it also represents the magnitude of the untapped development potential. Their own capital being inadequate, the only possible way to develop them is through special financial assistance from the centre.

From the viewpoint of yield also, the argument is rather restrictive in so far as it takes into account only the current returns, whereas economic development being a long-term phenomenon is concerned with higher yields over a period of time. Whether the returns to investment are lower or higher depend also on the length of the time allowed. Further, public policy is always concerned with net social yields, which are gross social yields less social costs. The social costs in poorer States would be lower because of the existence of unemployed and under-utilised resources.

New investment in backward States will produce large changes in the organisation of economic activity and in the economic structure of the state over a period of time. Partial analysis, in terms of which the criticism of financial transfers to backward States with low fiscal potential is usually cast, fails to take account of such changes. The misdirected application of partial analysis to the problem of developing countries is now widely recognised:

Thus it can be concluded that the objective of equalisation does not come in conflict with national growth. In fact, in a developing federal country-balanced regional development is desirable. The objective of federal fiscal transfers in a developing country should be to achieve equalisation in such a manner as to result in growth of all the lagging regions resulting in maximisation of overall growth.

It follows that equalisation grants may not always lead to inefficiency. Their effect may be quite the opposite. Thus, the foregoing discussion brings out that the objective of equalisation is economically beneficial, socially desirable and politically essential especially in a developing federation.

4.5 Indicators and Causes of HFI

Horizontal Fiscal Imbalances are the result of disparities that exists among the federating units in resources mobilised. The actual amount of resources mobilised, in fact depends upon three factors viz. Revenue capacity, Revenue efforts and administrative efficiency. Revenue raising capacity depends upon the per capita income, levels of socio-economic development, distribution of income (Poverty ratio), sectoral composition of State domestic product and so on. Levels of development and per capita income provide the tax and revenue base. People living below poverty line influence the tax base. Prominent primary sector with limited capacity to contribute to the exchequer reduces revenue capacity of a state.

To bring down these disparities and to achieve the objective of equalisation in a federation Federal fiscal transfers are resorted to.

However, while implementing the scheme of equalisation special care is needed about the size of the states, their levels of prosperity/development and need. If large states happen to be the rich states and small states happen to be the poor states, inter-governmental transfers from rich to the poor - on the one hand will be capable of satisfying the revenue requirement of the poorer states without putting undue strain on the richer states. The cost of being in a federation may be less than the gains of federation to larger states.

At the same time the smaller states may find it profitable to remain in the federation. On the contrary, if large states happen to be poor and backward while small states happen to be the rich, adequate fiscal adjustments cannot take place. The small rich states will not have enough surpluses to finance the large deficits of large poor states. In fact, any amount of resources transferred from the small state would be inadequate to meet the growing needs of the large poor states. Thus, the federal fiscal transfer mechanism may fail to satisfy the small rich states as well as the large poor states. Therefore, while effecting the principle of equalisation the size factor has to be kept in mind.

The states generally differ significantly in natural resources, level of development and fiscal potential, while they are required to provide about the same range of public services. As a result their needs for revenue reinforcement from the centre will vary. This adds another dimension to the problem of financial transfers. Generally the State with low level of development and relatively less fiscal potential, need relatively large amounts by way of central assistance. The states with relatively high level of development and large fiscal potential can maintain high standards of public services and of economic activities from their own resources. On this basis, we feel that the objective of federal fiscal transfers in a developing economy should be equalisation of general need of the States. [37] And two-factor (i) economic development and (ii) fiscal potential represent general need in turn. These transfers apparently seem to be similar to those recommended on the basis of inter- state equity in social services but their logic is different. [38] More about this and eligibility Index is given in the succeeding chapters.

4.6 Equalisation Assistance to Needy States

Equalisation assistance is designed to raise the level of public services in the poorer states to some national norms. Thus, to some, equalisation means, helping the states with below normal service level to attain the normal level. The possibility of achieving a national norm is enhanced if funds are given exclusively to the poorer states for raising the levels of services.

Once the objective of fiscal equalisation is accepted in principle and is considered necessary condition for meaningful and lasting devolution, it is important to guide the design of national policy. "As a first step, it is useful to state in concrete terms what exactly the objective of fiscal equalisation is to be. One such objective suggests itself. For those public goods and services considered appropriately provided by State Governments, it should be possible for all States to provide a minimum level of services without exceeding a maximum tax burden level." [39]

Equalisation objective can be achieved when each federating unit is enabled to provide a minimal level of selected services without imposing a tax burden on its citizens in excess of some nationally agreed upon maximum. This can be done through a national equalisation programme of inter-governmental transfer payment.

According to Hunter a national guarantee of minimum services at maximum tax burden establishes a general framework for designing an equalisation formula to allocate payments among States.

Yet another interpretation of 'equalisation' is in terms of transferring resources according to the size of the population. Larger the population larger is the transfer. Here population is taken to represent a generalised index of state differences in programme needs. The disadvantage of this 'basis' is that a state with larger population may be well advanced and may not be in need of heavy capital investments, while a state with lesser population may totally be lacking in basic infrastructure, and may have unutilised natural resources and hence in need of capital resources.

More appropriate interpretation of the term 'equalisation' would be in terms of equalisation of 'fiscal need'. [40] The term 'need' is used in a comprehensive sense. The state which occupies the lowest place in terms of physical indicators of development, representing productive sector, social infrastructure, economic infrastructure and financial infrastructure land at the same time has very low fiscal potential to mobilise resources, howsoever, measured, is considered to be the most needy state and vice-versa. Thus, need is measured by two factors: (i) the relative levels of realised levels of development and (ii) relative fiscal potential of the states. If the federal transfers help to reduce regional disparities in development level and fiscal potential (i.e. the needy states getting relatively more) the objective of equalisation would be considered as attained. This was the approach developed by the author. [41] The effective pursuit of the economic developmental objective in federal finance calls for an adequate amount of control and checks on the part of the federal government. This is to ensure that each state executes its part of the plan, exercises diligent economy in expenditure, and meets the tax effort required for it. Such exercises of federal control are bound to result in some measures of restrictions of state autonomy.

The basic premise of the development approach to federal finances is that guided public interference in the allocation of resources is desirable in order to promote economic development. If the poorer regions in a federation remain poor owing to lack of capital formation, it may be appropriate under this approach to devote some attention to the development of such regions. If such regions have the potential resources for development, some allocation of resources through fiscal measures, even though not maximizing the national product in the short run, may not be detrimental to such maximizing in the long run. Considering the acute shortage or capital resources, it is very essential to make the states to tap their own resources efficiently and use them economically. If the distribution scheme is comply based on equalisation of general need and neglects the resource mobilization factor, some of the poor and backward States might enjoy the benefits of central assistance without making any effort of their own at the cost of other states which could raise resources through their continuous effort. Therefore, along with equalisation, the scheme of distribution must make some allowance to the 'self help' factor and thus the objective of federal fiscal transfers should be to encourage the states to make more efforts towards resource mobilization.

4.7 Measures Adopted for Making Equalisation Payments

Federal Fiscal transfers to achieve fiscal equalisation gained lot of importance in older federations like Canada. Equalisation in the Canadian federation refers to the system of unconditional grants from the federal government to the governments of the poorer provinces, the stated intention of which is to enable the citizens of those provinces to enjoy services of comparable quality to those enjoyed in the richer provinces, without having to pay higher taxes for them. [42]

Equalisation is a program under which the federal government makes annual payments to provinces that have relatively low capacity to raise revenues with which to finance public services. [43] The eligibility of a province for getting equalisation payment is determined by comparing its fiscal capacity to a national standard, so as to close the gap. This comparison is done according to a 'formula' that is set out in legislation approved by the parliament. The comparison is carried out in a standardised way so that exactly the same criteria are applied in all provinces. Equalisation payments are unconditional and are entirely funded by the federal government. The purpose of equalisation payment in Canada is to meet the requirement of the Constitution Act 1982, Section 36, and sub-Section 2 of Part III.

Equalisation in Canada takes the form of equalising the fiscal capacity of recipient governments. A distinction is made in the literature between fiscal capacity equalisation and fiscal performance equalisation. Fiscal capacity is a measure of the ability of a political jurisdiction to raise revenue, and comparisons are usually made by reference to income. [44] Fiscal capacity equalisation seeks to achieve what is called "horizontal fiscal balance," by transfers which ensure that the poorer provincial governments have enough revenue to provide services comparable to the other provinces without having to impose higher taxes. There is no requirement that recipient provinces must provide the services provided by other provinces; indeed, they may choose not to increase services but to reduce taxes instead.

Fiscal performance equalisation is directed to the equalisation of the tax effort of provinces, on the revenue side, or, on the expenditures side aiming at equalisation of the level and pattern of spending of recipient governments. Tax effort is a measure of the revenue collected by a government in relation to its fiscal capacity. Fiscal performance equalisation involves specification of performance criteria or conditions, with the intention of harmonising taxation or spending policies of the recipient governments. It therefore implies a loss of freedom of action in decision making for recipient governments. [45]

Equalisation in Canada focuses on the relatively low-yielding revenue bases of the poorer provinces, and supplements these bases so that all provinces have the resources to finance a satisfactory level of public services. The supplement required to sustain a "satisfactory level of public services" is determined by measuring the gap between the per capita revenue yields of the poorer provinces and the other provinces.

The basis for calculating "equalisation entitlements" of the poorer provinces has varied over the years, according to how the bench mark yields are selected. It has varied from the per capita yield of the highest two provinces, to the average per capita yield for all provinces, the average per capita yield of the middle five ("representative") provinces. Two important changes were made in the equalisation formula in the original 1962 arrangements. The first related to resource revenues. Henceforth 50% of the 3-year average of provincial revenues and taxes from natural resources would be eligible for equalisation. The second, the new provision geared equalisation to the national average level of revenues rather than to the average revenues in the top two provinces.

After 1962, the formula of equalisation payment changed a number of times and schemes like RNAS 1977 (Representative National Average Standard) and Representative Five Province Standard (RFPS) 1982 were incorporated. In the new agreement, the per capita tax yield for each province was equalized to the average per capita level of the two highest-income provinces. Although equalization applied to the yield from only three revenue sources (personal income tax, corporation income tax and succession duties), it was extended to other revenue sources in subsequent five-year periods. Till 1990, 33 provincial revenue sources were equalised. If a province's revenue from some sources exceeds the representative average standard, the surpluses would be added to the deficiencies, and the equalisation entitlement would be the net amount. However, there is a minimum equalisation payment to a recipient province, set as a percentage of the previous year's payment and since 1987 the average yield of the "representative" provinces indexed to the gross domestic product.

4.8 Present Equalisation Payment Programmes

The Federal Provincial Relations Division, in the paper brings out the following assumptions and features of equalisation payment program. [46]

1. In the equalisation program on an overall basis, provinces will be able to provide comparable levels of public services if they have reasonably comparable revenue per capita post equalisation;
2. No explicit attempt is made to quantify per capita differences in respect of the costs of and/or needs for public services. It is generally agreed that estimates of this kind would be extremely difficult to make;
3. Equalisation is not intended to redress income disparities between individuals;
4. Equalisation is also not intended to redress or address regional economic disparities;
5. It is concerned only with reducing revenue disparities among the public sectors and governments of different provinces.

It is contended that there are other federal programs targeted at the needs of individuals and the needs to stimulate regional activity in the private sector, which complement these other programs. It is also contended in the paper that equalisation payments results in increasing the revenue raising capacity of the poorer provinces.

4.9 Methodology of Equalisation Payments

In order to determine the equalisation payment to provinces an objective comparison of provinces each year in respect of their relative capacities to raise revenues from taxes. This is done by estimating the potential revenues that each province could derive by levying a 'model' or 'representative' provincial tax system and comparing the amount with a specified standard of revenue raising capacity. This involves the following three steps:

1. Determining the revenues which are taken into account in the model tax system;
2. estimating the potential revenues of each province from that system if levied on a standardised (i.e. uniform) basis; and
3. Comparing the resulting estimate of revenues in each province with revenues based upon the program "standard".

Presently, the model tax system includes all of the various taxes that provinces levy together with "Quasi/taxes. There are in all 33 such items. As these revenues provide a comprehensive coverage of revenues under provincial control, this is usually referred to as the "representative tax system" (RTS). More about RTS is given in Chapter 6.

In order to make an objective comparison of revenue raising capacities of provinces, it is necessary to estimate the revenues that each province would derive from all of the taxes included in the RTS. This cannot be done by comparing actual revenues of provinces because actual revenues depend upon tax rates as well as the 'productivity' of the tax bases to which rates are applied and tax rates tend to vary significantly from one province to another. In order to make standardised comparisons the assumption therefore is made that each tax is levied at a uniform rate on a uniformly defined tax base in each province. The method is explained in detail in the paper prepared by the Federal Provincial Relations Division Ottawa. According to the paper, [47] the RTS makes standardised estimates of revenue separately for each of the 33 revenue sources. The estimates focus on two key concepts for each tax - the base and the rate. [48]

The tax base is an economic variable to which the tax rate is applied. It is the key element of the RTS.

The tax rate for each tax is an average of the actual rates of all provinces for that source i.e. the "national average rate of taxation", computed with the reference to the data used for actual revenues and for the defined tax base.

The estimates of revenues for each province that are derived by applying the average tax rates to the uniformly defined tax bases are therefore standardised estimates which should reflect differences in tax base productivity. Calculations are done separately for each of the 33-revenue source in the RTS and then added to arrive at an aggregate total for each province. This aggregate is then put on a per capita basis.

Once the total per capita revenue of each province from the RTS have been estimated, it is necessary to compare the total with a revenue raising bench mark or standard to determine whether the province qualities for equalisation and if so by how much.

The standard of equalisation which has been used since 1982-83 is known as the 'five Province Standard'. It is based upon the estimated average per capita revenues that five 'representative' province would obtain from the RTS. The Five representative provinces are: B.C. Saskatchewan, Ontario, Quebec and Manitoba. These are considered to be 'idle rich' provinces. The province with highest per capita revenue raising capacity i.e. Alberta and the four of the provinces with lowest per capita revenue raising capacity i.e. Atlantic Provinces are left out.

If a given province has an estimated revenue raising capacity, which is higher than the standard, it is ineligible for equalisation. On the other hand, if a given province has a revenue raising capacity which is lower than the standard it is eligible and will have an entitlement that is equal to its per capita shortfall from the standard multiplied by its population.

The document further mentions "it should be noted that since the equalisation standard is the same for all provinces, the provinces that qualify for equalisation in a fiscal year are all raised, through the program, to an exactly equal per capita level of revenue raising capacity. Hence they are said to be "equalised".

Thus in calculating equalisation payment following steps are involved. The illustration is taken from the document. [49]

Step 1: Revenues to be Equalised

(1) total revenues of 10 provinces from tobacco 1987-88 = $2080 Million

Step 2: Potential Newfoundland Revenues from Source

(2) Newfoundland tax base (No. of Cig. sold in province): 832.7 Million

(3) National average tax rate for cigarettes

$$= \frac{\text{total Revenue of 10 province}}{\text{total number of cig. sold in 10 province}}$$

$$= \frac{\$2080 \text{ million}}{55{,}728 \text{ million cigarettes}} = 3.73\ \text{C per cigarette.}$$

(4) Potential Newfoundland revenue from applying national average tax rate to its own base

= 832.7 million x 3.73 x = $31085000

Step 3:

Comparison of N.F's potential revenues with revenues it would derive if it had a tax base as productive as the Average for the five standard provinces.

(5) Standard province potential revenues per capita:

Cigarette consumption in 5 standard province x 3.73 c/ Population of 5 standard province

= $83.36

(6) Newfound land potential revenue per capita

= 31085000 / NF Pop 568100 = \$54.72

(7) Newfound land per capita shortfall from standard

= \$83.36 - \$54.72 = 28.64.

(8) Newfoundland equalisation entitlement for tobacco

= NF per capita shortfall x population

= \$28.64 x 568100 = \$16271000.

In the above manner revenue shortfall or surplus is worked out for each of the 10 provinces and for each of the 33 revenue items.

In the above method the emphasis is laid on providing equal revenue to all the provinces. However equalisation of revenue may not always ensure horizontal fiscal balances because the states may differ from each other in terms of their fiscal need, in cost of providing goods and services, in terms of realised levels of development, fiscal Potential and so on. Therefore federal fiscal transfer scheme requires to be based on several measures of fiscal need. In various federations various criteria are adopted. In India, population is taken as a measure of need, Along with this per capita income, economic backwardness. Taxable capacity, are also taken as indicators of fiscal need. In order to make sure that recipient states do not get a free ride. And to make them fiscally more responsible tax efforts and efficiency in expenditure are also included in the scheme of federal fiscal transfers.

Within this framework however, three other preliminary questions must be answered: [50]

1. What public services/responsibilities are going to be considered relevant when constructing the fiscal equalisation formula i.e., what activities are considered to be solely State responsibilities?
2. What are appropriate measures of a State's resource requirements necessary to provide the minimum level of services in question, i.e., how is States "resource needs to be measured, including taking account of geographic variations in the price level of the services?
3. How is fiscal capacity to be measured?

There is no patented solution to the sorting out exercise required to evaluate State's resources needs. Resource needs are related to the responsibilities assigned to different layers of government. In fact government (Federal and State) is required to provide pure public goods. This is the first responsibility of any government. Government is also considered to be best suited for semi-public or merit goods which have large externalities. However, there are certain items of expenditure over which there is no general agreement. There are certain private goods and services provided by the government, mainly to help the needy and disadvantaged in some manner.

If provision for the needy is considered solely a national responsibility then a fiscal equalisation program aimed at the fiscal problem of federalism need not take these responsibilities into account. There would be no need to consider the resource requirements of providing for the low income needy when answering the question what minimum level of services should States be able to provide their citizens. The only responsibilities factored into the equalisation equation in this instance would be those upon which there is wide agreement such as education, police etc. If on the other hand, it is determined that welfare is most appropriately a State Responsibility, then a major components of the resource requirements considered in computing equalisation payments would be the number of needy in each State.

"Another possibility is that welfare is concluded to be appropriately a shared responsibility between the Federal and State Governments. In this case, the solution to the fiscal problem of Federalism is more complex but there is still clear direction on how the problem should be attached. A general fiscal equalisation program would in this case be designed exactly if welfare were to be handled entirely by the Federal Governments excluding considerations of State resource needs in the welfare area," [51] then in order to address the problem raised by fiscal disparities in providing for the poor under a co-operative Federal/State welfare venture, the cost sharing arrangements would be designed to permit all States to provide a minimum level of welfare benefits without excluding an agreed upon tax burden on their citizens.

These criteria need to be applied very carefully. The database and a good measure of these criteria are essential to ensure that the objective of equalisation is achieved.

The succeeding chapter explains one of the criteria often used in the scheme of federal fiscal transfers, namely, taxable capacity bring down horizontal fiscal imbalances. The various quantitative techniques used for measuring taxable capacity and tax efforts are discussed and illustrated with actual situation.

End Notes and References

1. R A Musgrave, The Theory of Public Finance, McGraw Hill, 1959, Chap. VIII, p. 160.
2. Ibid.
3. R A Musgrave, The Theory of Public Finance, Mc. Graw Hill, 1959, Chap. VIII, p. 160.
4. J M Buchanan, "The Pure Theory of Government Finance: A Suggested Approach", Journal of Political Economy, Vol. L, VII, Dec. 1949, pp. 96-505.
5. J M Buchanan, "Federalism and Fiscal Equity", American Economic Review, Vol. XI, Sept. 1950, pp. 583-99.
6. J M Buchanan, "The Pure Theory", Op. cit., p. 496.
7. J M Buchanan, "The Pure Theory", Op. cit., p. 501.
8. J M Buchanan, "Federal and Fiscal Equity", Op. cit., p. 501.
9. J M Buchanan, "Federal Fiscal Grants and Resource Allocations", Journal of Political Economy, No. 3., Vol. LX. 1952, pp. 208-217.
10. Adebayo Adedji, Nigerian Federal Finance: Its Development Problems and Prospects, Hutchinson Educational Ltd., London, 1969, pp. 14-15.
11. Ibid.
12. Ibid,
13. J F Graham, Fiscal Adjustment and Economic Development: A Case Study of Nova Scotia, University of Toronto Press, 1963, p. 178, quoted by Adebayo Adedji, Op. cit., p. 15.
14. For example, tax payer X in region Y, whose b=#600 and t=#400, has a fiscal residuum of #200 on the other hand, tax payer N in region M, whose b=#2000 and whose t=1800 also has a fiscal residuum

of #200. Where t = taxes and b = benefits. See Adebayo Adedji, Ibid. p.15.

15. A Scott, "The Economic Goals of Federal Finance", in Public Finance, Vol. XIX, No.3, 1964, p.254.

16. R A Musgrave, "Approaches to Fiscal Theory of Political Federalism", Public Finance: Need, Sources and Utilisation, A Report of the National Bureau of Economic Research (Princeton University Press, 1961), pp.97-122; comments pp.122-33, p.98. .ls2

17. Charles, Tiebouts, "A Pure Theory of Local Expenditure", Journal of Political Economy, October 1956, pp.416-24.

18. A Breton, "A Theory of Government Grants", Journal of Economics and Political Science, Vol. XXI, No.2 , May 1965, pp. 175-87.

19. Economic Theory has a fairly defined criterion - the Pareto optimum - for determining the most efficient level of private goods. The output of public goods is not amenable to this criterion. According to Tiebout "there is no way in which the consumer can avoid revealing his preferences in a spatial economy". His formulation shows the way by which the most efficient level of output of public goods can be derived from the individual preferences. This applies only to those public goods which are produced by the sub-national governments. Its basic hypothesis is that there is a large number of sub national governments, producing more or less the same public good and the individual has a choice to 'buy' from any one of them. The individual can exercise his choice by moving from one government to another. Given the assumption of consumer rationality, the choice actually made in favour of a particular government can be construed to have revealed the individual preference. See for details Charles Tiebout, Op cit. pp.416-24.

20. Albert Breton, Op. cit, pp. 175-87. .ls2

21. B P Adarkar, Principles and Problems of Federal Finance, P S King and Son Ltd., London, 1933, Ch, XII, p. 215.

22. R N Bhargava, "The Theory of Federal Finance", The Economic Journal, Vol. IXIII, 1953, pp. 841-97.

23. R N. Bhargava, Ibid. pp. 90-91.

24. R N. Bhargava, Op. cit. p. 93.

25. H W Singer, "The Theory of Federal Finance: A Comment", The Economic Journal, Sept. 1953, p. 726.

26. R. N. Bhargava, "The Theory of Federal Finance: A Rejoinder" Op. cit., 1954, pp. 407-408.

27. Louis Lefeber, "Regional Allocation of Resources in India", Pricing and Fiscal Policy: A Study in Method (ed), P. N Rosenstein Rodan, London, George Allen & Unwin Ltd., 1962, p. 22.

28. Scott, Op. cit., p. 416.

29. Scott, "A Note", Op. cit., p. 416.

30. Scott, "Federal Grants and Resource Allocation", Op. cit., pp. 534-38.

31. J M Buchanan, "Federal Grants and Resource Allocation", Journal of Political Economy, Vol. IX, 1952. p. 209.

32. J M Buchanan, Ibid., p. 215.

33. Buchanan, "A Reply", Journal of Political Economy, Dec. 1952 - Vol. IX, pp. 537-38.

34. Ibid., pp. 537-38.

35. J M Buchanan, "A Reply", Op. cit., p.538.

36. M L V Haq, The Strategy of Economic Planning : A Case study of Pakistan, Oxford University Press, Karachi, 193, p. 130.

37. Rao, Hemlata, (1974) Centre State Financial Relations and the Problems of Financing Regional Development", Ph.D. dissertation, Delhi School of Economics, Delhi university, Delhi.

38. Ibid.

39. Lawrence H. Hunter, "The Desirability and Feasibility of Fiscal equalization in a federal system of Governments," Federal State Local Fiscal Relations Technical Paper, Vol.1, office of State and Local Finance, Department of Treasury, Sept.1986, P.25 (17-39)

40. Rao, Hemlata, (1974) op. cit. also see Hemlata Rao, (1994)Federal State Financial Relations, Ashish publishing House, New Delhi, Chapter VII,pp187-210

41. Rao, Hemlata ,(1974) and (1994) op cit,

42. Official statements usually do not specify "of equal quality." The statement in Section 32 (2) of the Constitution Act 1982 says "reasonably comparable levels of public services at reasonably comparable levels of taxation."

43. Federal Provincial Division, Ottawa, The Fiscal Equalization Program, October 1990.

44. D. G. Davies, International Comparisons of Tax Structures in Federal and Unitary Countries (Canberra: Centre for Research on Federal Financial Relations, 1976), 28-29.

45. For a full discussion of the different approaches to equalisation, see Russell Mathews, Revenue Sharing in Federal Systems (Canberra: Centre for Research on Federal Financial Relations, 1980).

46. Ibid.
47. Ibid.
48. Ibid, p. 3.
49. Ibid, p.5.
50. Ibid.
51. Ibid. p. 28.

5

TAXABLE CAPACITY AND TAX EFFORT OF FEDERATING STATES

Section 1

5.1 Taxable Capacity and Tax Effort Criteria

Reduction of Horizontal Fiscal Imbalance requires the federal fiscal transfer schemes to pursue the objective of Equalization. This objective in a scheme of federal fiscal transfers should recognize the underlying differences in the capacity of the states to raise funds from their tax resources for financing their expenditure and investment programs. To achieve this objective, it becomes imperative to help those states which are having low taxable capacity. States with low taxable capacity, in fact, need more funds for providing social and economic services as well as to undertake developmental works for achieving rapid economic growth.

Apart from `equalization' another important consideration in a sound federal fiscal transfer scheme is for `relative-tax-efforts'. To induce federating units to make higher resource mobilization efforts warranted by their capacity is one of the important objectives of a federation. Optimal resource transfer from the federal to the states imbued with such objective is however, a vexing problem. Recognizing this, the First Finance Commission (1952) of India had rightly observed that the extent of self help of a state should determine the eligibility for as well as the amount of help from the centre.

Different views prevail regarding the inclusion of tax-effort criterion in the distribution of grants. One view is, "In a truly federal system, each constituent unit must be free to decide upon its own level of public services to be provided and the level of resources it wishes to mobilize given its taxing powers and the transfers it receives. If punishment or reward is introduced through the mode or design of transfers, the choices of the sub-central governments will be interfered with. That will be contrary to the federal spirit". [1]

However this is not a very serious objection for tax-effort as a criterion of fiscal devolution. In the absence of any such efficiency criterion, a tendency to have a `free ride' by the inefficient states may go up. Residents of one state then may be forced to contribute to meet the expenses of another state, which is reluctant to tax its own people. This also goes against the basic principles of federal formation. [2] Further in the event of absence of any such `efficiency' measure as `tax-effort, there would be a tendency among the states to incur huge expenditure without raising resources adequately from their own sources and attract more federal fiscal transfers.

A state by improving its tax-efforts, relative to its tax potential, in fact, achieves some major national objectives. It wields the tax weapon to reduce spending and thereby check inflation, thus, falling in line with the national objective of maintaining price stability. Further, a state mobilizes more resources needed for larger development effort under the Five-Year Plans, which again is a national objective of utmost importance.

Inclusion of tax-effort as a criterion of federal fiscal transfers is helpful in reducing the possibilities of rewarding the states which lax in their tax-efforts and penalizing those who exert adequate tax-efforts. Besides, it helps the process of economic development by including the states to tap all possible sources of revenues.

Thus, both taxable capacity and tax efforts are very important criteria. However, the usefulness of these criteria depends entirely upon their accurate measurement. If taxable capacity or `effort' is wrongly construed or arbitrarily measured, it may defeat the very purpose of including these criteria in the scheme of devolution. Hence, proper 'measures' are very important.

5.1.1 Meaning of Taxable Capacity and Tax Effort: According to Mathews R L and Sweeney, "A fiscal unit's taxable capacity in particular to a revenue source may be defined as the amount of tax the unit can raise by applying a standard rate schedule to its own revenue base. A fiscal unit's severity of taxation in relation to the revenue source (or its tax effort) may be defined as the ratio of the revenue it actually collects from that source to its taxable capacity". [3]

A simple and lucid definition of the term fiscal capacity or taxable capacity is given by the Advisory Commission on Inter-governmental Relations (A.C.I.R.) According to the Commission, "fiscal capacity is a quantitative measure intended to reflect the resources which a taxing jurisdiction can tax to raise revenue for public purposes". [4]

According to this definition, available taxable resources would indicate the taxable capacity or potential. Defining `tax-efforts' ACIR expressed, "Tax-effort is a closely related measure quantifying the extent to which a government actually uses its capacity to raise revenue through taxation". [5] If two states are having equal fiscal capacity but state `x' collects more tax revenue than state `y', then the former is said to be making higher tax-effort. For purposes of this definition it is not important that `x' is able to export a large portion of its tax to other states. All taxes paid to state `x' are counted as part of x's tax-effort since they represent utilization of its tax potential.

5.1.2 Measures of Taxable Capacity and Tax Effort: Broadly, there are two different measures of tax potential/capacity and tax efforts and these are:

- Income measure and
- Tax yield measure.

In the first, income is taken as the measure of tax potential out of which state and local taxes can be paid and other non-tax resources flow to the government. In the second, taxable capacity means the resources i.e. estimated amount of tax revenues any state would produce, when subjected to various levels of taxation and comparison of these results with calculations for other states gives a measure of relative taxable capacity. By comparing the tax yield with the potential calculated in either way tax efforts are estimated.

A. Income Measure of Taxable Capacity and Tax Effort: Most of the taxes are paid out of current income. "Unless a community is drawing down its capital stock, its income is a measure of its capacity to meet both public and private needs" states the A.C.I.R. Thus, income is a broad measure of capacity. Various forms of income measure of fiscal capacity and tax-effort are developed. One very commonly used measure of tax-effort is the tax-income ratio:

TE = T/Y

Where TE is the Tax Effort, T = Actual Tax revenue and Y = GDP or SDP. Y is taken as the fiscal potential available to a country or state and `T' is the tax yield. Thus, in this measure tax-yield represents the severity of tax.

There have been a number of measures used for the purpose of making comparative study of tax effort based on `income approach'. Some of the measures widely used are: [6]

1. Tax income ratio T/Y
2. Incremental tax-income ratio $\Delta t/\Delta y$
3. Income Elasticity of tax revenue $(\frac{\Delta T}{\Delta Y} \cdot \frac{T}{Y})$
4. Modified T'/Y' ratio to reflect relative taxable capacity and tax efforts.

In the last method, a ratio between tax-effort and capacity is worked out. The relative taxable capacity is arrived at by the proportion of per capita state income to the average per capita income of all states. In the same way relative tax effort is worked out by taking the proportion of per capita revenue for every given unit of income to all state average per capita tax revenue for a given unit of income. This method was used by R L Mathews [7] and T.A. Sweeney and also by K V S Sastri (1966). [8] The various measures discussed above are based on `income approach'. Underlying assumption is state\national income is the measure of fiscal capacity.

However the fiscal capacity of a state depends not only on income but also on inter-state shifting of state and local taxes. Besides, fiscal capacity is influenced by a number of other factors like structural composition of the economy, level of consumption, price variation, distribution of income and so on which do not get reflected in the tax-income ratio. Thus, taxable capacity depends not only on income produced but also on income accrued. Besides it is also related to wealth. Hence a proper tax-effort measure has to be based on a comprehensive measure of fiscal capacity. Although taxes are generally paid out of the income stream at some point, individual income is by no means the only (or even the principal) basis on which state and local taxes are assessed.

Considering the inadequacy of the income measure of fiscal capacity, many studies were taken up to measure fiscal capacity and tax-efforts based on relative tax-yield approach.

B. Tax-Yield Approach to Measuring Fiscal Capacity and Tax Efforts: Under the tax yield approach, fiscal capacity is defined as the level of taxation that would occur, given certain assumptions as to tax bases and the average intensity of use of the bases by all countries/states in the sample. As noted earlier apart from `income' many other factors influence tax-yield. An allowance, therefore, has to be made for all such major factors. "This can be done either by adjusting the actual tax ratios for variations in the tax capacity factors or by estimating the amount of taxes that could be collected through the use of the potential bases available to the states". In the former approach, regression analysis is used to estimate or measure the influence of capacity factors on the tax-ratio. In the latter approach, a model tax or representative tax system is applied to potential bases to estimate the relative taxable capacity.

C. Regression Analysis Approach: This approach is an improvement over the traditional tax-effort measure namely tax-income ratio, where income was used as a measure of fiscal capacity. The regression approach also called a stochastic approach establishes that in addition to aggregate incomes, the denominator in the tax-ratio, other factors affect a country's taxable capacity.

Regression approach takes into account the effect of several capacity indicators on tax capacity and tax-efforts. For this purpose, the average degree of relationship between the tax-ratio and what are identified as the taxable capacity factors may be derived through multiple regression analysis. Since in this regression equation only the tax capacity factors would be included as independent variables, it is not intended to, and will not explain the total variations in the tax-ratio (minus the stochastic element). The difference between the actual tax-ratio in a state and that estimated for it on the basis of the tax capacity may be attributed to tax-effort. Tax-effort then could be measured in one of two ways:

Some expression of the residual variance can be taken as the measure of tax-effort and the states could be ranked according to the values of this expression,

Alternatively, the estimated tax-ratio can be taken to represent the relative taxable capacity which a state would have had if it had used its capacity to an average extent. Thus a comparison of actual tax-ratio for a state with its estimated ratio will show whether the state is making average tax-effort or above or below average tax effort. The ratio of actual tax-effort to the estimated one would be the index of tax-effort. The tax performance of the several different states can be compared on the basis of these indices: an index equal to 1.0 signifying the average tax-effort

Alternatively, in the regression equation one can take exclusively the indicators of tax-efforts such as the average tax-rates, extent of exploitation of tax base and cost of collection per unit of tax collected. The resulting tax-ratio would measure tax effort, while the residual would reflect the taxable capacity. A major constraint of this approach is the non-availability of comparable data on indicators of tax-efforts across the states.

As the overall tax-ratio is employed in the above regression analysis method of deriving fiscal capacity and tax effort, it has been called the aggregate regression approach. This method was applied by a number of scholars. [9]

The most important component in the regression method of measuring `taxable capacity' is to give a proper specification of the model. This requires identification of determinants of taxable capacity of a state. Once the determinants are identified, tax-function needs to be specified. The selection of the form of equation: whether OLS or log linear would depend upon the nature of the data. It is also important to choose a desired model for estimation of tax function. There are various models being developed for this purpose. The notable models are:

Stochastic Model: where cross section data are used to estimate tax yield. Several determinants exclusively determining `capacity' are chosen and tax-ratio or per capita tax is regressed upon these determinants. While the estimated yield measures `capacity', the residual i.e. the difference between the actual and estimated yield gives a measure of tax-effort. This method fails to distinguish residual variations due to factors affecting tax-effort from that due to random disturbances arising out of sampling fluctuation.

Panel data Model: The purpose of this model is to overcome the shortcomings of stochastic approach. This method helps not only identification of common traits in the tax behavior of the states but also to segregate the effects of state specific factors from that of pure random disturbance factors. Ninth Finance Commission had used this method in their first report. [10]

Panel data model has certain advantages over the conventional model. [11] Basic logic of the two models is similar as both require identification of the determinants at the first step, followed by tax-function specification, form of regression to be used, including the use of dummy variables and so on.

D. Representative Tax System Approach: Second approach analyzing tax-yield is popularly known as Representative Tax System Approach (RTS). This method is applicable at individual tax level. Major proponents of this measure are Advisory Commission on Inter-Governmental Relations. Subsequently, various improvements were suggested by scholars like, Akin (1973), Bahl (1972), Manvel (1971), and so on. This method is explained in Chapter 6.

Both the Aggregate Regression Method and R T S method are commonly used to measure capacity and efforts and both have their own relative merits and demerits. The applicability of R.T.S method depends upon the availability of adequate and reliable data on the tax bases and actual tax rates. In the absence of such information, aggregate Regression Approach is considered as suitable. This approach does not require highly disaggregated data and also takes account of the inter dependence of the tax bases. As the Ninth Finance Commission (1989) rightly observed [12] some times, the effective rates itself can vary with the size of the tax base (the effective tax rate may be higher in a more developed state than in a less developed state), which is captured in the regression approach. In regression approach the estimates are not derived by relating tax revenue to the actual or proxy tax bases, but only to macro-capacity indicators. A major weakness of the regression method is that the residual error is taken to represent tax-effort. The residual error may also contain random factor. The R.T.S method relates the tax revenue to individual tax bases or their proxies and therefore, the logic of the method is more transparent. But, this method is riddled with the complex problem of non-availability of comparable, reliable and adequate data on tax base and rates, and also item-wise tax-yield across the states. In the absence of such information any attempt to estimate tax-wise yield, results in disaggregated level regression approach only.

Illustration of the Methodology for the Estimation of Taxable Capacity and Tax-Efforts [13]

The illustration of the measures of taxable Capacity and Tax Efforts are taken from study conducted by Rao (1993). To illustrate the application of the above measures, in this study, she adopts a regression approach to measure taxable capacity and tax-efforts of Indian states. To be precise an aggregate regression method, using a panel data model of fixed effect type with changing intercept is adopted. The three important elements of this approach are:

- Identification of determinants of capacity variable and the criteria for the selection of determinants.
- Specification of the regression model and its modifications.
- Estimation of Taxable Capacity and Tax efforts.

5.1.3 Determinants of Taxable Capacity: Before a tax function is specified, it is essential to identify various factors that determine the taxable capacity of a state. Obviously, all those variables, which form the tax base of different taxes, emerge as important determinants. However, it is not always easy to identify the actual tax base and therefore one may have to use proxy variables or factors which generally influence the tax base and hence the tax-yield. In regression approach, we use certain determinants of aggregate taxable capacity instead of using the actual tax base.

There could be a long list of variables, which could emerge as determinants. But it is not possible to include all the determinants in a tax-equation. Some may have to be dropped due to non-availability of data or inadequacy of data, while some may have to be dropped due to their low explanatory power or due to high degree of multi-colleniarity with other variables. Further more, one has to restrict the number of determinants to a moderate size, when we have only a limited number of observations as in the present context. The important determinants of `taxable capacity' which are used by various scholars are:

1. Per capita income
2. Degree of openness
3. Degree of monetization
4. Size distribution of income/consumption expenditure
5. Per capita consumption expenditure
6. Sectoral composition of income
7. Extent of urbanization
8. Levels of development

Most of the studies that estimated relative taxable capacity and tax-efforts pertained to inter-country or international analysis. We shall briefly examine the above variables as determinants of taxable capacity.

A. Per Capita Income: Most commonly used independent variable, estimating taxable capacity, is per capita income. It is justified on several grounds. Per capita income is a measure of the level of prosperity and development. As early as in 1961, Williamson [14] established relationship between revenue share and stage of development. His results showed that there was a significant positive relationship between the tax-ratio and per capita income. Hinrich [15] also established in his study of 40 countries a strong relationship between tax-ratio and per capita income. Lotz and Morss, Bahl and many others also found per capita income as an important determinant of taxable capacity.

In fact, most of the taxes are paid out of current income and hence income forms an important tax base. Further, per capita income is also a measure of development, which also influences taxable capacity. Hence, per capita income is a universally accepted variable in the analysis of 'taxable capacity 'whether at inter-national or intra-national or intra-state levels. The hypothesis is that per capita income and tax yield are positively related so that an increase in per capita income results in an increase in tax-yield.

B. Degree of Openness: Openness is measured as the sum of imports and exports as percentage of GNP. This variable, though important for inter-country studies, cannot be used for intra-country or inter-state differences within a country.

C. Degree of Monetization: This determinant as measured by the supply of currency and coinage, is not relevant for state level analysis, as inter-state differences in the level of monetization is not expected to be significant enough to influence the variations in taxable capacity.

D. Size of Distribution of Income/Consumption: It is held by some that distribution of personal income or in the absence of data on income distribution, distribution of consumption expenditure has a significant bearing on the taxable capacity. If a state's per capita income is high but the distribution is highly skewed so that a larger portion of population is concentrated in the lowest range of income/consumption, the taxable capacity of the state would be low. If income/consumption is more evenly distributed, a larger portion of population will come under the tax range and thus a larger tax yield would result. Even when inequality is very high, and the Tax system is regressive though more number of people comes under the Tax net, the taxable capacity will be low, because the disposable income of the people coming under tax net will be very low.

A major problem with this determinant is the lack of data on the distribution of income or consumption. In India NSSO [16] conducts quinquennial survey of household consumption, of late even annual surveys are being conducted. These data can be used to measure inequality in consumption expenditure to reflect inequality in income distribution. The hypothesis in case of 'inequality' variable is, higher the inequality, lesser will be the taxable capacity.

Thus a fall in inequality level is expected to result in an increase in tax yield. How significant this relationship is depends upon the level of consumption expenditure and the nature of taxation, i.e. progressive or regressive since most of the state taxes are indirect taxes, which are regressive, in nature, a negative relationship is expected between the extent of inequality and tax yield.

E. Per Capita Consumer Expenditure: This is an important factor determining the taxable capacity of Indian states. It is hypothesized that higher the per capita consumption expenditure higher is the taxable capacity. When we take per capita income, the data available on state income relate to 'income originating concept'. It is very likely that in spite of high 'income originating' income accrual to a state may be low and vice versa. This aspect is partially captured when per capita consumption is taken into consideration. Further, if we analyze the state tax structure, a very significant part of tax-revenue comes from sales tax. A major part of sales tax comes from consumption goods and intermediate goods and hence per capita consumption expenditure emerges as a good explanatory factor for inter-state variation in taxable capacity.

Consumption expenditure as a determinant has some weaknesses. [17] Firstly, state taxes are levied not only on consumer expenditure but also on producers' goods and transactions. NSS consumption estimates take into account only final consumptions by households. Obviously, a lot of intermediate transactions that attract taxes like sales tax do take place everyday which lie outside the purview of household consumption.

Secondly, consumption expenditure of the higher income groups is grossly under estimated in NSS estimates, especially in the Indian economy where concealed income form a sizeable proportions of total expenditure, and

Thirdly, the cash components of total consumer expenditure differ between states. NSS estimates do not provide any information about it.

As regards the first limitation, we can reasonably assume that the sales tax levied on producers' goods is shifted on to the products produced with the raw materials and machinery and which is ultimately paid by consumers of that product. [18] Regarding the second, we may assume that underestimation, if any, of the richer income group will be of more or less the same magnitude in all the states and in an estimation of relative taxable capacity such differences are not of much importance. In fact, the third limitation of the consumption variable is removed when we take consumption expenditure along with variables like adjusted per capita income i.e. income minus per capita expenditure, urbanization and sectoral composition of income.

F. Sectoral Composition of Income: The sectoral composition of income in an economy has a definite bearing on the taxable capacity, especially in a country like India, where distinction is maintained between agricultural and non-agricultural sectors for purposes of taxation. In India, at the state level, tax-revenue from agricultural sector is almost negligible. A few taxes on agricultural sector are land revenue and agricultural income tax, which have become insignificant. There are various studies such as by Ved. P Gandhi [19] which, show that the incidence of taxation on agricultural sector is very low in India. Therefore, the tax-yield varies across the states, depending upon the composition of state domestic product. Thus, cetris-paribus a negative relationship is postulated between tax yield and agriculture share of income and a positive relationship between non-primary i.e. secondary and tertiary sector proportion in the income. In a country where there is no distinction for tax purposes between income generated from agriculture and non-agricultural sector, the sectoral composition of income is not important as a determinant. However, if tax-structure is such that it makes one sector to pay more and the sectoral incidence is unequal, then in spite of having equal per capita income the tax-yield would vary depending upon the sectoral composition of income. Further even if there is no distinction between the sectors for tax purposes, a state with larger agricultural sector has lower capacity because:

- the income of agricultural wage earners is relatively low,
- the profit margin tends to be low, and
- such enterprises are not as amenable to tax administration as

enterprises in other sectors of the economy.

If a state is in the very early stages of development and the secondary and tertiary sectors are not well developed, tax-yield that accrues to a state will depend mainly on per capita income, levels of development and also on the shares of agricultural and secondary sector.

G. Urbanisation: Extent of urbanisation is often linked with the level of development. Urbanization is measured by taking the proportion of urban population to total population. Higher urbanization indicates higher levels of living in state compared to a state with predominant rural sector. This also indicates higher level of consumption of durable commodities, and services, which have higher tax potential. It is comparatively easy to collect taxes in urban areas than in rural areas. Considering these features, it is hypothesized that a state with higher level of urbanization has higher taxable capacity.

H. Levels of Development: This is also considered as an important determinant of taxable capacity. Levels of development of a state is high, if it has better socio-economic infrastructural facilities, high productive sectors like industries, mining, commerce, etc., resulting in availability of higher level of consumer goods and-services. All these positively influence the tax yield. Level of development is a determinant of tax base. Higher the level of development, higher would be the tax base and hence higher taxable capacity.

The problem with this determinant is the lack of a comprehensive measure of development. In an earlier study Rao [20] had developed a composite index of development and had used it in the tax function.

Based on the above considerations, explanatory variables need to be included in the specification of tax equation.

If a choice is to be made between two equally acceptable variables from *a priori* reasoning, it can be argued that the variable that explains a greater portion of the variance should be chosen on the grounds that it is simply a better predictor of the inter-state taxable capacity differences.

In the choice of variables to include in such a model, the approach may be 'normative' or `positive'. Under normative approach, it may be argued that X1 or X2 are relevant indicators of taxable capacity and that they should be included in the estimation equation, regardless of variations explained and regardless of weather or not they are significant. In such a case, the regression analysis is used primarily to assign weights to the tax bases in the taxable capacity equation. [21]

If, on the other hand the approach is positive, the argument is that the "average" behavior of countries as measured by the (statistical) relationship between the observed tax-yield and hypothesized taxable capacity factors - reveal their propensity to use a particular base and subsequently reveal the surplus inherent in that base. In such a case goodness of fit would be a reasonable criterion for choosing bases that provide the most binding constraints on taxable capacity, or alternatively in identifying those components of the economic structure where taxable surplus is the highest. It also follows that variables that are not significantly related to per capita tax would be excluded from the equation that is used to estimate taxable capacity. The approach taken in our paper is positive and the objective of the regression analysis is to identify the factors that reflect such constraints or surpluses.

Specification of the Model:

Keeping in mind the above considerations for including variables in the tax-function equation, initially we selected the following list of variables and from these we selected the final short list.

1. Per capita SDP
2. Per capita annual consumption expenditure excluding taxes
3. Sectoral composition of SDP:
   - Secondary sector share,
   - Tertiary sector share.
   - Non primary sector share (secondary+tertiary sector combined)
   - Primary sector share
4. Extent of urbanisation
5. Levels of infrastructural development

6. Gini Coefficient, measuring consumption inequality.

The dependent variable selected is per capita tax yield. From the above list of determinants, which appear to be equally acceptable on *a priori* reasoning, finally we retained only those variables, which satisfied the criteria outlined above.

Statistical Method:

In order to estimate taxable capacity and tax-efforts first the 25 states were put under two categories based on the size (area, population etc.). The first category consisted of the following 15 major states: (1) Andhra Pradesh, (2) Assam, (3) Bihar, (4) Gujarat, (5) Haryana, (6) Karnataka, (7) Kerala, (8) Madhya Pradesh, (9) Maharasthra, (10) Orissa, (11) Punjab, (12) Rajasthan, (13) Tamil Nadu, (14) Uttar Pradesh and (15) West Bengal.

The second set consisted of very small, newly formed and special category states viz, (1) Arunachal Pradesh, (2) Goa, (3) Himachal Pradesh, (4) Jammu & Kashmir, (5) Manipur, (6) Meghalaya, (7) Mizoram, (8) Nagaland, (9) Sikkim and (10) Tripura.

The taxable capacity of the above states has estimated by using the panel data model. For the 15 major states data have pooled from 1983-84 to 1990-91, and for 10 states data have pooled for three years i.e. from 1987-88 to 1989-90. Thus, in all there were 120 observations, for 15 states and 30 observations for 10 states. These 15 states showed much of disparities in the levels of development and diversity in the natural endowments. Keeping in mind these diversities in the analysis, first a statistical test has conducted to determine to what extent the tax function was homogeneous across the group of states, and the need to minimize hetrogeneity if any by employing dummy variables either for the intercept or slope or both. F' test was done for this purpose. First the equations for individual states were obtained separately and then 15 states data were pooled over a period of 8 years. Thus, the following regressions were obtained: [22]

1. Regression equations one for each year having a cross section of 15 states,
2. 15 regression equations one for each state having eight year

time series data, and

3. One regression equation for time-series and cross section pooled series i.e. for 15 states and 8 years.

The tests for such structural effects showed that the parameters of tax function did differ among states and therefore there was need to include intercept dummies for states. The tests did not indicate the need for time dummies. Even the need for slope dummies did not emerge as significant. A similar test could not be effected for 10 minor states due to lack of data for adequate number of years.

To capture the structural effect, initially we used 15 state dummies, running the equation through the origin. However, the dummy coefficients were not found significant for all the states. Hence, alternatively, instead of using separate dummy for each state we grouped 15 states, by taking the three year average per capita income, into the following three groups.

1. High Income States: Punjab, Haryana, Gujarat, and Maharashtra
2. Middle Income States: Tamil Nadu, Andhra Pradesh, Karnataka, Kerala, and West Bengal
3. Low Income States: Assam, Bihar, Madhya Pradesh, Rajasthan, Uttar Pradesh and Orissa

Keeping the low income state dummy as reference, two dummy variables one for high income level and the other for middle income states [23] were introduced in the equation, mainly to capture the effect of differential levels of prosperity or development. The effect of a particular income group may operate in two ways. First even with identical marginal impacts of different determinants or explanatory variables, taxable capacity may be higher or lower in a given group i.e. intercept or constant term in the estimating equation may vary among the above three income groups. Second, the marginal impact of each of the independent variables may also vary among the different income groups i.e. the regression coefficients of explanatory variables may be different in each region (slope variation).

A panel data model is specified hypothesizing a functional relationship between inter-state disparities in tax capacity and its various determinants as mentioned beforehand. We are using panel data for controlling individual heterogeneity of the states. It also gives more informative, more variability, less collinearity among the variables, more degree of freedom and more efficiency. In the case of panel data model, the error term U_{it} is a composite residual consisting of time invariant state specific components μ_i, and it captures various characteristics of the states, which are not observable but have a significant impact on the state's tax capacity, and state invariant time specific fixed effects λ_t, and a disturbance term ε_{it}, which is assumed to be serially uncorrelated with mean zero, and is possibly heteroscedasticity. So, the behavioural equation for the panel data model can be specified as:

$$Y_{it} = \delta + \sum_{i=1}^{k} \beta_k X_{kit} + \mu_i + \lambda_t + \varepsilon_{it} \qquad \text{..................(1)}$$

Where δ is a scalar, x'_{it} is 1 × k and β is k × 1. i = 1........ N; t = 1...... T. We will assume that the equation (1) follows a two-way error component model.

The fixed effect model adopted here assumes that the slope parameters of the tax function are the same across the states. [24] The time effect is ignored in the models as the tests showed that there was no need to have time dummies. The fixed effect model assumes that the variations of the parameter vector across the states arise because of basic structural, socio-economic differences among the states, and that these structural differences remain fairly stable over the sample period. In this fixed effect model we have specified that only the intercept parameter varies across the group of states and the slope parameters are common.

Statistical analysis based on `linear' form and also `log-linear' form brought the serious problems of serial correlation/auto-correlation over time-series and cross-section pooled data. [25] To correct for auto-correlation we have used `search method' and derived equations after removing auto-correlation effects, and these equations are used for the final estimation of taxable capacity of Indian states.

In order to test for the need for capturing structural effects through dummy variables, we applied `F' test. The estimation involves the following steps:

(1) We have obtained separate regression equations both across the regions as well as over the period.

(2) From each regression equation, we have calculated the error sum of square, which denoted by ESS_i . Where i = 1, 2, ….., 8 and the Total Sum of Square for pooling (TSSP) = $\sum_{i=1}^{N} ESS_i$.

Where N = 8, similarly for 15 states, error sum of square can be written as

$$\sum_{i=1}^{N} ESSi \text{ for eight period of time.}$$

N = 15

(3) In the third step, we have obtained PESS (Pooled Error Sum of Square) for pooled series.

(4) $$F = \frac{PESS - TESS1 / Pk - k}{TESS1 / n - Pk}$$

Here, PESS = Pooled error sum of square, TESS1= Total sum of square for 8 years,

k = Coefficients used in the equation including intercept, P = Number of years and

N = Total number of observations.

(5) If the calculated F > table value of F then time specific effect is significant. That implies that we will reject the null hypothesis of intercept parameter being constant over the period of time.

In the similar manner, for the fifteen states:

$$F = \frac{PESS2 / Sk - k}{TESS2 / N - Sk}$$

Where, K = Coefficients, S = No. of States, N = Total No. of observation (states x time). If calculated F > critical value of F, state specific effect is significant otherwise not. Similarly in case the time or state specific effect is found to be significant, there is need to use dummies otherwise not. Keeping in view the above test, first we used fifteen states dummies. Since these were not found to be significant for number of states, we used state group dummies instead of individual dummies.

Section 2

5.2 Empirical Analysis and Statistical Results (Based on Panel Data Model)

5.2.1 Estimating Equation: The taxable capacity is a function of six major factors:

1. Level of prosperity and material well being as measured by per capita state domestic product.
2. Per capita income net of per capita household consumption per annum measuring savings and non-household consumption
3. Sectoral composition of income produced.
4. Level of consumption expenditure per capita per annum
5. Extent of urbanisation, measuring concentration of consumption, level of development etc. and
6. Extent of inequality in consumption expenditure.

First a simple correlation matrix was derived separately for 15 states and 10 states. It may be observed from Table 5.1 Correlation matrix for 15 states that each of the above mentioned variables is significantly related to the level of per capita tax. It may be seen that almost all the variables are significantly and positively correlated with tax yield, except for the last variable viz, inequality in consumption, which has a negative correlation;

In formulating a single estimate of taxable capacity, these factors some how should be combined into a single equation so as to permit an estimate of the effects of taxable capacity of, for example, a small differences in the level of consumption, given the differences in other variables held constant.

The specific hypotheses to be tested on these partial regression coefficients are that taxable capacity is negatively related to the inequality index and positively to all other variables. The relationship is assumed to be linear. In our model we included the above mentioned six variables as explanatory variables and per capita tax as the dependent variable. Level of development is also an important determinant, however, this effect is captured by other variables like per capita income, urbanization, non primary sectoral share and consumption level etc, and hence we did not include it. Further, a reliable development index is not available.

Table 5.1: Correlation Matrix for Fifteen States

	X1	X2	X3	X4	X5	X6	X7
X1	1.000						
X2	.918	1.000					
X3	.859	.959	1.000				
X4	.719	.795	.594	1.000			
X5	.583	.356	.359	.155	1.000		
X6	.711	.527	.547	.250	843	1.000	
X7	-.104	-.175	-.069	-.373	.226	.360	1.000

Note: X1 = Per capita Tax, X2 = Per capita income PY, X3 = Income net of H.H consumption (PY-PACE), X4 = Per capita Annual Consumption Expenditure (PACE), X5 = Non-Primary Sectoral income % share, X6 =Percentage share of urban population and X7 = Inequality in consumption expenditure.

If we look at the variables, justified on *a priori* ground, we find that two of the variables viz SDP per capita and consumption per capita, have some problem. Conceptually, expenditure is a part of income and hence, if both per capita income (PY) and per capita expenditure (PACE) are used in one equation, one of the variables becomes less significant and the potential result is a biased estimate of the regressions coefficient. In an analysis of taxable capacity at state level, both `income' and `expenditure' exert influence on tax yield. If we drop `consumption' we shall be dropping one of the most significant determinants of a major tax like sales tax. On the other hand if we drop `SDP' per capita, we are neglecting an important determinant of other taxes like, motor vehicle tax, property tax, profession tax, taxes on transaction and excise etc. This drives one to consider both the determinants in one equation. However Per capita consumption cannot be used along with per capita income without modifying the latter, as that leads to specification error. Avoid any such error, we derived a new variable income net of per capita consumption expenditure by subtracting per capita expenditure from per capita income (Table 5.2).

Table 5.2: Determinants of Taxable Capacity for Fifteen Major States (Equation 1)

Independent Variables	Fixed Effect with Group Dummy
PACE	0.07123* (9.39)
PACE – Ptax	0.1207* (10.89)
NPSI	2.7161* (3.51)
Urbanization	4.6647* (2.81)
Inequality Index	- 112.07 (-1.332)
Dummy for HIG states (D_1)	- 272.09* (- 4.86)
Dummy for MIG states (D_2)	- 276.994* (- 4.84)
Adjusted $\overline{R}^2 = 0.9637$; D-W statistic = 2.039; N = 120	

Source: Author's own calculation. Notes: (1) The values in parentheses below the coefficients show the t-statistics. (2) *, Show the 1 per cent level of significance respectively. (3) PACE = Per capita Annual Consumption Expenditure with tax, Ptax = Per capita tax, NPSI = Non Primary Sectoral Share of Income in percentage, HIG = High Income Group, MIG = Middle Income Group.

Here what remains after excluding per capita consumption expenditure is the non-household consumption expenditure plus savings. These two are important determinants of taxable capacity. However, this type of modification of a variable has limitations. First of all the data source for `Income' and `consumption' are different. While `income' figures are obtained from the C.S.O. the `consumption' data are from the sample surveys conducted by the N.S.S.O. Conceptually, `SDP' estimates are based on `income' generating concept while `consumption `data are based on income accrual concept. Consumption data as given by the N.S.S.O are of vital importance in the study of consumption behavior. But they do not provide directly with clear evidence on the relationship of aggregate consumption to aggregate income.

However, considering the fact, that no other estimate of `consumption expenditure' at the state level is available and that both consumption and income are important tax bases at the state level, with all these limitations, we have used PACE along with adjusted income in equation. As may be seen from equation (1) all the regression coefficients are highly significant at 1% level, $\overline{R}^2$ is as high as .9637, and D.W statistics 2.039 shows that there is no problem of serial correlation. Thus, the above equation provides a very good fit. Hence, we estimated taxable capacity and tax efforts of 15 major states by using equation (1).

In order to make a comparison we also derived an equation, consisting of per capita income and per capita expenditure along with other variables. It is given in equation 2 (Table 5.3).

Table 5.3: Determinants of Taxable Capacity for Fifteen Major States (Equation2)

Independent Variables	Fixed Effect with Group Dummy
PY	0.07165* (10.89)
PACE – Ptax	0.0353* (2.205)
NPSI	2.632* (3.67)
Urbanization	3.9002* (2.51)
Inequality Index	- 99.01 (-1.263)
Dummy for HIG states (D_1)	- 251.69* (4.83)
Dummy for MIG states (D_2)	- 241.145* (- 4.65)
Adjusted $\overline{R}^2 = 0.968$; D-W statistic = 2.04; N = 120	

Source: Author's own calculation. Notes: (1) The values in parentheses below the coefficients show the t-statistics. (2) *, Show the 1 per cent level of significance respectively. (3) PY = Per capita Income, PACE = Per capita Annual Consumption Expenditure with tax, Ptax = Per capita tax, NPSI = Non Primary Sectoral Share of Income in percentage, HIG = High Income Group, MIG = Middle Income Group.

Statistically, the two equations i.e. equation (2) with SDP per capita and equation (1) with adjusted SDP per capita, have more or less the same $\overline{R}^2$, (.96) Even the regression coefficients of almost all the variables are comparable except for `X6' for which T-value declined from 10.823 to 2.205 in the second equation. The statistical results presented in equation (1) not only are consistent with the hypotheses developed here but also make some intuitive sense.

In order to have an estimate of taxable capacity and tax-efforts of 15 major states, without resorting to assumptions and limitations as in the case of equation (1). We have selected another combination of determinants, where only one of the two viz. income or consumption is used along with the other variables. The equation using per capita income along with sectoral composition of income, urbanisation and inequality in consumption, gives a very good fit. The equation after correcting for auto-correlation with `search' method is given in Table 5.4.

Table 5.4: Determinants of Taxable Capacity for Fifteen Major States (Equation 3)

Independent Variables	Fixed Effect with Group Dummy
PY	0.08422* (25.28)
NPSI	2.849* (3.94)
Urbanization	3.0884* (2.01)
Inequality Index	- 129.02** (-1.64)
Dummy for HIG states (D_1)	- 220.66* (-4.32)
Dummy for MIG states (D_2)	- 196.90* (- 4.05)
Adjusted $\overline{R}^2 = 0.967$; D-W statistic = 2.04; N = 120	

Source: Author's own calculation. Notes: (1) The values in parentheses below the coefficients show the t-statistics. (2) *, **, Show the 1 per cent and 10 per cent level of significance respectively. (3) PY = Per capita Income, NPSI = Non Primary Sectoral Share of Income in percentage, HIG = High Income Group, MIG = Middle Income Group.

In the above equation, all the four determinants are highly significant and are with the expected signs. The $\overline{R}^2$ is also quite high and D.W statistics shows no problem of auto-correlation.

Thus, it provides a very good fit and is superior to equation 1 as it does not require correction for specification error. However, here we miss an important tax-base variable i.e. consumption expenditure.

The Ninth Finance commission in its first report had used a panel data model of fixed effect type with changing intercepts and had induced in the equations three determinants viz, per capita SDP, the proportion of non-primary sectoral income to total SDP and the Lorenz ratio of consumer expenditure distribution. Following, the Ninth Finance Commission, we have also worked out taxable capacity of 15 major states by using the same determinants in another equation. The equation after correcting for serial correlation is given in Table 5.5.

Table 5.5: Determinants of Taxable Capacity for Fifteen Major States (Equation 4)

Independent Variables	Fixed Effect with Group Dummy
PY	0.0866* (27.46)
NPSI	3.7013* (6.28)
Inequality Index	- 53.866 (-0.77)
Dummy for HIG states (D_1)	- 217.058* (-4.22)
Dummy for MIG states (D_2)	- 196.62* (- 4.013)
Adjusted $\overline{R}^2 = 0.966$; D-W statistic = 2.048; N = 120	

Source: Author's own calculation. Notes: (1) The values in parentheses below the coefficients show the t-statistics. (2) *, Show the 1 per cent level of significance respectively. (3) PY = Per capita Income, NPSI = Non Primary Sectoral Share of Income in percentage, HIG = High Income Group, MIG = Middle Income Group.

The above equation is comparable with the one worked out by the Ninth Finance Commission. Except inequality variable, all other variables in the model are statistically significant at one per cent level. All of them have expected signs and there is no problem of serial correlation.

5.2.2 Statistical Results: For estimating taxable capacity and tax-efforts, we used four equations i.e. 1, 2, 3 and 4 by replacing the actual values of explanatory variables for the years 1990-91, for the 15 major states we obtained estimated taxable capacity and by taking the ratio of the actual tax-yield and estimated yield we estimated tax-efforts of the states. These measures are given in table 1.3. By using these equations, the states may be ranked not only according to their taxable capacity but also according to their tax-effort. The ranking is presented in the columns next to the columns with taxable capacity measures and tax-efforts estimates. Tax-effort index number above 1.00 indicates an above average tax-effort. Specifically the figure shown for a state is an estimate of the per capita tax yield that corresponds to the present definition of taxable capacity indicators and to the average practice of the states in the sample.

It may be observed from Table 5.6 that the estimated tax yields resulting from equation 1 and 2 are similar, the difference is marginal, so also the measures of tax-efforts.

Since all the equations are statistically good and the variation in the results is not significant, and the explanatory variables are acceptable on a priori ground one can adopt any one of the equations for final estimates of taxable capacity and tax-efforts. Other things being equal, the final selection of the equation should be guided apart from the overall explanatory power of the model as revealed by $\overline{R}^2$ one should look at the explanatory power or statistical superiority. [26] Taking variables, which provide more comprehensive tax base in an aggregate tax analysis model, the first equation emerges as the best.

Equation 1, after modifying the per capita income variable, gives the best model $\overline{R}^2$ is as high as .96, and D.W statistics 2.04 shows no problem of serial correlation. That apart, the explanatory variables are significant at 1% level. Even the variable measuring inequality is acceptable as it is significant at 20% level. There is theoretical justification for each of the explanatory variable included in the equation.

Table 5.6: Taxable Capacity and Tax-efforts of 15 Major States Based on Alternative Equations (Amount: Rs. in Crore)

States	1990-91	Equation	Rank	Tax	Effort RK	Equation	Rank	Tax	Effort RK
	Actual	1	Eqn.1	Effort	Eqn.1	2	Eqn. 2	Effort	Eqn.2
Andhra Pradesh	407.6	391.787	9	1.0404	7	396.466	9	1.0281	7
Assam	192.48	241.734	13	0.7962	14	243.947	13	0.789	14
Bihar	135.03	162.749	15	0.8297	12	160.383	15	0.8419	12
Gujarat	593.97	564.743	3	1.0518	6	567.058	4	1.0475	6
Haryana	670.91	560.706	4	1.1965	3	572.701	3	1.1715	3
Karnataka	530.35	431.697	7	1.2285	1	443.713	6	1.1953	1
Kerala	467.8	408.749	8	1.1445	4	405.196	8	1.1545	4
Madhya Pradesh	271.18	280.254	12	0.9676	9	278.327	12	0.9743	9
Maharashtra	665.04	662.501	2	1.0038	8	667.539	2	0.9963	8
Orissa	216.05	189.683	14	1.139	5	194.459	14	1.111	5
Punjab	651.51	713.411	1	0.9132	10	714.465	1	0.9119	10
Rajasthan	284.17	331	10	0.8585	11	322.349	10	0.8816	11
Tamil Nadu	569.37	474.152	5	1.2008	2	482.883	5	1.1791	2
Uttar Pradesh	232.65	283.224	11	0.8214	13	279.421	11	0.8326	13
West Bengal	320.82	433.808	6	0.7395	15	429.288	7	0.7473	15

Contd...

States	Eqn.3	Rank	Tax	Effort Rk	Equn.4	Rank	Tax	Effort Rk
		Eqn.3	Effort	Eqn.3		Eq. 4	Effort	Eqn.4
Andhra Pradesh	401.121	8	1.0162	7	402.709	8	1.0121	8
Assam	252.374	13	0.7627	14	271.637	12	0.7086	15
Bihar	156.652	15	0.862	12	167.023	15	0.8085	13
Gujarat	570.514	4	1.0411	6	561.845	4	1.0572	5
Haryana	580.801	3	1.1551	4	591.588	3	1.1341	4
Karnataka	455.912	6	1.1633	3	450.975	6	1.176	2
Kerala	379.52	9	1.2326	1	381.864	9	1.225	1
Madhya Pradesh	271.861	12	0.9975	8	260.38	13	1.0415	6
Maharashtra	678.041	2	0.9808	9	671.802	2	0.9899	10
Orissa	198.965	14	1.0859	5	208.633	14	1.0356	7
Punjab	721.012	1	0.9036	11	719.299	1	0.95058	11
Rajasthan	300.621	10	0.9453	10	285.393	10	0.9957	9
Tamil Nadu	487.881	5	1.167	2	484.588	5	1.175	3
Uttar Pradesh	274.424	11	0.8478	13	274.574	11	0.8473	12
West Bengal	432.258	7	0.7422	15	435.065	7	0.7374	14

The second equation suffers from specification error and problem of multicollinearity. In the third equation, one of the important proxy base of the most important state tax i.e. per capita consumption expenditure is left out. And in the fourth equation, apart from leaving important determinants, we final that even out of the variables is insignificant. Hence, considering the theoretical justification for the explanatory variables, statistical norms, looking at the estimated values of taxable capacity and efforts based on alternative equations, we have selected equation 1 for final estimate of taxable capacity and tax efforts of 15 major states.

In order to arrive at the final taxable capacity and tax effort indices, we first estimated these two for three years starting from 1988-89 to 1990-91 and then worked out 3 years average taxable capacity and 3 year average tax efforts and the states were ranked and grouped on the basis of their three year average performance. The reason for taking 3 years average lies in avoiding any error in estimation due to any abnormal situation faced by any state and to obtain stable estimates.

The results are presented in Table 5.7 the last 4 columns present estimated fiscal capacity and respective ranks, and estimated tax-effort and respective ranks the advantage of taking an average is clear from the table.

In order to have a closer look into the divergence between the two rankings i.e. based on 1990-91 estimates and 3 years average estimates of Tax-effort, we have used a graphical method.

The Diagonal line is the line of perfect agreement between the two rankings. The placements of states away from the line show the extent of disagreement between the two estimates. Farther a state falls from the line, the larger the divergence. As the diagram shows, only Punjab, Rajasthan, Bihar and UP fall on the line of perfect agreement. While most of the other states are quite close to the line. However the states of Karnataka, Kerala, Haryana, Tamil Nadu, Orissa and AP are scattered away from the line.

Juxtaposing the diagram along with the facts in table, some interesting cases may be highlighted. Karnataka, which occupies first place in 1990-91 drifts to 3rd place when average tax-effort is

Table 5.7: Taxable Capacity and Tax-effort of Indian States from 1988-89 to 1990-91 and 3 Years Average (Amount: Rs. in Crore)

Equation 1

	Tax Yield 1988-89					Tax Yield 1989-90				
States	1988-89 Actual	1988-89 Est.	Rank Capa..	Tax Effort	Rank Effort	1989-90 Actual	1989-90 Est.	Rank Capa...	Tax Effort	Rank Effort
Andhra Pradesh	341.02	303.867	9	1.12	3	375.04	331.471	9	1.1314	3
Assam	133.3	189.67	13	0.7	15	155.77	228.254	13	0.6824	15
Bihar	102.52	117.923	15	0.87	11	111.73	135.982	15	0.8217	12
Gujarat	480.92	452.236	4	1.06	6	544.74	515.181	3	1.0574	5
Haryana	522.79	459.015	3	1.14	2	584.39	495.161	4	1.1802	2
Karnataka	401.11	361.798	6	1.11	4	447.74	396.905	6	1.1281	4
Kerala	381.77	324.068	8	1.18	1	435.85	364.973	8	1.1942	1
Madhya Pradesh	215.94	199.294	12	1.08	5	249.21	239.234	12	1.0417	6
Maharashtra	519.58	530.53	2	0.98	8	584.75	613.054	2	0.9538	10
Orissa	148.21	156.955	14	0.94	9	172.59	170.417	14	1.0128	8
Punjab	544.94	550.894	1	0.99	7	630.8	634.829	1	0.9937	9
Rajasthan	219.23	257.704	10	0.85	12	256.81	272.692	10	0.9418	11
Tamil Nadu	373.72	408.27	5	0.92	10	459.99	452.112	5	1.0174	7
Uttar Pradesh	159.02	214.091	11	0.74	14	184.28	252.727	11	0.7292	14
West Bengal	272.6	351.301	7	0.78	13	297.9	391.956	7	0.76	13

Contd...

	Tax Yield 1990-91					Average Tax Yield				
States	1990-91 Actual	1990-91 Est.	Rank Capa..	Tax Effort	Rank Effort	Average Actual	Average Estimate	Rank Capa..	Average Tax Effort	Rank Effort
Andhra Pradesh	407.6	391.797	9	1.0403	7	374.55	342.38	9	1.094	4
Assam	192.48	241.734	13	0.7962	14	160.52	219.89	13	0.73	15
Bihar	135.03	162.749	15	0.8297	12	116.43	138.88	15	0.8383	12
Gujarat	593.97	564.743	3	1.0518	6	539.88	510.72	3	1.0571	5
Haryana	670.91	560.706	4	1.1965	3	592.7	504.96	4	1.1737	1
Karnataka	530.35	431.697	7	1.2285	1	459.73	396.8	6	1.1586	3
Kerala	467.8	408.749	8	1.1445	4	428.47	365.93	8	1.1709	2
Madhya Pradesh	271.18	280.254	12	0.9676	9	245.44	239.59	12	1.0244	8
Maharashtra	665.04	662.501	2	1.0038	8	589.79	602.03	2	0.9797	9
Orissa	216.05	189.683	14	1.139	5	178.95	172.35	14	1.0383	7
Punjab	651.51	713.411	1	0.9132	10	609.08	633.04	1	0.9621	10
Rajasthan	284.17	331	10	0.8585	11	253.4	287.13	10	0.8825	11
Tamil Nadu	569.37	474.152	5	1.2008	2	467.69	444.84	5	1.0514	6
Uttar Pradesh	232.65	283.224	11	0.8214	13	191.98	250.01	11	0.7679	13
West Bengal	320.82	433.808	6	0.7395	15	297.11	392.36	7	0.7572	14

Structural model of Taxable Capacity panel data model, 120 observations, 15 states and eight years from 1983-84 to 1990-91.

taken note of. While Kerala improves its position from fourth place to second, first place of Karnataka is replaced by Haryana, when its average performance is taken into consideration. Similarly Tamil Nadu, which gets second place in 1990-91, goes down to occupy 6th place on its average performance.

A state, due to some abnormal favorable situation may be able to score high in a particular year (may be good arrear collection etc) or a state may show lower yield due to some year specific changes. In order to smoother such variations, it is preferable to take 3 year average.

Based on the average capacity, the states are put in the following three groups:

- **High Capacity States:** Punjab, Maharashtra, Gujarat, Haryana.
- **Middle Capacity States:** Tamil Nadu, Karnataka, West Bengal, Kerala, Andhra Pradesh
- **Low Capacity States:** Bihar, Orissa, Assam, Madhya Pradesh, Uttar Pradesh and Rajasthan.

In Table 5.8, States are grouped according to tax effort and Tax Capacity Characteristics.

It is interesting to observe that tax-efforts made by different states is irrespective of the taxable capacity available to them. It is not true that only rich states make higher tax-efforts and the low income states lag behind. States like Orissa and M.P though low capacity states have made above average efforts to raise resources, while states like Punjab and Maharashtra have recorded below average tax-effort in spite of having high taxable capacity. Even states with middle capacity like Tamil Nadu, Karnataka, Kerala and A.P have made higher tax efforts, while West Bengal falls far below expectation.

While estimating taxable capacity of states, the question of `prohibition policy' arises. When we normatively assess total tax-revenues, the potential revenue from state excises are implicitly included even in the case of states where prohibition is in force. Whether a state wants to follow a prohibition policy or not is left to the state concerned. It is same as a state opting for introducing profession tax or not or any other tax. Center cannot be made to bear the cost of prohibition in a particular state and hence no adjustment is made while calculating the fiscal capacity of states with prohibition policy.

Table: 5.8: Distribution of 15 Major States: Tax Efforts and Taxable Capacity Performance

	Taxable capacity & Tax effort		
	High Capacity	Middle Capacity	Low Capacity
High Tax Efforts	Gujarat (5,3)	Tamil Nadu (6,5)	
	Haryana (1,4)	Karnataka (3,6)	
	Kerala (2,8)	Orissa (7,14)	
	A.P. (4,9)	M.P. (8,12)	
Low Effort	Punjab (10, 1)	West Bengal (14, 7)	Bihar (12, 15)
	Maharashtra (9,2)		Assam (15,13)
			U.P. (13,11)
			Rajasthan (11, 10)

Note: Figures in parentheses are the rank of the state relating to tax effort and Tax capacity respectively.

5.2.3 Estimates of Taxable Capacity and Tax Efforts of Ten States

Group II consists of ten states, which are very small in size, some of them are newly formed and belong to special category, Most of these states were either union territories or they formed parts of some major states. For these states, detailed reliable data on all the explanatory variables on time series basis are not available. Even structurally most of these states are not comparable with major states. Some of the minor states are not even as big as a district of a major state-both in terms of area and population. Even the economic structure is slightly different. In most of these small states, proportion of tertiary sector is large. Even the composition of tertiary sector is different from the composition in the major states bulk of the tertiary sector is accounted for by general administration unlike by trade & business, transport, Hotel etc in the major states.

It is rather surprising to find that in spite of relatively higher share of tertiary sectoral income, its correlation with tax yield is negative. It may be seen from Table 5.9 displaying correlation matrix that the correlation between tertiary sector and tax yield is just .0106. It appears that bulk of the income generated in the tertiary sector flow out of these states and hence is not available for tax purposes.

An examination of the correlation matrix brings forth strong correlation between tax-yield and level of development, per capita income, secondary sectoral share, and primary sectoral share (negative). Hence we have tried to estimate tax function for these states by including the above four explanatory variables. The results have estimated after correcting for serial correlation (Table 5.10).

In the above model 2.1, all the regression coefficients are significant, adjusted $\overline{R}^2$ is also reasonable and the DW statistic shows that the problem of serial correlation is not very serious. However, the expected negative sign does not appear in the case of primary sectoral share.

This could be due to multicolleniarity problem between primary and secondary sectoral income - which showed as high as -.8707 correlation. Therefore, we dropped secondary sector from the model 2.2. In the above model, after dropping secondary sectoral share, the regression coefficient pertaining to non primary sector became less significant and at the same time adjusted R^2 also declined.

When we drop primary sectoral share from the equation and retain secondary sector share, the level of development becomes insignificant and adjusted $\overline{R}^2$ value goes down, which has been specified in model 2.3.

Table: 5.9: Correlation Matrix for Ten States

	A1	A2	A3	A4	A5	A6	A7	A8	A9
A1	1.000**								
A2	.4103	1.000**							
A3	.6080**	.1385	1.000**						
A4	.7624**	.1069	.7178**	1.000**					
A5	.7629**	.4918*	.6147**	.7813**	1.000**				
A6	-.3419	-.0695	-.2054	-.2988	-.2098	1.000**			
A7	.6466**	.1447	.9532**	.7310**	.6117**	-.4918*	1.000**		
A8	.3926	.4976*	.5159*	.3773	.6255**	.0041	.4577*	1.000**	
A9	-.8707**	-.8058**	-.4696*	-.5527**	-.7607**	.2595	-.4980*	-.5233*	1.000**

Note: No of observations = 30; 1-tailed Significance: * - .01 ** - .001; A1 = Secondary Sector share, A7 = Derived income, A2 = Tertiary Sector share, A8 = Urbanization, A3 = Per capita Income, A9 = Primary Sectoral share, A4 = Per capita Tax, A5 = Development Index and A6 = Per capita annual consumption.

Table 5.10: Determinants of Taxable Capacity for Ten States

Variables	Model 2.1	Model 2.2	Model 2.3
Constant	- 585.807 (- 3.23)	- 228.55 (- 1.46)	- 239.077 (- 4.02)
Per capita Income	13.21 (2.79)	0.0623 (3.67)	0.0620 (3.97)
Secondary Sector	0.0541 (3.46)	---	7.185 (1.77)
Development Index	1.426 (1.47)	2.136 (2.07)	0.708 (0.72)
Primary Sector	5.47 (1.99)	0.079 (0.032)	---
Adjusted $\overline{R}^2$	0.821	0.76	0.80
D-W statistic	1.66	1.64	1.70

Source: Author's own calculation; Note: The values in parentheses below the coefficients show the t-statistics.

In fact, none of the above three models (model 2.1, model 2.2 and model 2.3) appear to be very good. Among the three, model 2.1 appears to be the best as $\overline{R}^2$ value is the highest, all the coefficients are also significant. Using model 2.1 we estimated taxable capacity and Tax efforts of 10 states for the year 1989-90.

However the estimates and the grouping are not very satisfactory, as they are based on an equation, which has certain limitations. Considering the fact that these minor states are essentially heterogeneous in character and their data base is very poor, we agree with the observation of the Ninth-Finance Commission (1988) that "it would not be appropriate to judge them on the same yardsticks as applied to the major states".

The Ninth Finance Commission did not attempt to estimate the levels of under taxation or over taxation in the base year; they just applied the normative rate of growth of tax revenue for this moderated rates of growth of tax revenues for these states were derived by multiplying `group' income elasticity of taxes with the rates of growth of SDP.

As may be seen from Table 5.11, when we use model 2.1 i.e. percentage share of secondary sector, per capita income, development index and proportion of non primary sector, due to the problem of multicollinearity changes the sign of primary sector gets changed and also becomes significant. Hence, the resulting estimate is a biased one.

The states are ranked above according to their estimated taxable capacity and tax efforts by using the above three equations. It may be seen from the Table, that state of Tripura emerges as a state having the lowest taxable capacity and emerges as making highest tax effort, when model 2.1 or 2.2 are chosen. However, when secondary sector is dropped, Tripura occupies sixth place with regard to tax-effort index. Barring this one state, the ranks obtained by other states on tax effort index, recorded marginal changes, by one or two places when different equations are used. Thus for example Arunachal Pradesh which occupied 9th rank on equation obtained 10th rank on model 2.2. The rank coefficient of correlation between model 2.1 and 2.2 is as high as 88 between model 2.1 and model 2.3 is as high as .963 and between model 2.3 and model 2.2 is as high as .836. Even the index values, except for Tripura, are not significantly different between the different models based on the taxable capacity and tax-efforts the states are grouped into four categories-using model 2.1.

- **High Capacity high effort:** Goa, H.P, Sikkim
- **High Capacity low effort:** Nagaland
- **Low Capacity High effort:** Meghalaya, Tripura, J & K
- **Low Capacity low effort:** Mizoram, Manipur, Arunachal Pradesh

The above estimates, both for 15 states and 10 states, do provide a base for comparing the relative Taxable Capacity and tax-efforts. The minor states are different in socio-economic structure from the major states and hence, the two sets of estimates cannot be compared. However, within the broad groups estimates for different states are comparable.

Table 5.11: Taxable Capacity and Tax Efforts of 10 States: 1989-90

States	Actual tax yield Per capita Rs.	Model 2.1					
		Rank	T.C	Rank	T.E	Rank	T.C
Arunachal Pradesh	29.00	(10)	96.86	(9)	.2994	(9)	102.29
Goa	538.23	(1)	476.76	(1)	1.128	(4)	479.18
Himachal Pradesh	289.71	(3)	257.91	(2)	1.123	(5)	204.95
Jammu & Kashmir	184.58	(5)	152.11	(5)	1.21	(6)	145.68
Manipur	77.18	(8)	117.39	(7)	.65	(8)	159.72
Meghalaya	195.06	(4)	103.58	(8)	1.88	(2)	128.58
Mizoram	36.86	(9)	130.69	(6)	.28	(10)	150.72
Nagaland	112.45	(6)	160.36	(4)	.70	(7)	132.52
Sikkim	293.00	(2)	217.97	(3)	1.34	(3)	171.41
Tripura	85.12	(7)	18.70	(10)	6.21	(1)	95.11

Contd...

States	Model 2.2				Model 2.7		
	Rank	T.E	Rank	T.C.	Rank	TE	Rank
Arunachal Pradesh	(9)	.28	(10)	105.24	(9)	.27	(9)
Goa	(1)	1.12	(5)	429.94	(1)	1.09	(6)
Himachal Pradesh	(2)	1.41	(3)	223.29	(2)	1.29	(5)
Jammu & Kashmir	(6)	1.26	(4)	131.71	(6)	1.40	(4)
Manipur	(4)	.48	(8)	127.84	(8)	.60	(7)
Meghalaya	(8)	1.51	(2)	130.45	(7)	1.49	(3)
Mizoram	(5)	.24	(9)	154.39	(5)	.238	(10)
Nagaland	(7)	.84	(7)	200.46	(3)	.56	(8)
Sikkim	(3)	1.71	(1)	182.01	(4)	1.61	(2)
Tripura	(10)	.89	(6)	25.98	(10)	3.27	(1)

One common objection to this method lies in the fact that all such regressions contain a stochastic or random error term. However, this can be reduced by modification of the equation in terms of a `Panel data' model. Nevertheless, ascribing all unexplained variations in the dependent variable to tax-effort is likely to confuse between stochastic or random error and tax-effort. Secondly, an a priori assumption of this method is that the independent variables included in the estimated equation are those that affect only taxable capacity and explain the variations in it fully. As rightly pointed out by Chelliah and Sinha, [27] "This assumption may not be fulfilled entirely there may be factors that simultaneously affect taxable capacity and tax-efforts. For example, the per capita income variable does affect the capacity to pay taxes, but it may also influence the tax effort through its impact on the demand for public services".

Another limitation of the regression approach is that if the specification of the model is not correct, it loses its validity of the conclusions drawn. Further, the interpretation of the statistical results is not free from the usual econometric problems such as least square bias, multicollinearity, hetroscedasticity etc. Further, as pointed out by Chelliah, Sinha, the aggregate regression approach deals only with the overall tax-ratio i.e. the ratio of sum of all taxes levied to the SDP, it does not explicitly bring out the relationship between individual taxes and related economic structure variables.

This has led to think of an alternative system of measuring fiscal capacity and need, which is popularly known as Representative Tax system and Representative Expenditure method. These are discussed in the succeeding chapter.

5.3 Conclusions

In the foregoing analysis we have brought out the importance of the two criteria viz. taxable capacity and tax-efforts in the scheme of federal fiscal transfers aiming at achieving objectives of equity and efficiency. The problems of vertical and horizontal fiscal imbalances are sought to be corrected through various types of grants. In India grants-in-aid of revenue under Article 275 (1) is one such provision aiming at achieving equalization of revenue. In fact, the Finance Commissions have endeavoured to use both tax-devolution and grants-in-aid to correct these imbalances and to bridge the resource gap at the state level. Considering the need for including the states to mobilise more resources on their own, the `self help' factor is also considered important. Thus, keeping in view the perspectives of a dynamic fiscal federalism, along with the objective of achieving equalization, objective of promoting continuous process whereby the states at various levels of development keep continually progressing with disparities among them getting narrowed down progressively with their own self help, is also given importance.

In order to achieve this twin objective of equalization and `incentive' appropriate criteria are needed. Equalization refers to equalization of `fiscal need' and this is measured with the help of three factors like, total population, levels of development and taxable capacity. While to satisfy the objective of `Incentive', criterion of `tax-effort' is advocated. Thus, a federal fiscal transfer scheme aiming at `equalization' of fiscal need and reward to self-help effort should take into consideration the following four criteria:

1. Population
2. Levels of development
3. Taxable capacity, and
4. Tax-efforts

Suitable weights may be assigned to these four criteria and based on that share of individual states may be determined.

An important issue while adopting these criteria relate to their respective measures. As far as `population' is concerned, there is no problem of measurement, as quantitative estimates of population are available from various census reports. The level of development can be measured either by its proxy measure viz., State Domestic Product or a composite index of development based on physical indicators. The other two criteria i.e. taxable capacity and tax-efforts needed suitable measures. In the foregoing we have described the various measures and also developed a measure based on `panel data' model for estimating taxable capacity and tax-efforts of Indian states. There is need to give weightage to both the criteria so that states with low capacity but high tax-effort get the maximum, while states with high capacity and low-effort get the minimum grants. These two criteria should be used along with `population' and `levels of development' in order to meet the objective of achieving equalization of fiscal need. A weightage of 10% to taxable capacity and 10% to tax-efforts is considered suitable to help the states with low capacity and high efforts.

Owing to the various shortcomings of the regression approach to measure taxable capacity alternative measures like RTS and RES were developed. These are discussed in the following chapter.

End Notes and References

1. Chelliah R J, M G Rao, T K Sen, "Background paper", Seminar on Issues before the Tenth Finance Commission oct-nov-1992, mimeographed. p. .9.
2. Musgrave R A "Approaches to Fiscal Theory", in Need sources and utilization, NBER 1961. p. 103.
3. Mathews, R L & T A Sweeney, "Concepts and Measures of Taxable Capacity and Tax efforts" in State and Local Taxation (ed) Mathews R L, Canberra 1977, pp 94-124.
4. Advisory Commission on Inter-governmental Relations (1962) Measures of State and Local Fiscal Capacity & Tax Efforts October 1962. p. 3.
5. Ibid.
6. Some of the notable studies using income Approach are those by Frank, H S (1959), Aaron H (1965), Richard Bird (1964), K V S Sastri (1966).
7. Op cit.
8. Sastri K V S (1966), Federal State Financial Relations in India, Oxford.
9. Notable studies employing regression method are those by Lotz & Morse (1960), Hinrich (1966), Roy Bahl (1971), Plasschaert (1962), Thorn R S (1967), Kilman shin (1969), Chelliah R J, (1971) Ninth Finance Commission First Report and so on.
10. The Finance Commission (1988) First Report
11. Sarma J V M, " Panel Data Models and Measurement of States' Tax Effort in India," Journal of Quantitative Economics, Vol 7, No 1 January 1991, 145-164.
12. Ninth Finance Commission (1989) p. 105.

13. Rao Hemlata.(1993) Taxable Capacity, Tax Effort And Forecasts Of Tax Yield of Indian States.(Study sponsored by the Tenth Finance Commission), ISEC, Bangalore, Mimeograph.

14. Williamson J G, "Public Expenditure and Revenue" the Manchester School of Economic & Social Studies, Vol XXIX 1961 pp 43-56.

15. Hinrich (1966) Op cit.

16. N.S.S various rounds (38th, 42nd, 43rd, 44th & 45th).

17. Jose Sebastians, "Sales Tax-Efforts of States", Artha Vignan, Sept, 1992, v.34. No.3 pp. 302-3.

18. Chelliah & Lall (1978).

19. Ved. P. Gandhi, Tax Burden On Indian Agriculture 1960. Rao Hemlata, "Incidence of Taxation of Agricultural Sector" EPW Sept 11 1971.

20. Rao, Hemlata, Centre State Financial Relation in India, Allied, New Delhi, 1981.

21. Bahl Roy, "A Regression Approach to Tax Effort and Tax Ratio Analysis, "IMF staff Papers, (1971) p. 583-84.

22. For details see Rao, Hemlata (1993).

23. N-1 Dummy used to avoid multicollinearity and subsequent dummy variable trap.

24. We can also use all the three different models, namely Fixed Effect model, Random Effect model and simple pooled OLS model using equation 1. Furthermore, keeping the fundamental difference between Fixed Effect model and Random Effect model in mind, we can chose the appropriate model out of this two alternatives by using Hausman's specification test.

25. Since we have used both cross section and time series data, the serial correlation revealed by Durbin Watson statistics, may not be exclusively due to time effect. Even cross section data can affect such estimates. In order to check this, we calculated `D' statistics for each state by taking the time series data. We also reshuffled the cross-section data and then estimated `D'. These tests, however, revealed the presence of `auto-correlation' problem. Hence, we applied `Search Method' to correct for serial correlation.

26. A suggested method for selecting the best model is to estimate regression coefficient dropping one of the observations randomly, and repeating this for 3 or 4 observations Then one should compute ESS and look for the di-square. Compare such estimates using different equations. Compute chi-square, which ever model gives the lowest rank order chi-square can be selected.

27. Chelliah R.J.8 Narain Sinha, Measurement of Tax Efforts of State Governments 1973-76, NIPFP. 1982 p. 6.

6

REPRESENTATIVE TAX SYSTEM APPROACH

6.1 Representative Tax System (RTS) Approach

In the previous chapter, we have developed Measures of Taxable Capacity and Tax-efforts of Indian States by using a multiple Regression approach. As discussed earlier this method, has its own merits and demerits. Keeping in view the shortcomings of the Regression approach, an alternative measure is generally recommended which is known as Representative Tax System Approach. Major proponents of this measure are Advisory Commission on Inter-Governmental Relations, U.S., Subsequently various improvements were suggested by scholars like, Akin (1973), Bahl (1972), Manvel (1971), and so on.

6.1.1 Genesis: The issue of fiscal equity first emerged in 1920s in the US when the problem of distributing State aid to District Schools emerged. The equity concept adopted by several States was known as foundation grants. "The policy goal was to ensure that all school Districts were able to provide a specified minimum level of spending per capita (i.e. the foundation spending level) with equal local tax burden. The grants allocation formula was," as follows: [1]

$$g_i = e^* - t^* b_i \qquad (6.1)$$

Where

g_i = the per capita grants to the ith school districts

e^* = the foundation level of spending per pupil

t^* = the minimum level of tax effort local school districts are expected to undertake to finance the local share of the foundation expenditure level) and

b_i = the per capita tax base of the ith school district.

The formula can be interpreted as measuring revenue gap,

Where: e^* is the desired per capita expenditure level and t^*bi, represents the revenues a local school district could generate if it were to exploit its local tax base at an exogenously determined rate, t* .

Thus, this formula measures revenue gap e*

This can also be interpreted to represent expenditure needs and t^* bi as reflection of the district's ability or fiscal capacity. According to Fastrup, "this interpretation of t*bi was the starting point for developing the RTS measure" (proposed by Selma Mushkin and Alice Rivlin, ACIR 1962).

The Representative Tax System method defines "tax capacity" as the absolute amount of revenue that each state would raise if it applied a nationally uniform set of tax to a common set of tax bases. The system is "representative" in that national average tax rates are applied in each state to standardized tax bases. Because the same tax rates are used for every state, estimated tax yields vary only because of differences in the underlying bases. The tax capacity measure is not concerned with whether an individual state imposes a low or high tax burden compared to other states. The capacity measure pertains only to the level of economic resources in any state, resources that by common practice may be said to be potentially taxable whether or not the particular state actually taxes those resources and regardless of the intensity with which a state utilizes those taxable resources.

To put it in a simple way, the RTS method defines a state's "tax capacity index" as its per capita tax capacity divided by the average for all states, with the index for the average set at 100. A state with an index of 120,for example, would have a capacity 20% above average, and one with an index of 80, a capacity 20% below average. The tax capacity indices thus provide a measure of the relative taxing abilities of the states.

The RTS measure is defined in the context of the US as "the revenue yield that would result if each State and Local fiscal system were to tax each of 26 statutory tax bases at national average rates." This is expressed as:

Where:

RTS = the ACIR measure of fiscal capacity for the ith State – Local system ($ per capita)

t_j = US average effective tax rate on the jth tax base and
b_{ij} = the ith tax base for the ith State

Under RTS, instead of using one statutory tax base, 26 tax bases are used and t^x is set at the national average rate for each individual tax base.

The RTS method essentially involves identifying actual tax bases or their suitable proxies for individual taxes and then calculating an effective tax rate for each tax as a ratio of actual tax-revenue to the actual or proxy base. A normative tax rate is then derived from these effective tax rates over the observations. This gives the measure of taxable capacity. Individual tax potential can then be summed across states to arrive at the aggregate tax potential.

As in the case of regression method, in R T S method also, by measuring actual aggregate collections against aggregate capacities so derived an index of aggregate tax-effort is derived. Since RTS uses standardized rates applied to standardized bases, the resulting tax-effort measures give comparability among states that simple comparison of statutory rates do not.

The simplifications of the Representative Tax System estimates are a response to two competing policy requirements: (1) the need for a more accurate measure of fiscal capacity than per capita income, and (2) the desirability of a fairly simple, timely, and understandable measure. While maintaining the methodology of the original RTS, the simplified version reduces its complexity so that it can be consistently updated. Although less comprehensive than the average financing system, the simplified RTS accounts for most of the tax sources used by state and local governments and provides a broader measure of fiscal capacity than resident per capita income.

The ACIR staff has studied various measures of fiscal capacity and has suggested the Representative Tax System as an alternative approach to personal income. The Commission issued its first information report on this topic in 1962, presenting the rationale for and procedures necessary to develop the Representative Tax System, using this approach to estimate "tax capacity" or "tax wealth" for each state (using its combined state and local governments).

6.1.2 Extensions of the RTS Approach: The second ACIR report (1971) amplified the initial ACIR study of the RTS in two ways – by extending the procedures and estimates to selected individual local areas and by including non tax revenue sources (i.e., user charges, fees, utility revenues, etc). This system referred to as the "average financing system" built upon the Representative Tax System methodology to account for state/local revenues other than taxes. In addition, this study extended the system to include 747 counties and 218 metropolitan areas and was much more complex and extensive than the original study that computed capacities only on a state-wide basis.

Although the RTS has not yet been used in the U.S. grant system, Canada has incorporated the concept into its revenue equalization program. The fiscal capacity measure, provided by the Federal Provincial Fiscal Arrangements Act of 1967, is based on the Representative Tax System with some modifications. The purpose of the Canadian program is to equalize revenues among the provinces, and the capacity index used is built up from 29 revenue sources – including taxes and non-tax sources of provincial revenue.

6.1.3 Simplified Representative Tax System: Building upon the ACIR reports, Robert Reischauer and Kent Halstead simplified the RTS methodology so that it can be updated annually or biennially, while maintaining the system's basic structure. Incorporating their modifications, as well as some other refinements, the ACIR Taxation and Finance staff had re-examined the system and developed the another set of tax capacity estimates in 1979.

In order to produce the less complex measure of tax capacity, the core of the original ACIR methodology was retained, but the scope was narrowed. The tax capacity estimates are based only on taxes, thereby excluding non-tax charges and fees, as well as a number of minor taxes. Also, the estimates were for states and their local governments combined; no estimates were developed for sub-state jurisdiction. By condensing the amount of time and effort required to develop state indices, timely and regular reports on state-area tax capacity could be produced.

6.1.4 Definition of Tax Effort: Mathematically, the tax effort index for a state is created by dividing the state's actual tax collections by its estimated tax capacity and multiplying by 100. The result may be interpreted as a measure of how much that state chooses to exploit all its potential tax bases relative to other states. If a state has a tax effort beneath the national norm, it will have an effort index under 100. An index of 115, for example, indicates that tax effort is 15% above the national average.

Tax effort, like tax capacity, can also be measured for each tax. The individual tax effort measures test how intensively a state uses each tax compared to all other states. Because the RTS uses standardized rates applied to standardized bases, the resulting tax effort measures give comparability among states that simple comparisons of statutory tax rates do not. For every state, sales tax effort, for example, is measured relative to retail sales excluding food and drugs whether or not a state actually exempts these or other items from the tax. A simple comparison of statutory sales tax rates is biased because it does not take into consideration the great variation in the composition of the various state sales tax bases.

6.1.5 Illustration of RTS Method: All bases that are commonly subject to state and local taxation are used in the RTS calculations of tax capacity. In order to illustrate the method of RTS, example is taken from, "1982 Tax Capacity of the Fifty States." An information report, Advisory Commission on Inter-governmental relations, Washington D.C. M-142. The study provides breakdowns of the 26 bases included, as well as the amount of nationwide revenue each base generates and the average tax rates for each base. The estimated total state-local tax yields reflect the actual intensity of use of the various tax bases on a national basis, avoiding the error of introducing arbitrary weights by simply adding together billions of dollars in property values, millions of dollars in income, and so forth.

For each tax base, the representative tax rate is applied in every state regardless of whether a given state actually levies that tax. If this were not done, tax capacity would be understated in states that choose not to employ a full spectrum of taxes.

The Representative Tax System method has five basic elements:

- the revenue coverage,
- the classification of revenue into separate sources,
- definition of a standard tax base for each revenue source,
- the definition of a standard tax rate for each revenue source and
- the estimation of R T S revenue for each state.

6.1.6 RTS Method Step by Step: Each step of the RTS method is described and illustrated below.

Step 1

Compute 26 representative tax rates according to the nationwide tax collections of all states and localities and the nationwide tax base amounts.

The Report (1985) brings forth the 1982 representative general sales and gross receipts tax rate of 6.7% was obtained by dividing the $60,405,983,000 state and local general sales and gross receipts tax collection by national retail sales of $895,447,955,000 (excluding food and drugs).

Step 2

Determine the hypothetical yield for each tax in each state by applying the representative (average) tax rate to that state's actual tax base. This hypothetical yield is the capacity under that particular tax.

Step 3

Determine the tax capacity for each state by adding together the hypothetical yields for each of the 26 taxes.

Step 4

Determine the tax capacity for each state. Tax capacity (i.e. the yield from applying the representative rates to the tax bases in each state) is simply divided by state population.

Step 5

Determine for each state's tax capacity index by dividing its tax capacity per capita by the national average tax capacity per capita.

6.1.7 RTS and Aggregate Regression Methods: Both the Aggregate Regression Method and RTS method are commonly used to measure capacity and efforts and both have their own relative merits and demerits. The applicability of RTS method depends upon the availability of adequate and reliable data on the tax bases and actual tax rates. In the absence of such information, aggregate Regression Approach is considered as suitable. This approach does not require highly disaggregated data and also takes account of the inter dependence of the tax bases. As the Ninth Finance Commission (1989) rightly observed [2] some times, the effective rates itself can vary with the size of the tax base (the effective tax rate may be higher in a more developed state than in a less developed state), which is captured in the regression approach. In regression approach the estimates are not derived by relating tax revenue to the actual or proxy tax bases, but only to macro-capacity indicators. A major weakness of the regression method is that the residual error is taken to represent tax-effort. The residual error may also contain random factor. The RTS method relates the tax revenue to individual tax bases or their proxies and therefore, the logic of the method is more transparent. But, this method is riddled with the complex problem of non-availability of comparable, reliable and adequate data on tax base and rates, and also item-wise tax-yield across the states. In the absence of such information any attempt to estimate tax-wise yield, results in disaggregated level regression approach only.

RTS method involves identifying actual bases or suitable proxies, and then calculating an effective tax rate for each tax as a ratio of actual tax revenue to the actual or proxy base. A normative tax rate is then derived from these effective tax rates over the observations and applied to the actual or proxy bases used. This yields the taxable capacity or the tax potential. Individual tax potential then can be summed across taxes to arrive at the aggregate tax potential. By measuring aggregate capacities derived, an index of aggregate tax-effort can then be arrived at. It is believed that under RTS method more disaggregated picture of the economies of the states could be brought into the computation of relative capacities, and hence the advantages or disadvantages that the several states enjoy or suffer from, in terms of availability and value of potential bases could be more explicitly taken into account.

6.1.8 Advantages of RTS Method over Other Measures: The RTS provides a sophisticated yet understandable approach to measuring state-local fiscal capacity (the ability to raise revenues to provide public services). It strikes a balance between two extremes; it is neither so theoretical nor difficult to develop that it loses its institutive appeal in a political forum nor so simplistic and rooted in the current tax practice of any state as so to provide no policy guidance. Although the RTS has been criticized as being too complex, it provides measures of fiscal capacity which is much more accurate and useful to both state-local and federal officials than the measure most commonly used, the per capita income of the residents of each state.

The RTS estimates provide a truly unique form of tax policy guidance to state-local officials because they enable interstate comparison of tax capacity and utilization on a disaggregated tax – by-tax basis. As illustrated in the lower graph on each page of Appendix B, policymakers can see at a glance how, relative to other state is under- utilizing or over – working a certain tax. No-where else is this form of valuable comparative information made a available to state and local policymaker.

The RTS also can be a useful tool for federal policymakers. Indices of interstate fiscal disparities are used in equalizing formulas for numerous federal grant programs including General Revenue Sharing, Medicaid, and Vocational Education, to name just a few. Because the RTS is a far wealth than per capita income, it can provide a better basis for accomplishing interstate fiscal equalization. Three major advantages of the RTS in this regard stand out.

The first major advantage of the RTS over per capita income is that it provides a more accurate measure of fiscal capacity. This advantage occurs not only because the RTS takes into account a broader range of tax bases but also because it implicitly and effectively captures the extent of states' tax exportation opportunities – the ability to collect taxes from nonresidents.3 the ability to export taxes depends, for example, on how much of a state's tax base lies in industries which can pass on taxes (such as severance taxes) to nonresidents, and on the amount of taxes (such as sales taxes in tourist areas) a state receives which are paid directly by nonresidents. In sharp contrast, per capita income ignores tax exportation and there by understates the tax capacity of a rich base state.

By capturing a state's ability to export taxes to nonresidents, RTS has an advantage not only over the per capita income method but also over other approaches to measuring fiscal capacity, such as using a more comprehensive definition of income, which attempt to measure and adjust for tax exportation directly.

The major advantage of the RTS is that it is far more sensitive to changes in the economic and fiscal conditions of state that affect their tax bases than is the per capita income measure.

Although analytically complex, the Representative Tax System is a straight forward way of adding together each state's tax bases on a commensurate basis. By combing a wide variety of taxable resources – such as income, property, retail sales, and motor fuel – the Representative Tax System generates a broad index of a state's tax capacity. As a measure of fiscal capacity, this system has the major advantage that, for each source of tax revenue actually used, it measures the economic activity subject to the tax. Unlike resident per capita income, the RTS method has the decided conceptual appeal that it does not rely solely on one measure of economic activity; it provides a measure of the multiple resources claimable by state and local governments through a variety of taxes.

6.1.9 RTS: A Critique

A. Experimental Modifications to the Methodology: The standard RTS tax capacity index has been criticized as a measure of fiscal capacity on several accounts. One criticism is that the RTS excludes non-tax revenue sources such as user charges and royalties from leases of republic lands. Another is that the tax bases used in the calculation of capacity are treated as being independent from a state's tax rates, when, in fact, they may be highly interrelated. The first problem is straightforward- many states receive significant revenues from user charges, and some states receive large payments from public and leases, such as from oil and gas producers. These additional revenue sources can be easily included in the RTS calculations.

The second problem is more complex. The RTS uses tax bases that are observed under current state tax practices as a measure of what the bases would be if the states all levied the same tax rate. In the past we have ignored any possible interaction between a state's own tax rate and its observed tax base. However, the theoretically appropriate tax base, but the unobserved base that would exist if a state, in fact, levied the national average tax rate. In the results that are presented below, this interaction effect has been estimated for the general sales tax base. Further research on the interaction of other taxes and bases clearly seems warranted.

RTS measure has many plus and minus points criticisms have centered on the use of statutory tax bases and the ad hoc fashion by which the RTS captures the phenomenon of tax exporting.

These criticisms of the RTS led researchers to advance other measures of fiscal capacity that attempt to control for the inter-dependence between tax rates and tax bases by fitting regressions between actual State-Local revenues and statutory tax bases, and using the estimated coefficients to weight the statutory tax bases instead of using average rates. [3]

The above simplifications ease the task of estimating tax capacity and allow the measures to be easily updated because most of the data are published regularly.

B. Conceptual Problems: Several conceptual criticisms of the Representative Tax System have been registered. According to John Akin, the "most serious fault" of the ACIR methodology is its failure to recognize the interrelated nature of the various tax bases. Stated simply, no consideration is given to the possibility that the capacity to tax a given base will be affected by the size of another tax base. For example, the capacity of a state to tax residential property depends upon the income of the state's residents; thus a state with high income has a greater capacity to tax property than does a low income state. This conclusion is based on the assumption that the final incidence of the tax is borne by homeowners who pay their property taxes out of current earnings. Similarly, the capacity of a government to levy business property taxes depends upon the net income of a state's firms.

A second drawback of the Representative Tax System is its failure to account for the possibility that many of the revenue bases upon which such an index is grounded are not independent of government action. Reischauer raises the point that deliberate government policy, such as tax rates, zoning and subsidies, affect the size of the tax base. He cites numerous examples where state law inherently reduces or expands the size of a tax base. Such cases include the exclusionary zoning of commercial-industrial activity or of apartments; legalized horse and dog racing, which provide a base for pari-mutuel taxes; legalized gambling, which improves a state's amusement, liquor and sales tax bases; liberal incorporation laws, which attract a larger corporation tax base.

To the extent that a state makes a conscious decision based on a trade-off between revenue and other social, environmental, psychological, and pecuniary costs, the RTS is not neutral with respect to state policy.

The size of a state's tax base is also affected by the state's choice of tax rates which raises problems for the Representative Tax System. Theoretically, the Representative Tax System seeks to answer the question of how much revenue each state could generate if it taxed all of its bases at national average rates. Unfortunately, if all states taxed at the national average rate (for each tax base), the distribution of each tax base would certainly be different. This criticism is fairly serious, for it implies that the use of existing tax bases creates a systematic bias by understanding the tax capacity for states with above average tax rates, and vice versa. Reischauer points out that a solution to this dilemma "is an impossibly difficult task, for researchers can only guess at the locational patterns of business, industry, sales and population that would result if all jurisdictions had the same institutions and legal (and fiscal) frameworks." The significance of this criticism is mitigated, however, by the fact that personal income (as a measure of fiscal capacity) inherently suffers the *exact same form* of systematic bias for the identical reasons. In other words, personal income, as well as other tax bases, tends to gravitate away from high tax rate states.

The RTS method, though better than the Aggregate Regression method, suffers from severe data constraints. In order to estimate taxable capacity, it is very important to have reliable, consistent and comparable data on, commodity-wise tax-yield and commodity-wise actual tax base. This is important to workout the average affective rates of tax. Data on the bases are rarely available with the necessary degree of desegregations. For example, in India the indirect tax system is very complex. In the case of sales tax alone there are difference in the points of levy, the number of taxable points, and nominal rates of tax. In such situation, obtaining data on the tax bases as also the tax-yield from each of the tax rate categories becomes virtually impossible. Hence, the tax bases are aggregated into some manageable groups and tax base proxies are employed where ever the actual tax base data are not available. When actual tax base data are not available, or item wise tax-yield figures are not available for purposes of estimating capacity, proxy bases are relied upon and tax bases are aggregated into some groups, the use of simple average effective tax rate imparts a bias against some states. For example if all consumption of goods are taken as one category of sales tax base, given that the nominal rate on necessary goods like food grains and lower than the rates on more expensive consumption items such as dry fruits etc, and further that the proportion of consumption of the former in poorer states would be higher, using a uniform average tax rate for all consumption goods might work against these states. Therefore, while calculating taxable capacity, instead of taking average tax rate, alternatively one can employ cross-section regression average tax-rates.

The use of a representative set of tax rates for capacity measurement in no way implies that a state should use the representative rates in practice, nor do the tax capacity estimates depend on the actual set of tax rates employed by a state. The state exhibit a wide diversity in the tax instruments they use and the rates they apply. The RTS measures tax capacity independently of the tax mix or level a state employs, even if a given tax base is not taxed at all. Because the rates chosen are independent of the rates used by a given state, the system gauges tax capacity without regard to whether a state has generally high or low levels of taxation. The common set of tax rates used by the RTS reflects the typical behaviour of all states and is not meant to be ideal or prescriptive.

Section 2

6.2 RTS in India

The RTS method, though better than the Aggregate Regression method, suffers from severe data constraints. In order to estimate taxable capacity, it is very important to have reliable, consistent and comparable data on, commodity-wise tax-yield and commodity-wise actual tax base. This is important to workout the average affective rates of tax. Data on the bases are rarely available with the necessary degree of desegregations. For example, in India the indirect tax system is very complex. In the case of sales tax alone there are difference in the points of levy, the number of taxable points, and nominal rates of tax. In such situation, obtaining data on the tax bases as also the tax-yield from each of the tax rate categories becomes virtually impossible. Hence, the tax bases are aggregated into some manageable groups and tax base proxies are employed where ever the actual tax base data are not available. When actual tax base data are not available, or item wise tax-yield figures are not available for purposes of estimating capacity, proxy bases are relied upon and tax bases are aggregated into some groups, the use of simple average effective tax rate imparts a bias against some states. For example if all consumption of goods are taken as one category of sales tax base, given that the nominal rate on necessary goods like food grains and lower than the rates on more expensive consumption items such as dry fruits etc, and further that the proportion of consumption of the former in poorer states would be higher, using a uniform average tax rate for all consumption goods might work against these states. Therefore, while calculating taxable capacity, instead of taking average tax rate, alternatively one can employ cross-section regression average tax-rates.

Chelliah and Sinha [4] in their study chose to employ an arithmetic average effective tax rate. While in the second report of the Ninth Finance Commission effective rates based on regression coefficients were employed.

Another major study employing the technique of RTS was done by Rao (1993). [5] In order to estimate taxable capacity based on the RTS method, in this study, Rao first explored the possibilities of adopting the typical RTS method using arithmetic average rates. Recognizing the practical constraints, due to non availability of data on item wise tax-yield and the respective tax-base data in value terms, a regression coefficient method was adopted. The important step involved in calculating taxable capacity based on RTS method was to identify proper tax base. This necessitated an examination of tax base of individual taxes.

In the above study, for illustration, just three important state taxes viz, general sales tax state excise duty and motor-vehicle tax, which account for more than 85% of total state's own tax receipts were selected.

6.2.1 Sales Tax: There are two types of sales taxes whose proceeds accrue to the states viz, general sales tax and central sales tax. The latter is levied by the centre and hence while measuring relative tax-efforts it has to be taken out. Hence, only general sales Taxes were considered in the study. Sales taxes on petroleum products and purchase tax on sugarcane were also included under general sales tax. Ideally, these Taxes should be treated separately. But it is very difficult to do so, as in many states, yield from the latter two taxes are merged with the general sales tax (GST). Rao explained, "In order to identify the tax base of sales tax one has to classify the goods on which sales tax is levied into two categories viz. i) consumer goods and ii) producer goods." The tax base for consumer goods is the total consumption expenditure in value terms, while the tax base of producer goods is the value of the input used by industries in the state. However, item-wise tax-yield figures were not available for all the commodities and in all the states. Hence, The ratio of the yield of the two categories of goods based on commodity wise statistics were worked out and these proportions of yield to commodity-wise statistics were applied to derive the actual yield of the GST in the several states.

There was problem with regard to tax base of producer goods viz, value of input used by industries in the states. Such information was not available and hence a proxy base like SDP originating in the industrial sector of a state was considered.

Apart from GST (Including sales Tax on motor spirit and purchase Tax on Sugarcane) two other important Taxes taken for illustration in the study were: Motor vehicle Tax and State Excise Duties. Data pertaining to item-wise tax-yield from taxes on motor spirit was not available. Moreover, tax-yield and tax rates varied from item to item. In the absence of such disaggregated information, the total tax-yield from motor spirit was taken. Even this information was not available for all the states, as it was merged with general sales tax in some of the states. Since, item-wise petroleum tax yield was not available, an aggregate consumption of petroleum products in the state was taken as the potential tax base for the tax. Here again we face data problems. Information on petroleum consumption is available only in quantities and not in value terms. In order to arrive at tax base of petroleum tax, one has to estimate the consumption in value terms by multiplying the total quantity of petroleum products consumed by zonal prices. Even this information is not readily available. Similarly, total purchase of sugarcane by sugar factories in a state is the potential base for purchase tax on sugarcane. However, we could not get data either on sugarcane tax yield or its base for all the states. Since, in most of the states, these two taxes are merged with GST we did not take either base separately. Taxes on petroleum or on purchase of sugarcane separately are not available and preferred to take total general sales tax including these two taxes.

6.2.2 State Excise Duty: State excise duty is levied on all kinds of alcoholic liquor, opium, hemp and other narcotics. State thus collects taxes from country liquor, Indian made foreign liquor, beer and narcotic products. Apart from this government also collects revenue from issue of licenses etc. Bulk of the yield, however comes from the consumption of various types of liquor. Hence consumption of liquor by type provides a good tax base. But, we have the problem of non-availability of data. In the absence of any detailed, comparable state-wise data on consumption of liquor by type, one can take demand for alcohol or production of alcohol as a proxy base along with other proxy bases. Since, these data available only in physical quantity and state-wise price data is not available, this cannot be used to derive an arithmetic average rate. However, the quantity of production of alcohol may be tried as a determinant in a regression model. Along with this one has to depend on indirect determinants of state excise like SDP, urbanization and so on while measuring taxable capacity.

6.2.3 Motor Vehicle Tax: Tax-yield data available at the state level is highly aggregative in nature. This tax is levied on different types of vehicle like, two wheelers, mopeds, four wheelers, light vehicles, trucks, buses and so on and the rates are substantially different. For RTS method, it is desirable to have vehicle category wise tax-yield data-but such information is not available. Even data on number of vehicles in each category according to range of laden weight, seating capacity etc is not available. Hence, one cannot work out average effective tax rate based on traditional RTS method and instead has to resort to regression coefficient method alone. In this study, therefore, we have taken two sets of equations. In the first, we considered proxy variables like PACE, NP sectoral percentage, adjusted, income etc, and in the second, we took, category-wise number of vehicles as explanatory variables.

6.2.4 RTS Method: An Illustration: Once the potential tax base is identified in value terms it becomes easy to work out taxable capacity based on RTS method. For illustration, an example is given here, working out taxable capacity and Tax-effort made by states in terms of sales tax, based on the popular R.T.S method, for the year 90-91. The results are shown in Table 6.1.

Table 6.1: Effective Rates and Average Effective Rates of General Sales Tax,1990-91

State	Sales Tax	Tax Base Sec SDP Rs. in Crore**	TACE Rs. in Crore	Total Tax Base	Effective Tax Rate	Average Rate X Base	Tax Effort	Rank
Andhra Pradesh	1198.73	9173	14684	23857	5.02	722.87	1.652	5
Assam	243.49	1928	4658	6586	3.69	199.55	1. 220	9
Bihar	385.24	8103	16803	24906	1.55	754.65	.510	15
Gujarat	1430.22	16395	9719	26114	2.80	797.25	1.878	4
Haryana	177.74	5383	4385	9768	1.82	295.97	.60	14
Karnataka	1088.32	6564	9158	15722	6.92	476.07	2.286	1
Kerala	800.77	4173	8725	12898	6.21	390.81	2.049	3
M.P.	600.22	8006	14039	22045	2.72	667.96	.898	13
Maharashtra	2552.57	32831	18781	51612	4.94	1563.84	1.632	6
Orissa	336.64	2926	6019	8945	3.76	271.9	1.24	8
Punjab	416.73	7698	6365	14063	2.96	426.11	.977	11
Rajasthan	616.58	4356	11842	16198	3.81	491.00	1.255	7
Tamil Nadu	1787.86	16349	12115	28464	6.28	862.45	2.073	2
Uttar Pradesh	1286.08	13666	30376	44042	2.92	1334.47	.964	12
West Bengal	979.63	11087	15842	26929	3.63	815.95	1.20	10

Sec.=secondary sector, average rate = 3.93, ** Based on Annual Survey of Industries, 87-88.

If item-wise and commodity-wise (sub-heading-wise) tax yield data and their potential tax base data are available for all the states, one can calculate taxable capacity and tax efforts of the states by using the RTS methods as applied in the US or Canada or as shown in the illustration. However, in the Indian situation, availability and quality of data for this purpose is very poor and hence, it is very difficult to arrive at capacity measure by using the typical RTS method. Alternatively, one can use regression method to arrive at average effective rate.

For purposes of using the regression method at disaggregated level, one requires the data on tax-yield by major heads, and data on the proxy bases of that particular tax.

Statistical estimates of taxable capacity of 15 major states pertaining to selected taxes are analyzed in the following section.

6.3 Statistical Analysis of Taxable Capacity and Tax Efforts of 15 Major States based on Modified RTS Method

In the foregoing section, we have brought out the severe data limitations which a researches faces in applying RTS method. In spite of all the limitations set above, in this section an attempt is being made to examine the possibilities of estimating taxable capacity and tax-efforts of 15 major states by using regression coefficients for effective average rates. This tasks involved, identification of appropriate proxy base, availability of data relating to tax yield and selected potential base and finally choosing a model to derive effective tax rates.

6.3.1 Tax Bases and Their Proxies: After examining the nature, type and quality of data available across the states and for the selected years, for purposes of measuring taxable capacity of states with regard to sales tax, we selected the following variables.

1. ADTSDP = Total State Domestic Product net of Total annual Household Consumption
2. TACE = Total annual household consumption expenditure
3. NP % = Percentage share of non-primary sectoral income
4. URB % = Urbanization
5. Prin = Price Index

6. Sec % = Secondary Sectoral income share.

Keeping in view the statistical requirements and the theoretical arguments for selecting the tax bases, finally we selected three variables viz,

1. ADTSDP
2. TACE
3. NP %

In order to derive the regression coefficients, we pooled time-series and cross section data pertaining to 15 states over 3 years viz 1988-89, 1989-90 and 1990-91. In this model we have assumed that the intercepts and slopes remain common across the states and over the selected period.

The dependent variable, sales tax included taxes on petroleum products and purchase tax on sugar cane and excluded central sales tax. The equation after correcting for auto correlation on the basis of maximum likelihood Estimation method reads as follows.

$$ST_{it} = \alpha + \beta_j \sum_{i=1}^{m} X_i + u_{it} \qquad (1)$$

Where, ST = Sales Tax, α is intercept, β is the slope coefficient of explanatory variables (X_i), j = 1, ..,3 ; m = 1,2,3 (Table 6.2).

Table 6.2: Results of Pooled Regression for Modified RTS Method (Equation 1)

Explanatory Variables	Coefficients
Constant	-1469.56* (6.53)
TACE	0.00027* (4.74)
ADTSDP	0.0003* (5.55)
NP	28.0313* (7.13)
Adjusted $\overline{R}^2 = 0.93$; D-W statistic = 1.94; N = 45	

Source: Author's own calculation. Notes: (1) The values in parentheses below the coefficients show the t-statistics. (2) *, Show the 1 per cent level of significance respectively. All variables were found to be significant less than 1% level.

By replacing the actual values pertaining to the above determinants for the year 1990-91, we derived the estimated yield of sales tax for all the 15 states for the year 1990-91 and based on this states were ranked according to their taxable capacity and Tax-efforts (Rs. in crores). These values are displayed in Table 6.3.

Table 6.3: Sales Tax: Actual Taxable Capacity and Tax Efforts (yield Rs. in lakh)

State	Sales Tax Yield (A)	Estimated Yield (B)	Tax Effort A/B	Rank
Andhra Pradesh	1198.78	1060.92	1.129	6
Assam	243.49	164.90	1.4	3
Bihar	585.24	602.42	.97	10
Gujarat	1430.22	1277.78	1.119	7
Haryana	177.74	444.49	.40	15
Karnataka	1088.32	1023.09	1.063	9
Kerala	800.77	696.54	1.14	4
Madhya Pradesh	600.22	737.12	.814	11
Maharastra	2552.57	2393.40	1.066	8
Orissa	336.64	157.49	2.13	1
Punjab	416.73	590.06	.70	14
Rajasthan	616.58	399.74	1.54	2
Tamil Nadu	1787.86	1583.21	1.13	5
Uttar Pradesh	1286.34	1587.89	.810	12
West Bengal	979.63	1264.71	.77	13

6.3.2 State Excise Duty: For purposes of estimating taxable capacity and tax-efforts in terms of state excise duty, we tried to get data on its appropriate tax-base viz, consumption of liquor by type. However, this information was not available for the concerned years and for all the states. We also tried to use, demand for alcohol as the proxy base, even this data was deficient and hence we had to depend on the proxy bases.

First we examined various determinants as proxy base such as, sectoral composition of income, price index, urbanisation and so on finally, keeping in view the statistical requirements, we finally selected two variables, which were found significantly influencing the excise tax yield. The determinants are: Total State Domestic Product and Implicit Price index. The equation after correcting for auto- correlation is given in Table 6.4.

Table 6.4: Results of Pooled Regression for Modified RTS Method (Equation 2)

Explanatory Variables	Coefficients
Constant	-490.57* (-2.70)
TSDP	0.0001* (5.67)
PI	2.5128* (2.79)
Adjusted $\overline{R}^2 = 0.64$; D-W statistic = 1.81; N = 45	

Source: Author's own calculation. Notes: (1) The values in parentheses below the coefficients show the t-statistics. (2) *, Show the 1 per cent level of significance respectively. (3) TSDP = Total State Domestic Product, PI = Price Index.

The estimated taxable capacity and tax effort based on the above equation is shown in Table 6.5.

Table 6.5: State Excise Duty: Taxable Capacity and Tax Efforts

State	Actual Tax Yield	Estimated Yield	Tax Effort	Rank
Andhra Pradesh	727.980	459.512	1.580	2
Assam	13.040	144.925	.089	15
Bihar	108.000	333.150	.324	13
Gujarat	12.000	343.406	.0349	12
Haryana	286.350	191.893	1.492	3
Karnataka	429.690	295.853	1.452	4
Kerala	175.410	187.425	.935	8
Madhya Pradesh	300.830	380.830	.789	10
Maharastra	542.310	649.274	.835	9

Contd...

Orissa	45.640	143.320	.318	14
Punjab	435.780	223.498	1.9498	1
Rajasthan	260.460	258.891	1.006	7
Tamil Nadu	434.860	319.120	1.363	5
Uttar Pradesh	724.790	622.951	1.163	6
West Bengal	164.290	401.372	.409	11

6.3.3 Motor Vehicle Tax: After sales tax and state excise duties, motor vehicle tax is the third important state tax from resource mobilization point. In order to know the potential tax base, it would be ideal to have tax-yield data by vehicle type and also information about the type of vehicles. As we have explained that the tax-yield data at the disaggregated level is not available, therefore, we could not estimate tax yield by type of vehicles. We have run two equations one based on indirect proxy variables as determinants such as SDP, urbanisation etc and the other taking the type of vehicles as the determinant of tax base (Table 6.6).

Table 6.6: Results of Pooled Regression for Modified RTS Method (Equation 3)

Explanatory Variables	Coefficients	t
Constant	-135.48*	-2.36
TACE	0.00029*	1.9
NP	2.9167*	3.13
Ad SDP	0.000023	1.6
Adjusted R^2 = 0.68; D-W statistic =		

Source: Author's own calculation. Notes: (1) The values in parentheses below the coefficients show the t-statistics. (2) *, Show the 1 per cent level of significance respectively. (3) TACE = Total Annual Consumption Expenditure, NP = Non primary sectoral income in percentage, Ad SDP = SDP adjusted for TACE.

In the above equation except X3, all others were found to be significant at 1 per cent level. Even X3 was significant at 10% level. R^2 was around .68. The estimated values based on equation 1 are given in Table 6.7.

Table 6.7: Motor Vehicle Tax Equation: 1990-91

State	Actual Tax Yield	Estimated Yield	Tax Effort	Rank
Andhra Pradesh	185.790	111.520	1.665	3
Assam	12.74	30.5408	.417	15
Bihar	85.00	74.8678	1.135	5
Gujarat	95.75	134.585	.711	9
Haryana	35.78	56.352	.635	10
Karnataka	192.43	111.022	0.577	11
Kerala	74.14	86.9887	.853	8
Madhya Pradesh	74.95	84.6267	.886	7
Maharastra	204.32	227.703	.897	6
Orissa	52.29	29.6908	1.76	2
Punjab	37.43	67.4760	.554	12
Rajasthan	107.51	52.9756	2.029	1
Tamil Nadu	227.34	168.721	1.347	4
Uttar Pradesh	85.42	163.976	.5209	14
West Bengal	71.76	132.358	.542	13

In equation 6.4 we have taken different types of vehicles as the independent variables. Motor vehicles of different types, ranging from two wheeler to trucks, are taxed at varying rates and hence it is not possible to take the total number of vehicles as the potential base of this tax. The composition of total vehicle is very important. Two states having equal number of total vehicles will have different taxable capacity if in one, two wheeler's account for 70% of total vehicles and in the other heavy vehicles account for 70% of the total.

Keeping in mind the difference in tax rate structure the Vehicles are grouped into the following categories.

X1. Two wheelers

X2. 3 Wheelers + Four Wheelers

X3. Buses

X4. Trucks, Trailer Tractors and others

X5. Total vehicles

In order to derive estimated tax yield from Motor vehicle tax based on RTS method using regression coefficients as effective rates, we used the following.

$$MV = f(X1, X2, X3, X4) \tag{4}$$

Where X_j are defined above and j = 1,2, … 4.

A double log function has been fitted in order to estimate the equation (4). By using the above function we derived the following results (after correcting for auto correlation) (Table 6.8).

Table 6.8: Results of Pooled Regression for Modified RTS Method (Equation 4)

Explanatory Variables	Coefficients	T
Constant	3.963	-3.9
X1	0.988	8.5
X2	0.0023	0.01
X3	0.5576	2.9
X4	-0.8541	-6.36
Adjusted $\overline{R}^2 = 0.184$; D-W = 1.85		

Source: Author's own calculation. Notes: (1) The values in parentheses below the coefficients show the t-statistics. (2)*, Show the 1 per cent level of significance respectively.

It may be observed that in the above equation `Bus' does not emerge as significant determinant similarly the vehicles under `others' category have negative sign, though with highly significant coefficients. Theoretically, we expect a positive effect of `Bus' and other heavy vehicles on Tax yield.

Taxable Capacity and Tax-efforts estimated for 89-90 based on the above equation after correcting for the auto correlation are displayed in Table 6.9.

Taking the aggregate of actual and estimated Tax-yield worked out on the basis of equations.1,.2 and.3 tax-effort of 15 major states are worked out. The estimated values are given in Table 6.10. The tax effort index derived on the basis of Representative Tax System and Regression method are not comparable as the RTS method consists of only 3 of the state taxes while in the other model we have taken the aggregate tax-yield consisting of all the state taxes.

Table 6.9: Taxable Capacity, Tax Efforts and Ranks Motor Vehicle Tax:1989-90 (Rs.in crores)

State	Actual Tax	Based on Estimated Yield	Tax Effort	Rank
Andhra Pradesh	193.45	152.78	1.26	4
Assam	11.74	15.96	.737	13
Bihar	75.00	79.83	.939	8
Gujarat	87.09	144.02	.604	15
Haryana	21.39	15.95	1.34	3
Karnataka	157.95	157.59	1.00	6
Kerala	69.92	81.45	.858	9
Madya Pradesh	72.39	108.85	.665	14
Maharastra	191.08	186.79	1.02	5
Orissa	43.90	59.62	.736	12
Punjab	39.35	47.85	.822	10
Rajasthan	99.21	54.05	1.835	1
Tamil Nadu	196.01	142.02	1.380	2
Uttar Pradesh	79.30	99.48	.797	11
West Bengal	54.98	57.39	.958	7

The RTS method, though, is very popular in countries like the U.S and Canada, does not do well in countries like India, owing to non-availability of disaggregated level of tax-yield data and information on potential tax base. In the absence of these two crucial elements of RTS, resorting to indirect determinants or proxies, and aggregation of tax-yield data give us biased estimates. When we use regression coefficients for arriving at average effective rates, instead of arithmetic average effective rate, the results are no

Table: 6.10: Tax Capacity and Tax Effort based on RTS (Total of 3 Taxes):1990-91

State	Sales Tax		State Excise duty		Motor vehicle tax	
	Sales tax yield	Estimated Yield	Actual tax yield	Estimated yield	Actual tax yield	Estimated yield
Andhra Pradesh	1198.78	1060.92	727.980	459.512	185.790	111.520
Assam	243.49	164.90	13.040	144.925	12.74	30.5408
Bihar	585.24	602.42	108.000	333.150	85.00	74.8678
Gujarat	1430.22	1277.78	12.000	343.406	95.75	134.585
Haryana	177.74	444.49	286.350	191.893	35.78	56.352
Karnataka	1088.32	1023.09	429.690	295.853	192.43	111.022
Kerala	800.77	696.54	175.410	187.425	74.14	86.9887
Madhya Pradesh	600.22	737.12	300.830	380.830	74.95	84.6267
Maharastra	2552.57	2393.40	542.310	649.274	204.32	227.703
Orissa	336.64	157.49	45.640	143.320	52.29	29.6908
Punjab	416.73	590.06	435.780	223.498	37.43	67.4760
Rajasthan	616.58	399.74	260.460	258.891	107.51	52.9756
Tamil Nadu	1787.86	1583.21	434.860	319.120	227.34	168.721
Uttar Pradesh	1286.34	1587.89	724.790	622.951	85.42	163.976
West Bengal	979.63	1264.71	164.290	401.372	71.76	132.358

Contd...

State	Total of 3 taxes	Total of 3 taxes	RTS tax effort	Rank
Andhra Pradesh	2112.55	1631.95	1.2945	3
Assam	269.27	340.37	0.7911	12
Bihar	778.24	1010.44	0.7702	13
Gujarat	1537.97	1755.77	0.8760	10
Haryana	499.87	692.74	0.7216	14
Karnataka	1710.44	1429.97	1.1961	4
Kerala	1050.32	970.95	1.0817	6
Madhya Pradesh	976.00	1202.58	0.8116	11
Maharastra	3299.20	3270.38	1.0088	8
Orissa	434.57	330.50	1.3149	2
Punjab	889.94	881.03	1.0101	7
Rajasthan	984.55	711.61	1.3836	1
Tamil Nadu	2450.06	2071.05	1.1830	5
Uttar Pradesh	2096.55	2374.82	0.8828	9
West Bengal	1215.68	1798.44	0.6760	15

better than what we get by using aggregate regression method. In fact, we are using more or less the same determinants except for one or two plus or minus, as one uses for the method given in the part one. Further, as disaggregated tax-yield data is not available even for regression method, what we estimate is the tax-yield by broad group of taxes, which serves no better purpose than the method outlined in part one.

End Notes and References

1. Jerry C. Fastrup, "Fiscal Capacity, Fiscal Equalization and Federal Grants Formula" in Federal State Local Fiscal Relations. Op. cit. p. 42-43 Vol. 1. 2 Ibid

2. Ninth Finance Commission (1989) p. 105.

3. See Akin, "Fiscal Capacity and the Estimating Methods of the ACIR," National Tax Journal, Vol. 26 (June 1973) pp 275-92); W. Douglas Morgan, "An Alternative measure of Fiscal capacity," NTJ, Vol.27 (June 1974) pp.361-6.

4. Op Cit.

5. Rao, Hemlata. (1993) Taxable Capacity, Tax Efforts and Forecasts of Indian States",(Study sponsored by the Tenth Finance Commission), ISEC Bangalore, Chapter II.2, pp. 96-69. Mimeograph.

7

EXPENDITURE NEEDS: ISSUES AND MEASURES

7.1 Introduction

Principle of equalization is accepted almost in all the federal countries in the scheme of fiscal transfers. The principle is based on the twin concepts of fiscal capacity and fiscal need. Estimation of expenditure need of a federating state is very important in implementing a rational intergovernmental transfer system. The Fiscal transfer system is required to off set revenue and cost disabilities and provide for the additional expenditures required to meet the requirements of the respective states. While to understand the concept of fiscal capacity is relatively easier, to define what constitutes need of a state and how that should be measures, is very difficult and is riddled with complexities.

The need of the federating states may be construed to indicate need for grants from the federal government to enable the federating state to provide comparable levels of services at a comparable cost. If a state has low fiscal capacity and the resources are not adequate to meet the constitutionally allotted functions, the federating state needs resources from the federal government. When fiscal need is interpreted in this manner, one usually arrives at the revenue gap approach to estimate revenue need i.e. to juxtapose the revenue resources with the expenditure requirements. The revenue need may vary from state to state due to various factors.

Expenditure need of a federating state needs to be looked at both from the demand side and from the supply side. Need of the state to supply public goods and services also depend upon the political philosophy pursued in the state. In a country, which has staunch faith in capitalism and believes in the least interference by the state in the economic activities, perhaps the supply side provides a strong ground for the differential need for resources by the federating states. If a federating state has low fiscal capacity and the cost of providing services is very high, the need for resources to be transferred from the federal to the state will be more. The public expenditure basically depends upon the unit cost of providing the service and cost of input purchase and also on the productivity of public expenditure. As a major component of input cost in the government sector is labour cost, the cost variation among states depends on the nature of labour market and the bargaining capacity of the government. Similarly, the cost of material purchases depends on the price variations among the states. This approach measures need for resources to provide a uniform level of services across the federating states with uniform level of taxation. However in a state with socialistic objectives or in a welfare state the need for resources required by the federating states will vary not only due to differential fiscal capacity to raise resources but more due to variation in the demand for goods and services resulting from the diversity and economic disparity factors.

Thus in a state with predominant market economy the expenditure need of the federating units vary due to supply conditions like cost differentials and price differentials but in a welfare state the need of the states depend upon the demand for public goods and services which vary according the economic disparity factor and diversity factors. Thus some of the important factors explaining need for resources for meeting the expenditure responsibilities of states are:

7.1.1 Environmental Factors: Variation in resource need arises due to variations in geographical features, social structure including demographic features and economic features like already realized levels of developments in the productive sectors, variations in the availability of economic infrastructure like transport, communication, power, water and so on, social infrastructure like availability of educational facilities or health facilities, hospitals, qualified Doctors, sanitation, drinking water, availability of financial infrastructure like financial institutions like banks, insurance, cooperatives and marketing infrastructure access to forward and backward markets and so on. Economic variations are due to historical factors, locational factors and due to variations in the skills to administer and execute rational policies and also due to variations in the quality of governance. Thus, need for resources to provide transport network in hilly region would be more due to the nature of the terrain in a State with plain lands. Similarly, a State which already has developed economic infrastructure like roads, power, irrigation etc., would need resources mainly for the maintenance of these assets, while a State which does not have adequate infrastructure would require more of capital resources for capital formation and asset creation. A State with strong primary educational institution may have to spend more on higher and technical education, while a lagging State may have to spend a lot even on primary education. [1]

Thus, Revenue need of the federating states may vary because of the differential levels of demand for public goods and services. And also due to the demand pattern showing preferences for certain type of goods and services. Thus the revenue need may be different due to population and its composition, levels of economic development, also due to natural endowments. Thus, economic disparities and diversities cause differential revenue need of the states.

7.1.2 Inter-State Price Level Differences: Expenditure need of the federating states may vary from state to state depending up on the variation In the unit cost of providing a service and the input differences. Hence two states with equal fiscal capacity may need different amount of revenue to provide comparable levels of services.

The prices of the goods and services purchased by State and local governments vary with climate, with distance from the point of production, between rural and urban areas, and as a consequence of State-local government policy. For example, State laws relating to the compensation of public employees vary widely, with major consequences for the costs of public services. Cost differences traceable to the policies of State and local governments must be abstracted from. The price of providing public goods and services very much depend, apart from political and administrative skills, on cost of living. Inter-State cost differentials, if significant mean that costly areas require relatively more resources to provide a standard set of public services when environmental factors are held constant. For example, it costs more to get coal for producing thermal power in a land located far off State than in a State where it is produced the cost of transport itself makes all the difference, in the resource need for generating thermal power.

However, too little information is available on the prices paid by the States and localities to permit estimation of a comprehensive index of the relative input costs of governments in all the States. However, to date, efforts to workout an acceptable cost of living and cost of government differentials and how they might be taken into account in federal aid formulae have not succeeded. Data constraints are one factor and other is political factor which have made it difficult to asses cost differentials. Hunter has expressed, "much has been written on this topic in recent years, but little on this topic in recent years, little progress has been made in developing acceptable need measure." [2]

Given that the actual policies of any one State are to be disregarded, variations in the costs of public services among the States depend on three general classes of factors:

1. The range and types of services that must, by law, be provided.
2. The prices of the inputs used to produce public services, such as wages and salaries, gasoline prices, and the cost of asphalt.
3. Factors that determine the scope of the services provided, such as traffic and the miles of highways that must be maintained.

7.1.3 Legal Requirements: The services for which a jurisdiction is responsible are a key consideration in the cost of government at the local level, where obligations prescribed by State law vary among the States and among different types of local governments. At the State level, however, requirements imposed by the federal government apply uniformly throughout the nation, and the States are essentially free to offer whatever arrays of services they may choose. Their choices are, of course, embodied in policies, from which the analysis must abstract, hence the first of the three types of factors is not germane in considering differences in the costs of public services that are not the result of the policies of the governments in a State.

An attempt to define need was made as early as in 1970 by Musgrave and Polinsky (1970). They defined needs as 'the cost of supplying average performance levels for the existing mix of State-Local programs'. This definition assumed all cost disabilities as legitimate, and treated them as sources of inequity. A limitation of this definition is that it does not differentiate cost disabilities due to factors within and beyond the control of the States. This definition points at the need for defining from the supply view point.

For a long time low fiscal capacity or per capita income was taken as a sole measure of need of a state. Government raises revenue through tax, non-tax and debt sources mainly to finance the goods and services to be supplied to the citizens. If the capacity is low state cannot provide an optimum level of goods and services. However, it was soon realized that the extent of goods (pure public, merit and private goods) to be provided by the states depends upon various factors. Fiscal need is identified with relative cost of providing a given level of a specific public service or public services in general. [3] Hence a new definition flows from the premise that a measure of revenue-raising ability alone is a seriously incompatible indicator of the overall ability of a State or local government to fiancé service responsibilities. Only when revenue raising capacity is related to the costs of the public service responsibilities of a government can it be said that its general fiscal situation is accurately represented." [4] A mere differential in the fiscal capacity is not enough to indicate the revenue requirements of the government. In a federal country federating states, due to wide disparities and diversities and cost and price differentials require different amount of revenue to meet the expectations of their citizens. Hence it is considered important to have some estimates of expenditure need to determine the revenue requirement of the states.

In the literature several measures of need have been used. In some studies for the purpose of formulating federal aid policies, generalized and categorical need measures were developed. Stephen Barro had developed an index of need as far back as in 1970, which was based on a weighted population method, where the weights represented relative magnitudes of service demands associated with different population groups. Centre for Governmental Research, used this measure. [5] Categorical need indicators were used for Medicare, vocational education etc. A number of poverty indicators were also considered. In some countries (including India) population is taken as a direct measure of need for resources.

Barrow (1975) used regression approach to identify benefiting population groups and to determine statistically the importance of each need-related population characteristic. Indexes of need were developed. with per-capita expenditures in four categories (education, welfare, highways and others) as the dependant variables and relevant population variables (Public school pupils per-capita, percent families with female head and children under 18, percent population in metropolitan areas and percent population in central cities) as independent variables. In the same study, Barrow constructed a need index based on the method of direct imputation – where expenditures in eight functional categories were assigned to various population sub-groups i.e. local school expenditures to public school pupils, spending for higher education to population aged 18-22 and spending for welfare to persons below the poverty level." [6]

In some federations attempts were made to develop some measure of need for example, the 'Commonwealth Grants commission' of Australia measures expenditure needs of each of the states for individual expenditure categories by calculating the differential cost with reference to a standard level. Important factors such as social and demographic composition of population, population density, urbanization and other physical cost disabilities are included for estimating the differential expenditure need. In some other federations low fiscal capacity (per capita income) itself is taken as a measure of need.

Some of the measures often used to estimate expenditure need are:

- Population;
- Levels of development along with some measure of fiscal capacity like per capita income or Fiscal capacity as discussed in the previous chapters;
- Representative expenditure Method;
- Assessment of expenditure need based on the cost and price differentials.

In fact a comprehensive measure of expenditure need has to take into consideration both the supply side factors and demand side factors into account. In the present day almost all the countries have mixed economy and welfare objective. Hence one has to estimate need of the state both from the point of demand and from the point of capacity to provide for such goods and services.

7.2 Studies Measuring Fiscal/Expenditure Needs of States

Rao, (1974) [7] made an attempt to measure fiscal need in terms of fiscal capacity and a composite index of development which had population and area as common denominators for most of the physical indicators of development. She developed the index of need on the ground that in a federation federating units have wide economic disparities and diversities. While all the states are required to provide about the same range of public services, they differ from each other in terms of their capacity to do so owing to diversity and disparity factors. This leads to differential levels of assistance sought from the centre. Usually states with low fiscal potential and low level of development need more resources from the federal government on the contrary rich and developed states can finance their expenditure programme, to a large extent from their own resources. This means the rich and developed states can provide high level of services out of their own resources or provide the level of services comparable with poor states, at a low rate of levies. Thus, they are in an advantageous position when compared to less developed and poor states. On this basis, objective of 'equalization' of general need for resources, may be accepted as the general objective of federal fiscal transfers. 'General Need' in turn is represented by two factors viz., levels of development or backwardness and fiscal potential. Higher the level of development (as measured by the realized levels of services and socio-economic infrastructure necessary for the growth of productive sector) and higher the level of fiscal potential lesser would be the need for public expenditure on socio-economic infrastructure, and higher would be the resources generated from own sources, thus lesser would be the need for resources from the federal government.

The term 'need' is used in Rao's study in a comprehensive sense the most backward state with very low fiscal potential is considered to be the most needy state and vice versa. Thus, need is measured by (i) relative levels of development and (ii) the relative fiscal potential of the state. If the federal transfers help to reduce regional disparities in development and fiscal potential, (i.e. the needy states getting more) the objective of equalization would be considered as achieved.

The federal fiscal transfers can be made either highly equalizing or moderately equalizing, depending upon the intensity of and variations in need among the states. The transfer model will be highly equalizing when the funds are transferred for raising the levels of development and fiscal potential of only those states which are ranked below the national average with respect to these two measures. On the other hand, the model would be moderately equalizing when the resources are transferred to all the states, but the amount thus transferred upon their relative backwardness and fiscal potential level i.e. the assistance would vary inversely with development and larger fiscal potential or in other words with low level of 'need' would get the minimum assistance and vice versa.

Highly equalizing scheme is suitable for a highly developed country where the number of less developed states or the extent of backwardness is limited. In such developed federations most of the states are self-sufficient and require little assistance from the federal government[1] hence, federal government can adopt a highly equalizing scheme. On the contrary, in a developing country, most of the states would still be in the developing stage. Even a relatively developed state is not fully developed in terms of its need and potential. In fact many of the developed states of a developing country are far backward when compared with an average or developed state of a developed nation. Hence, all states in a developing nation do require federal assistance, but the requirement for such assistance varies depending upon their fiscal need and fiscal resources. Therefore, in a developing federation a moderate equalizing scheme would be more suitable than a highly equalizing scheme.

Rao in her alternative approach supported a moderately equalising scheme.

7.2.1 Representative Expenditure Method: As explained in the previous chapter, the Representative Tax System (RTS) has invoked lot of interest among scholars to measure fiscal potential of a State in an objective manner. However, RTS is subjected to criticism.

RTS is criticized on the ground that it is flawed as a measure of fiscal capacity because it assumes implicitly that the costs of the service responsibilities of States depend solely on population. In response to the second criticism Robert W. Rafuse Jr. (Advisory Commission on Intergovernmental Relations (1990)) developed a Representative Expenditure (RE) method. The estimates of RE yields were intended to improve measure of the relative public service costs of the State. As such the use of RE in combination with the estimates of revenue raising ability (RTS) is expected to be a signification refinement in the measurement of fiscal capacity and fiscal need. s long back as in 1962 Mushkin and Rivalin, had expressed, "we have identified fiscal capacity of a State with the resources (measured by income or the yield of some combination of taxes) available to the State for Public expenditures. But little interest attaches to capacity, as such, unrelated to public needs.... We need a measure of State needs as well as State Capacity."

Therefore, the treasury report (US) defines fiscal capacity as the ability of a State or Local Governments to raise revenues relative to the cost of its service responsibilities. Cost of public service varies from State to State due to the following:

1. the nature of the services a State is legally required to provide e.g. provision of merit goods.
2. the prices of the inputs involved in the production of services such as wages, cost of raw material, cost of delivery of goods and services and so on.
3. factors that determine the scope of services that must be provided, such as number of students enrolled in public schools.

As the RTS yield for a State can be calculated by multiplying the estimate of the States tax base by the RTS tax rate, so the representative expenditure for a State can be derived by multiplying the State's work load measure by the national – average expenditure per unit of work load. [8] In other words, the Representative Expenditure procedure is that the actual State-local outlays for a function are distributed among the States in proportion to the values of the work load measure for the function.

RE is a relative and not an absolute concept. They are estimates of the expenditures that would be required (or the cost) to provide the average level of public services that actually prevailed nation-wide, in the year for which the estimates are calculated. It should be borne in mind that there is no implication that this actual service level is necessarily the correct or 'needed' level in any absolute sense. In Representative expenditure method key step is the identification of the best possible measure of the work load for each of the major functions or categories of State local expenditures. This is equivalent to the identification of proto typical tax base in RTS. In some studies work load is referred to as 'needs.'

The workload measure may be as simple as total population or more complex, comprising multiple variables equally or unequally weighted. However, the workload measures are limited to data availability. To illustrate: in order to measure RE with respect of elementary/secondary education, the "best measure of work load for local schools is a weighted average of the elementary (5-13) secondary (14-17) school age population net of private-school ennoblement at each level with special allowance for the number of children living in households with incomes below the poverty line." [9] Similarly for Public Welfare, the workload measure could be population living in households with income below the poverty line. Likewise, for each of the important government expenditure one can derive weights for measuring work load.

Representative expenditure measure is yet to be developed fully. As it stands today due to practical constraints, it is not a workable solution.

7.2.2 Estimating Representative Expenditures: The representative expenditure approach parallels that of the RTS. The crucial step is the identification of the best possible measure of the workload for each of the major categories of State-local expenditures. A State's workload for a service indicates its relative need for outlays on that function. To ensure that the workload measures are independent of the actual policies of the governments in a State, such program-client variables as enrollment in public schools and the number of people receiving welfare benefits are not used. [10]

Given the workload measure for a function, the representative expenditure per unit of workload is calculated by dividing the total of actual State and local outlays for the service by the U.S. total for the workload measure. A State's representative expenditure for the function is then arrived at by multiplying the representative outlay per unit by the state's workload. The result is an estimate of how much it would cost the governments in a State to provide the national-average (representative) level of the service.

A variety of general findings can be drawn from the estimates given in the Report. It is clear that population is an inferior measure of the relative cost to the governments of a State of providing a standard level of public services. Its use in a measure of fiscal capacity systematically overstates the capacities of States below the national average and understates the capacities of States above the national average. Fiscal disparities among the States are significantly larger than most measures available until now have suggested.

The differences among States in the cost of providing a common level of public services are substantial. They are smaller than the differences in own-revenue raising ability, by all measure currently available.

High Public service costs tend to be associated with low revenue-raising ability.

The actual spending of three out of four States with fiscal capacities below the national average is less than their representative expenditures.

The existing federal grant system, taken as a whole, tends to worsen fiscal disparities among the States. Therefore, the failure to allow for federal grants in a measure of State fiscal capacity results in systematic understatement of the magnitudes of fiscal disparities.

The report explicitly states, three points which deserve special emphasis in interpreting the results of the analysis. First, no implication should be drawn that the representative outlays are in any sense correct or "needed" in any absolute sense. The estimates merely show how much it would cost each State to provide the national-average level of each service.

Second, the estimates assume that every government produces the representative level of each service with the same efficiency. In other words, a given level of spending per capita (adjusted for differences in compensation costs) buys the same level of service in every State. Hence no inferences about operating efficiency can be drawn from the relationship between actual spending for a function and the representative expenditures.

Third, and a closely related point, the estimates are silent on the issue of performance. A dollar of spending (adjusted for differences in unit costs) in one State is assumed to yield the same quantity and quality of a service as it does in every other State. Although we know that public services are not of equal quality per dollar spent everywhere in the nation, it is, regrettably, impossible to take this into account because credible measures of performance are not available.

7.3 Measuring Expenditure Needs of States in India [11]

M.G. Rao et.al. [12] in their study take into consideration the variation in the input cost of providing the goods and services, and cost of input purchase and also the productivity of public expenditure.

The authors have adopted a normative approach for measuring need. They define expenditure needs as the normative cost of providing an average level of public services. In order to avoid any kind of value judgment on subjective standards like minimum level of services or reasonable level of services, average performance level as the equalization standard was adopted in the study. 'While choosing the average performance levels, it was also felt necessary to take into account the requirement of services arising from special characteristics of the population. Authors felt taking costs in a normative sense helps to take account of only those cost disabilities that are beyond the control of the State Governments.

The study differentiates between expenditure need and expenditure demand. In the above approach 'expenditure 'need' is conceptualized from supply side, in terms of providing an average level of a given service. While doing so, the attempt was to measure the need based on the actual expenditures incurred or the actual pattern of demand. In other words, the expenditure need is estimated on the basis of current resources and preferences of society. To the extent that the expenditure need is estimated on the basis of all-State average demand behaviour, assessment is done on the basis of average behaviour and this will differ from the actual expenditure pattern of individual States."

7.3.1 Methodology: The norms for estimating expenditure needs vary with the type of expenditures, in this exercise, as was done by the Ninth Finance Commission, States' expenditures are classified into three categories.

The first category comprises expenditure items whose needs depend on the stock of physical assets or financial liabilities. Maintenance expenditures and interest payments fall into this category. For determining expenditure needs for maintenance of physical assets like roads, buildings, public works and major, medium and minor irrigation works, engineering norms were considered as appropriate. Similarly, expenditure requirement in respect of interest payments depends upon outstanding loans and interest rates.

The second category of expenditure comprises irregular and non-recurring items. Items like refugee relief and rehabilitation, social security and welfare, famine and flood relief and elections are either not of recurring nature or even if they are, there is no regularity and therefore cannot be predicted in advance. Such items of expenditure have to be projected on the basis of broad judgments. Alternatively, the average of three/five years' all-State expenditures on those items as a ratio of GDP may be assumed to hold for the period of projection and that may be distributed on equal per capita basis for each of the States.

The regular and recurrent items of expenditure whose public service levels can be approximated by analyzing past trends fall into the third category. In the case of these items, revenue expenditure constitutes a substantial portion of total expenditure and represents, public levels of services. Expenditure variations in these items of expenditure can be explained in terms of factors influencing the quantity of services and unit cost of providing them. In other words, these items of expenditure are amenable to meaningful statistical analysis as regressions can be estimated to separate the effects of different factors representing quantity and cost of providing public services on the level of expenditures in different States. Separation of the effects of quantity and cost factors helps to estimate the expenditure required to provide the predetermined normative (average) standard of public services in each of the States.

In M.G. Rao's study on expenditure need is taken in a relative sense. Expenditure need is defined as 'justifiable cost of providing average standard of services'. The norm for equalization chosen is the all-State average. Expenditure need is estimated according to the norm determined on the basis of actual achievement of service levels rather than being imposed by an outside standard. The simplest method of measuring expenditure need is to express public services as expenditure per intended beneficiary population group and estimate the cost of achieving an average output level. In most cases, the relevant beneficiary group is total population, and expenditures are taken in per capita terms. In the case of education expenditures, however, the beneficiary population is the relevant age group in the population. Accordingly, primary education expenditure is taken per child in the age group 5-9, secondary education expenditure is taken per population in the age group 10-16 and for higher education the relevant age group is 20-24.

Having understood the logic of expenditure needs, the next step is to formulate the expenditure (cost) function by expenditure per beneficiary population on variables representing quantity and unit cost of providing public services. Variables representing unit cost differences, in turn, are differentiated in terms of those that are within the control of State Governments and those that are beyond their control.

In the next stage, the formulated models are estimated by pooling the data across the States and over time. The regression analysis quantifying the effect of quantity and cost factors on expenditures has been carried out separately for the 15 large States [13] and 10 smaller States. Separate regression analysis has been carried out for the two categories of States.

For estimating the regression equations, cross-section data for different States have been pooled for 6 years from 1992-93 to

1997-98. Thus, in the case of large States, the data of 15 States are pooled for the six years and in the case of smaller States the data of 10 States for each of the six years are pooled to estimate the regression equations. Before estimating the pooled regressions, yearly cross-section equations for each of the expenditure functions were estimated for both non-plan and total revenue expenditures.

This exercise is carried out only to have some idea about the behavioural aspects of the cost functions. These models have been helpful for formulating alternative pooled regressions. In the second stage, the pooled regressions are estimated for each of the expenditure functions for non-plan and total expenditures separately for the large States and for the smaller States. After experimenting with three alternative models, viz., for the simple pooled regressions, fixed effects models and random effects model, they finally settled for the simple pooled regressions with adjustments for heteroskedasticity, cross group error correlation and autocorrelation.

Since the formulated models are cost functions, the dependent variable was the public expenditure per beneficiary population. For most of the expenditure functions per capita public expenditure is taken as the dependent variable, whereas for the education, expenditures per population in the relevant age group is considered.

Another variable which was considered in the study was 'price differences' between the States. To isolate the effect of price variations between the States on public expenditures, the Ninth Finance Commission had estimated the index of price differences based on the information on prices of different commodities collected in various urban centres by the Labour Bureau, Shimla. In this study, authors applied the changes in prices recorded in different States (averaged for different centres) on the base year differences of 1986-87 to estimate price differences among the States. Estimated values of this variable, however, were available only for the 15 large States and, therefore, the variable had been employed as an explanatory factor only in equations relating to large States.

7.3.2 Shortcomings: The authors themselves recognized the difficulties in developing a measure of need. Several conceptual problems arise in the measurement. They expressed, "The problem is compounded by the fact that public expenditure is only an intermediate output and does not represent final output or outcome in terms of public services or its impact on society." [14]

Although equalizing expenditure per beneficiary (in the relevant population group) has the virtue of simplicity, this does not ensure equalization in the standards of these services among the States. This is because, it is not possible to clearly identify the beneficiary group for every expenditure category as there may be more than one beneficiary group of population. More importantly, even when beneficiary group is clearly identified, equal expenditures will not result in equal service levels if there are cost differences among the States. For estimating expenditure needs, it is necessary to identify and control various quantity and cost factors that cause differences in expenditure levels across States. This is very difficult owing to non-availability of data relating to all the states over a period of time on uniform basis.

When expenditure on specific group is taken as a dependent variable it poses problems e.g. expenditure on education according to age group. This may pose a conceptual issue. Educational service may be provided both by the public as well as by the private sectors. If private school expenditures were significant, the need for public education expenditures would be commensurately lower. In other words, taking only public expenditure as the dependent variable to measure expenditure need provides only a partial picture.

The above examination of various measures of 'fiscal need' bring out clearly that so far no satisfactory measure of fiscal need is yet developed. There is need to conceptualise already 'fiscal need' and develop a method to measure relative fiscal need of the federating states.

End Notes and References

1. Hemlata Rao (1974), Centre-State Financial Relations and The problems of Financing Regional Development in India, Ph.D. Thesis, Delhi University.

2. Hunter, Op. cit., p. 35.

3. Richard. A. Musgrave and Peggy-B Musgrave, Public Finance in theory and Practice, Second edition McGraw-Hill 1966, pp 645-50.

4. Roberts W. Rafuse.Jr. "A Representative Expenditure Approach to the Measurement of the cost of the Service Responsibilities of States" in *Federal State Local Fiscal Relations* office of the State and Local Finance Department of the Treasure, Sept.1986 mimeograph. p. 135.

5. Fredrick J. Grasberger, Principal Investigator (Developing and Applying Analytical Tools to evaluate the distributional effects of Federal Grant-in-aid formulas and to improve formula performance. C.Jan.1980)

6. Stephen M Barrow, Equalization and Equity in General Revenue sharing: an Analysis of Alternative Distribution Formulas", Part-I (1975) Quoted in Hunter in Hunter Op. cit. P.37

7. Rao Hemlata, (1974), Centre State Financial Relations and the Problems of Financing Regional Development in India, Ph.D. Thesis, Delhi School of Economics, Delhi University,

8. Robert, W. Rafuse Jr., Op cit.

9. Ibid., p. 143.

10. For detailed estimates Refer, Robert .W. Rafuse, Op cit.

11. M.G. Rao, B. Kammaiah, Allen Roy, Measuring Expenditure Needs of the States, Study sponsored by the Eleventh Finance Commission Of India., ISEC, Mimeograph.

12. Rao et.al. Op. cit.

13. These include all non-special category States except Goa and Assam

14. Rao et.al. Op. cit.

8

MEASURES OF DEVELOPMENT AND INTER-STATE DISPARITIES

Section 1

8.1 Federal Fiscal Transfers and Economic Backwardness

In a federal country, there is need to protect the interests of all the federating states especially of the backward states. Precisely for this reason, weightage is given to the criterion of economic backwardness in the scheme of federal fiscal transfers. The rationale for transferring more resources to the backward regions is outlined in chapter on Horizontal Fiscal imbalances.

Uneven regional development results in numerous complications such as wastage of resources increase in public costs, social injustice, deceleration of economic growth, threat to national integration and political instability. In the era of `globalization', liberalization, while private investment (domestic, foreign) tend to flow to the regions which are already developed and have good marketing network and socio-economic infrastructure, regions, which are backward remain deprived of any fresh investments. There is an urgent need to tackle these problems. Otherwise, they will further aggravate the imbalances in the economy. Political, economic, social and ethical considerations also call for measures to attain greater parity in the levels of development. Reduction in disparities is also crucial to accelerate the growth of economy as a whole. This is particularly relevant for the underdeveloped economies. In fact, the growth can be maximized when the resources and growth potential of backward regions are used for enhancing productive capacities.

Hence it is important that while formulating any policy proper weights are assigned to different objectives. In a federal country, the need for a balanced approach towards growth and equity is all the more important. Reduction in Regional Disparities would pave way for greater national integration, increase in economic growth and political stability. On the contrary, if the disparities are widening, a sense of unfairness and injustice may kindle regional and parochial movements, as seen in many countries. The emergence of small states in India in the recent years is an example of the consequence of the continuous neglect of backward regions.

The above explanation justifies inclusion of Backwardness of a state as one of the criterion of federal Fiscal transfer scheme based on the objective of Fiscal need. However before including this criterion it is pertinent to understand the concept of development and the causes of backwardness.

8.2 Development Defined

In the literature on development economics, the term development has been used widely. But the conceptual framework and precise quantification of the term, "Development" bristles with complications. In fact, there is no clear or agreed definition of the term development. At one extreme development is understood to indicate long term material improvements, flow of goods and services, on the other extreme it is supposed to bring changes in social, cultural, political institutions and in the attitude of people. In fact a combined effect of the two extremes stated above determines the level of development.

Generally development is identified with the level of per capita real income. The UNO (1951) identified 'development' with the level of per capita income. Thus an under developed country is one "in which the per capita real income is low when compared with the per capita income of the U.S.A., Canada, Australia, and Western Europe.' Though, this definition focuses attention on a very important characteristic of underdevelopment viz., poverty, can by no means be considered wholly adequate. It may easily be open to a theoretical objection. A country may be poor and yet not underdeveloped in relation to its resources. The resources themselves are scanty and inadequate. These in turn are identified with the presence of better conditions of nutrition, housing, education, health, transport and so on. In the series of studies by

UNRISD (1976), Development is identified with the levels of living and levels of welfare.

According to Jan Drewnowski (1966), "Development is a process of quantitative growth of the social and economic reality which we can call either society or economy. Because of the close inter-relation of economic and social factors 'purely' economic development is possible. Consequently it is better not to speak of social development separately. It is a single process which is best called simply development." [1]

In the above definition, Drewnowski identifies socio-economic development with change in the quality of life and quantitative growth of various values. Quality of life can be improved by improving the conditions of health, nutrition, education, transport and communications and so on.

The Indian Planning Commission (1952) defined under-developed country as one "which is characterized by the co-existence in greater or less degree of unutilized manpower on the one hand and of un-exploited natural resources on the other." [2] This definition stresses upon one of the characteristics of underdevelopment i.e. the existence of idle resources. However, this criterion taken by it does not really indicate underdevelopment. In some of the developed countries also one can expect the existence of idle resources. This is especially so during the period of economic depression. Thus the definition of underdeveloped country as given by the Planning Commission is partial and also misleading.

In some of the studies 'development' level is assessed on the basis of stages of economic growth. If one examines the characteristics outlined by Rostow, one can observe that, countries with modern technology, high industrialization, having maximum availability of goods and services, are highly developed. Thus, in essence the availability of infrastructure, industrialization, modernization and new technology determine the levels of development.

All the definitions given above whether based on the concept of realised levels of development or the degree of the utilization of the available potential or stages of economic growth attained, or per capita income or availability of goods and services, point at material well being of the citizens of the State.

From the various definitions given above one can summarize and use the term 'development' to imply 'improvement' in the material well-being of the people in a region. Material well-being of a region or a country can be identified with the increase in the real production, availability of infra-structural facilities, social amenities and services like health, education, nutrition, etc., better employment opportunities, practice and adoption of new and modern technology and increased rate of investment and Consumption. Any change for betterment in these parameters indicates development.

8.3 Factors Causing Backwardness

Regional disparities are commonly found in all the countries - developed and developing. However, the nature and essential features of backwardness are not the same. Almost all countries have been attempting to develop their backward regions. The range of these measures and their application, however, is widely different. Success of the strategies for the development of backward regions very much depends upon the understanding of the nature of backwardness of a region.

In the context of a federation a region is identified with sub national governments like the states and the local bodies. Backward regions require the government intervention depending upon the nature and causes of backwardness. For the purpose of formulating development strategies for these regions, it is essential to know the basic causes of backwardness.

Causes of backwardness of regions can be classified as under:

8.3.1 Diversity Factor: Diversity due to resource endowment and natural resources lead to differential levels of development and those, which have structural disadvantages, tend to lose e.g. Northern part of Canada, which is Ice clad has natural disadvantage; similarly desert area may also be disadvantaged. There may also be partial disadvantaged regions like the forest regions, hilly regions and so on.

8.3.2 Special Problems: The second cause of backwardness could be associated with special problems of the region such as predominance of Tribal population, or the region may have frequent floods, famines, or it may be affected by drought.

8.3.3 Location of a Region: Backwardness of a region can also be attributed to Location factor. If a region lies in between two growth poles or very near to a growth pole it becomes a shadow region and in spite of all advantages tend to remain backward. Region may also have problems due to its location on the border of the country.

8.3.4 Under-utilization of Available Potential: Fourth cause of backwardness is the mismatch between the development potential and the level of its utilization. This mismatch could be due to several reasons: historical, political, economic, social and so on. These lagging regions generally are capable of reaching the standards of developed regions. They have development potential, which has remained untapped due to several factors. We may label these regions as economically and socially backward regions. In the context of formulating policies pertaining to federal grants and other assistance schemes it is the fourth factor causing backwardness that assumes special importance.

In this study the focus is on the fourth category of backward region. For this group of regions, as stated above, the cause of backwardness is the mismatch between the available resource potential and its utilization. In order to utilize these potentials there is need to attract investment. And for this the development of socio-economic infrastructure is very crucial. If backward regions are bestowed with good transport, communication, power, health, education, recreation, financial infrastructure, marketing net work to facilitate development of backward and forward linkages; investment and entrepreneur will flow automatically and the productive sectors will start growing. This requires huge amount of fiscal transfers from the federal government.

There are broadly four types of sectors which need to be developed in backward states. The first is the productive sector which comprises of agriculture and allied activities, manufacturing and other secondary activities and services. The second comprises of basic economic infrastructure like power, transports, communication, water and irrigation and so on. The third includes sectors like banking, cooperatives, and other financial services, and the last is social sector including, health, education, social welfare schemes for the deprived, aged, women and children, nutrition, drinking water and sanitation etc. Federal government can help the backward states in different ways. For example, in the productive sector, in the initial years of development the federal government may opt for direct investment in the productive sector either exclusively by itself or jointly with the states and private sector.

Section 2

8.4 Methodological Issues

Any policy aiming at helping the backward states requires the following Issues to be resolved:

1. Measures of development, Identification of backward States;
2. Analyze the trend and measure regional disparities;
3. Delineation of homogeneous States

The first issue is concerned with the measures of development; which involves selection of indicators, assigning weights and applying methods of aggregation.

The second issue pertains to grouping of States on homogeneous basis. This involves the study of typology and dimensions of development and also grouping of States according to the relative levels of developments.

The third issue i.e. to examine the trends in disparities is also important for a meaningful policy of reducing disparities, this requires a proper measure of disparities applicable across the states and over a period of time.

8.4.1 Measures of Development: Several techniques have been used in regional studies to measure the magnitude of regional development. The measurement of development may be based on single or multiple indicators depending on the purpose of the study and the nature of the data to be analyzed. When one is interested in the development of material output, an indicator like aggregate output in the form of gross material product or gross domestic product becomes an adequate indicator for regional analysis. Development indicators take into account social aspects also along with economic variables. There are two important measures of development:

- Monetary measure; and
- Physical measures.

This is presented in chart 8.1.

A. Monetary Measure: Per capita income is widely accepted as a general measure of development. It is customary to identify whether a region has been backward or advanced in terms of development using the estimates of per capita income. According to this measure, regions which enjoy higher per capita income are deemed to be more developed than States or regions with low per capita income. [3]

At the international level, the United Nations while determining whether a country is developed or underdeveloped uses per capita income (PCI) as a measure of development despite its sensitivity to the presence of very high-income groups. Besides United Nations, other global organizations like the World Bank, International Monetary Fund, International Labor Organization, etc. also use it for measuring development and comparing different countries. While carrying out the analysis of inter-country regional disparities, PCI as a single indicator has been used by several economists.

The 'per capital' income as a measure of development is defended on a number of basis. One defense of 'Income' is that it is an objective, value free indicator. It has also been argued on behalf of 'national income' as a development indicator that it could at least be quantified.

The 'income' measure, if one examines carefully is in fact heavily value loaded. Every type of product and service is assigned its own particular weight (many being zero). This weight is mainly determined by market forces, which reflect the county's distribution of income and wealth.

Chart 8.1

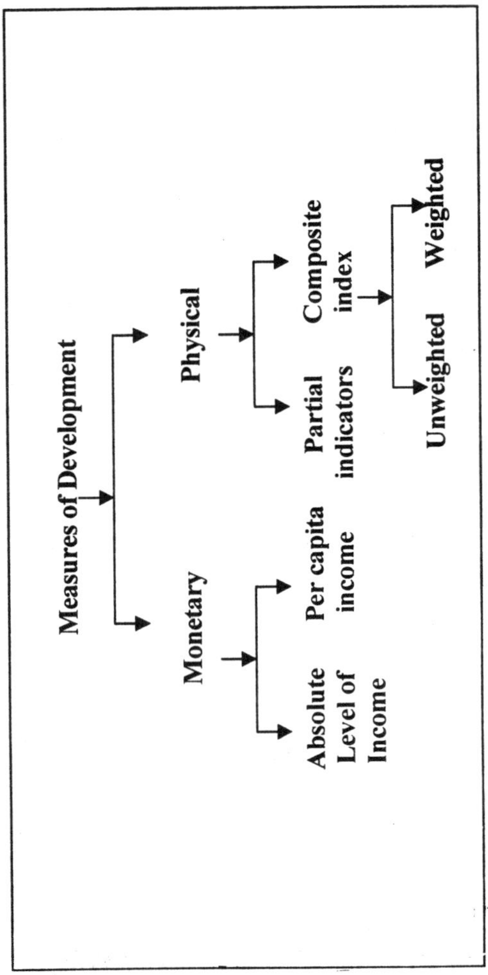
Measures of Development
Monetary
Physical
Absolute Level of Income
Per capita income
Partial indicators
Composite index
Unweighted
Weighted

Estimation of National Income also implies a set of judgments about what activities it should cover what are the 'final' products as against 'intermediate' products which are not considered intrinsically valuable and only produced because they make possible the production of other more desirable products.

Quite apart from theoretical consideration, where the per capita income is used in practice as a means of ranking countries, according to their general levels of development, the ranking obtained sometimes conflicts sharply with a common sense ranking e.g., Japan has much less per capita income than Venezuela. In fact, the classification of countries into 'developed' and 'developing' used in practice does not coincide with a breakdown according to per capita national income.

`Income' as an aggregative concept does not reflect structure and distribution. If it is used as a general measure, then different countries are equally developed if they have the same per capita income, whatever the contents of their development. [4] Yet some countries can have a well balanced economic development covering both agriculture and industry and a relatively healthy and well fed population, while others, with the same per capita income can be developed in only one limited part of economy and the mass of the population relatively untouched, may continue to live in traditional poverty.

Per capita income, which is normally used as a measure of development, gives at best, only a rough indication of relative level of the welfare of various regions. When development is seen as comprising both economic and social elements which tend to change together as a complex, univariate statistics for describing complex social processes provide a partial picture and are consequently found to be inadequate both as tool of analysis and as an input in policy making process.

Economist McGranahan disagreed with the usual practice of identifying development in terms of per capita GNP. He argued that "this is too narrow and not the way the word `development' is understood and used by most people...that other indicators can be found that in practice perform better in describing, estimating and predicting the totality of aspects that constitute development, and are therefore better indicators of development as a whole, than the per capita GNP." [5] In a similar vein, Drewnowski commented about the traditional economic variables such as GNP and all its derivations [6]...it is generally recognized that traditional economic accounting variables cannot legitimately be used for measuring improvement in social conditions, nor can they be considered satisfactory as objectives for development planning.

Thus, the use of per capita income as a single indicator of development is bound to narrow down the scope of analysis to a considerable extent. Development is to be seen as a web of several socio-economic activities, which cannot be comprehended by observing only one indicator, i.e., per capita GNP. Per capita income fails to reflect the inherent process of structural transformation of socio-economic development that has taken place in a country.

Finally there is a major problem of lack of data, unreliable and incomplete set of data and their non-availability at micro-levels and in backward regions.

Thus there are a number of problems which one encounters while using 'per capita income' as a measure of development and hence, though convenient, income is not a very satisfactory measure of development and at best it can be taken as one of the indicators of development.

B. Physical Measure: As explained above, measuring development in terms of per capita income is subject to several criticisms. They fail to reflect the up gradation in the quality of life that may have taken place due to economic development. In particular, there are several indicators of well being that are sensitive to distributional questions and less prone to difficulties of conceptualization, valuation and measurement as compared to income per capita. Social indicators have an additional advantage. They have upper limits, which mean that they cannot be skewed by presence of individuals whose characteristics are vastly different from the average, that is, unlike per capita income they are less sensitive to extremes in the distribution. This brings regional economists, to the question of appropriate indicators of development or backwardness.

The choice of indicators inevitably depends upon the purpose and the availability of data. There are mainly two approaches which are used for measuring development using physical indicators: partial or single variable approach and the multiple variable approaches. These are discussed below.

C. Partial Indicators or Single Variable Approach: In some investigations, differences in productivity, employment, industrialization, and mortality rate and protein consumption and so on, are taken as index of development. Some scholars have used variables like per capita electricity consumption, life expectancy, etc., but the analysis is univariate in orientation. If the purpose of the analysis is to examine a particular aspect or dimension of disparity, then it is better to deal with the univariate or single variable approach. For example, to examine the disparity in industrial development, one can use per capita power consumption.

However, they are only clues, and may well be misleading if used to compare nations of very different structure, genetic stock, dietary habits etc. unemployment is a very difficult concept to define in a non-industrial society.

D. Multiple variable approach or Composite measure of Development: A meaningful study of differences in inter-regional or inter-regional development levels should take into consideration various physical variables which have some bearing on the overall development.

It is normally observed that most of the variables applied in socio-economic development analysis are inter-related. In this sense multivariate data analytical techniques provide a solid ground to construct a composite index of development. Instead of using judgment or a subjective weighting pattern, this technique provides a weighting pattern derived from the data itself.

Multivariate analysis can simply be defined as the application of methods that deal with reasonably large number of measurements (i.e., variables) made on each object in one or more samples *simultaneously*. In this admittedly loose definition the important point is that multivariate analysis deals with the *simultaneous relationships among variables*. If interest centers on the association between two sets of variables, where one set is the realization of a dependent or criterion measure then the appropriate class of techniques would be those designated as *dependence methods*. If interest centers on the mutual association across all variables with no distinction made among variable types, one uses *interdependence methods*. Dependence methods seek to explain or predict one or more criterion measures based upon the set of predictor variables. Interdependence methods, on the other hand, are less predictive in nature and attempt to provide insights into the underlying structure of the data by simplifying the complexities, primarily through *data reduction*.

Having chosen a large number of indicators, the problem arises as how to combine the multiple indicators having different types of scales (or units of measurements) so as to give a common index of development which would reflect the true picture of development in the economy.

8.4.2 Construction of Composite Indices for Regionalization: The models and techniques for regionalization should emerge from the objectives of study and the theoretical frame within which the problem is posed. This is true even for the so-called positivistic approaches to regionalization undertaken to satisfy purely "cognitive enquiries" that regard "region" as a non-evaluative and non-hypothetical concept. That is because it is not possible even to apprehend or interpret anything we would want to call a "fact" independent of a theoretical framework. The justification of the assumptions technological or behavioral, that any model maker, has to be sought not in its mathematical logic but in the underlying theory, which, in some way is an abstraction of the real world.

The crucial stage in regionalization in a multivariate analysis is that of reducing a large number of variables into one (or a few) composite index, so that the geographical micro units (districts, taluks, etc.) can be compared, ranked or categorized. There exists no foolproof or value free method of obtaining a composite index for regionalization. There are four stages, not mutually exclusive, involved in this task and at each stage one cannot help making a series of judgments. These stages are

- the decision about the unit for which data are to be collected,
- selection of variables,
- compositing the variables, and
- Classification on the basis of homogeneity.

The problem of composition of indicators has two major aspects: elimination of the bias of scale and determination of weightage. It is always possible to handle the two problems together as weightage to the indicators may be so designed that the scale effect is eliminated simultaneously and vice versa. There are, however, distinct advantages in attempting to tackle them in two stages, as this would allow an analyst to probe deeper into the theoretical premise and examine, in greater depth, the assumptions of the techniques applied at each stage.

A. Search for a Standard Scale: The variables chosen for working out composite indices are measured in different units and hence in general, are not directly additive. It therefore, becomes necessary to convert them to some standard `units' so that the initial scale chosen for measuring the variables does not bias the results. It is; however, true that any method of scale conversion involves implicit weighting and the selection of a standard scale is never a value-free decision.

B. Conversion to a Discrete Scale: For eliminating the bias of scale, it has been proposed that the chosen variables (measured in ratio, interval or ordinal scale) be transformed into certain given discrete variable. Each observation may be assigned a value in the discrete scale on the basis of its relative position in the series. The method of ranking, popular among regional scientists for its simplicity and computational case, falls, in this category. When there are *n* observations, say, districts, there will be, under this scheme, feasible points in an n-dimensional Euclidean space, the axes corresponding to the districts. Each transformed variable will be assigned one of these points (depending on the relative position of the districts for that variable), the former will simply be an arrangement or permutation of numbers from 1 (one) to *n*.

This method has been dubbed as having "doubtful theoretical meaning", as it involves a shift in the origin and occasions considerable loss of information, i.e. unit difference in ranks do not reflect an equal difference in variable value. A variable after transformation, if represented as a point in *n*-dimensional space, would not be on the straight line joining the origin and the point corresponding to the original variable, owing to the shift in the origin. This implies that the ratio of two observations in the transformed series will not be the same as in the original series. The transformed variables being a permutation of certain fixed numbers (from unity) to n, in the case of the ranking method), the statistical properties of their distribution would be identical.

C. Standardization: The scale-effect can be removed by dividing the deviation of each observation from the mean by the standard deviation. This technique, widely used by Western geographers, imposes on variables conditions that might be sufficient, but not necessary to eliminate the bias of scale. Subtraction of the mean from observations of a variable leads to a shift in the origin and distorts their `relative positions'. Addition to or subtraction from two unequal observations of any constant, affects their earlier `relationship', whereas division or multiplication by any positive (finite) number leaves it unaffected when the variables are measured in a ratio scale. The method also has the disadvantage of equalizing variance and length of all the variables and these may be discrimination against variables having higher dispersion independent of scale.

D. Division by Standard Deviation: The observed values of a variable may be divided by the standard deviation of the series, which is an absolute measure of dispersion to obtain a new series with standard deviation as unity. This method does not lead to a shift in the origin although the criticism leveled against the method of standardization for equalizing variance would be valid in this also.

E. Normalization: A series may be made scale-free by

dividing it by its length. Points equidistant would then, represent the transformed indicators from the origin. The obvious drawback of this technique lies in its ironing out the difference in the length of vectors from the data matrix.

F. Division by Mean: If the observations for each variable are divided by the mean, one can get rid of the bias of scale without affecting the relative position of the districts in the series. This transformation does not disturb the `dispersion' of the variables since the coefficient of variation of the original series is retained as the standard deviation (which is equal to the coefficient of variation) of the transformed series. In social research, however, mean does not enjoy any `secular sanction' greater than any other parameter of the distribution; nor is there *a priori* justification for preserving the coefficient of variation of the original series as standard deviation of the new series.

G. Division by an `Ideal' Value: A value higher or lower than the mean, viz., national average, target parameter etc. may be considered to be the norm of a series. It should then be possible to suitably manipulate the coefficient of variation by dividing the series by this normative value. When norm is higher (lower) than the mean, the standard deviation of the transformed series will be less (more) than the coefficient of variation in the original series. This is understandable because a given difference put in relation to two unequal values has different significance.

8.4.3 Selection of Indicators: The major problem in the construction of general index is the selection of indicators. It is easy to load the concept of development with arbitrary, capricious or contradictory variables. The proper choice of indicators constitutes the crux of the methodology.

While selecting variables it is important to bear in mind the differences in the meaning of the concepts like diversity and disparity, which are quite often used in the same sense. Disparity arises as a result of failure to exploit the hidden development potentials of a region's "initial resource endowments, its latent comparative and absolute resource advantages, relative to another comparable region and is therefore, comprised of factors which are not natural or physiographic but human, institutional and historical-socio-political and/or economic technological. [7] The term 'diversity' on the other hand denotes differences in the initial resource endowments, largely of a natural or physiographic character, leading to territorial specialization and division of labor through exploitation of the resource advantages comparative as well as absolute. In this context the land utilization data reflects more of 'diversity' than 'disparity' and hence a mix of this data with agricultural development indicators like use of chemical fertilizers, mechanization etc., should be avoided. However, in a dynamic analysis, when changes over a period of time are taken into consideration, any changes in the land use pattern would reflect the direction of overall development.

Similarly, cropping pattern is a structural variable in a static analysis, while the change in cropping pattern over a time is an indicator of development. Here it would be noted that the 'change in the variables' over a period of time is an indicator of development and not the structure itself. Interpretation of the 'change' has to be done carefully after assessing its various impacts and implications either in a time series or a cross section analysis. In a number of studies, such differences between the diversity factors and disparities factors are totally ignored. In some other studies, natural phenomenon like Rainfall is also taken as an indicator of Development. Similarly in his study, M.L. Patel [8] attributes inter-regional disparities in agricultural development, to variations in the natural endowments and technological level of farming practices. He identifies land use pattern with natural endowment and tries to assess disparities in terms of this factor. According to him, since the geographical area of tribal area is 1.5 times more than the area of non-tribal area, the "Relative backwardness of tribal districts as compared to the non-tribal district may be attributed to over sizing of the earlier....". [9]

In some other studies the choice of indicators is not rooted in any defined analytical frame and is highly arbitrary and ad hoc. The distinction between the indicators relating to input and output of the system is sometimes ignored and both are merged together in the process of the composition of the index. Thus it is quite common to see agricultural production along with agricultural input indicator. Output is the result of the application of a combination of inputs. If output and input indicators are taken together, there would be duplication of information.

Sometimes, not quite so often, factors unrelated to the process of development are included as indicators of development. For example, the Bureau of Economic and Statistics, [10] Ahmedabad and also Karnataka and also the High Power Commission for Redressal of Regional Imbalances, Karnataka(2000) included in their set of indicators variables like density of population and cultivable area per capita and percentage of area under food crops. These cannot meaningfully be related to the level of development in their set of indicators.

Sometimes as Boudhayan Chatterjee [11] brings out, "under the influence of supposed value of neutral terms like modernization and 'social change' developed by the 'under developed' sociology of under development" determinants representing the basic forces of production are confounded with factors representing super structural effects.

`While selecting the indicators one should try to avoid the above pit falls. The indicators should be selected rationally and looking into its impact on development. Pooling of large number of indicators,-without examining the 'economic sense of the data; sometimes lead to paradoxical results. For example Das Gupta [12] in his work starts the analysis with 24 variables, but discovers components which are inefficient. Then taking the correlation matrix as guide he reduces the number of indicators to 15.

An indicator may be viewed as a combination of matters of fact (data) and matters of relation (theory), and can be constructed only through a "correct sequence between factual and logical order". Thus, an indicator should not be only a pure numerical figure but it should convey the implications of the underlying functional form in the given situation and be relevant for the theoretical framework adopted. According to McGranahan, [13]

"Economic and Social indicators are not simply statistics, and statistics are not ipso facto indicators, unless some theory or assumption makes them so by relating the indicator variable to a phenomenon that is not what it directly and fully measures". Indicators "should emerge from the analytical frame in which the term denoting the phenomenon has meaning and relevance". Therefore, the selection of indicators is a crucial step in empirical analysis.

A development indicator represents some aspects of development, such as industrialization, electrification, health and education. It may be a direct measure of an economic or social variable or, more often, an indirect measure of some non-measurable phenomenon. Drewnowski, for example, argued that indicators should be limited to, observable and measurable phenomenon. Irma Adelman and Cynthia Morris Taft [14] on the other hand make a case for a more flexible approach to the measurement of institutional phenomena, which would rely on expert judgment, on quantitative rankings, on reasonable explicit criteria of complex phenomena such as degree of political participation.

It is normally observed in the literature on selection of indicators, especially in the case of socio-economic development, that indicators represent both inputs as well as final output of the sector simultaneously. Actually, the characteristics of high growth rate and high development level as found in developed regions are essentially on account of the existence of a high level of development in the productive forces and favorable social conditions to use them in the process of production. A similar view was also expressed by Gothoskar [15] and he termed `real' development as the potential created for future growth. He said, "With this definition of `real' development, we will evolve indicators of real development from the indicators of `potential' created in the economy for future growth and development. However, their indicators would differ from country to country, depending on particular circumstances and objectives of economic plans."

8.5 Criteria for Selection of Indicators

The indicators are scaled dividing the variables suitably by population, geographical area of the State for uniform representation of data. In general, the following points are taken into consideration in the selection of the indicators:

1. Indicators that reflect the impact of implementation of government policies in socio-economic fields, particularly in the use of inputs are usually preferred.
2. Indicators that reflect natural diversities in geographical conditions, climatic conditions, natural resources, etc., are usually excluded.
3. All political and administrative indicators are excluded.
4. Besides, other things like accuracy of data, its availability, measurability and stability should also be considered as major pre-requisites.
5. Many indicators which may be desirable (or even very much needed) but data for which are not available across all the regional may be left out.

The main problem is with regard to how best to select indicators among the large number of available indicators. One way is to use regression analysis for selecting indicators, but the indicators pertaining to any sector are themselves interrelated and the problem of multicollinearity arises. As a result, the estimation process becomes uncertain. McGranahan suggested two ways of validation and selection of indicators:

- use of expert consensus; and
- use of correlation analysis technique and related multivariate techniques.

He commented: "The indicator that best correlates with the rest of the correlations, or, more precisely, has the highest average correlation with others, may be considered to be the best indicator of the group". Nancy Baster also expressed a similar opinion in the case of a representative indicator. Baster said, "a representative indicator is selected as `best' measure of a particular phenomena on the basis of some criteria such as closeness of correlation with other indicators of the same phenomenon" [16] Keeping in view the above suggestion, usually, `principal component analysis (PCA)', a multivariate technique is used for the selection of variables. The component loading, which is noting but the correlation coefficient between the derived variable and the original variable is used for selection. The development index is normally compiled on the basis of the first component; therefore the variables which yielded low values of the loadings are rejected outright. Keeping in view the loadings of the first component, the indicators with higher loadings only are considered. Generally indicators which had high loadings on the first component are selected. However, this procedure cannot be followed uniformly in all sectors due to various reasons.

In the case of economic and social infrastructure sectors, an additional consideration should be kept in mind, viz the need to maintain intra-sectoral balance in the selection of indicators. Economic infrastructure comprises sub-sectors such as transport, communication, post and telegraphs and power, whereas social infrastructure includes health, education and nutrition. Often, in view of the easy availability of data on some aspects the indicators selected relate mainly to one or two dimensions of social and economic infrastructure development. This should be avoided and an attempt should be made to give due or equal representation to various facets of development in these sectors.

While selecting indicators-one should also avoid duplication of information. For example, in the context of the formulation of the earlier Draft Fourth Plan (1966-71), the Planning Commission appointed a Study Group to review a set of indicators of regional development. The study Group recommended following 15 indicators which were accepted by the Planning Commission.

(a) Total population and density.
(b) Number of workers engaged (including all) as percent of total workers.
(c) Cultivable area per worker.
(d) Net area sown per worker.
(e) Percent of gross irrigated area to net sown area.
(f) Percentage of area sown more than ones to net sown area.

(g) Per capita gross value of agricultural output.
(h) Establishment and using electricity.
(i) No. of workers engaged in manufacturing per lakh of population.
(j) Mileage of surfaced road-(i) per 100 sq miles (ii) per lakh of population.
(k) No. of commercial vehicle registered in the district.
(l) Percentage of literates- (i) Male to total population; (ii) Female to total population.
(m) Percent of school going children.
(n) No. of seats per million population for technical training; and
(o) Hospital beds per lakh of population.

It may be observed from the list of selected indicators that many of them overlap with each others, e.g. separate treatment of males and females under literacy percentage may lead to high rank correlation. Another example here may be cultivable area per agricultural worker and net area sown per agricultural worker appearing as separate indicators.

Another, lacuna in some of the studies most frequently encountered is over-emphasis on one sector. In the 15 indicators given above including the sub-columns, 8 separate columns are provided for educational facilities as against one on 'per capita value of gross output' or one on 'hospital beds'. Similarly in the study by Iyengar and Sudarshan, [17] we find the predominance of Transport and Communication sector. They selected some 21 indicators out of which-8 indicators related to transport and communication, 5 to agriculture as against one indicator of education one of Banking. one of health and two indicators of electricity.

Thus the overlapping of indicators and under representation to any one sector lead to distorted picture of development and hence care should be taken to avoid these-two shortcomings while selecting indicators of development.

Care should also be taken while interpreting certain indicators. Generally speaking-Teacher-Student ratio or Institution-Student ratio is taken as indicators of educational development. However, the interpretation of these two indicators changes over two regions.

The number of students, per teacher may be very high in urban area merely because, number of teachers appointed is less thus here in this context the ratio reflects backwardness. On other hand in rural areas the number of students per teacher may be very low-because of thin enrolment of students thus once again pointing out educational backwardness. Thus while interpreting such indicators it is important, to bear in mind the situation prevailing in different regions.

For helping a state financially through grants, it is important to understand the typology and dimensions of development. This requires a study of sectoral backwardness It is essential to identify those sectors of the economy, which need greater attention for removal or minimizing the disparities in development. It is known that economic development affects various sectors of the economy differently. Therefore, the analysis of the levels of development and the disparities in development if carried out separately for different sectors, viz. agriculture, industry, economic infrastructure and social infrastructure is good. [18]

The main purpose of sectoral analysis is to help the policy maker in identifying the causes of disparities in overall development and to point out those sectors that need more attention for removal or minimizing disparities.

In short, selection of indicators should be done very carefully and judiciously. Therefore, while selecting indicators one has to be very cautious and judicious. Indicators should be understood and correctly perceived before using them in the analysis. In fact, selection of indicators is the most difficult job. In practice, one faces the major constraint of non-availability of reliable and desirable data for one's analysis purposes.

8.5.1 Assigning Weights: When development is measured by using several indicators, a problem of assigning weights arises as the indicators do vary in their relative importance.

There are several methods adopted to aggregate the indicators some have assigned weights and some simply pooled the ranks and derived Unweighted index.

There are a number of studies where composite index method

has been used e.g. Bennet takes 19 physical indicators for 31 countries [19] In India The Planning Commission also tried to use a composite index method. [20] In all these studies attempt was made to use the mix of variables and the procedure followed was to rank the units according to the absolute values of individual indicator and to pool the ranks together. Thus a serious shortcoming of some of these studies is that while combining various physical variables either they give subjective weights or have them without weights. Since the indicators vary in terms of their relative importance, assigning equal weights would not be justified. The weighting pattern used in the various indices produced so far on the basis of various physical variables has no theoretical justification, or even clear interpretation whatsoever.

While constructing a composite index, it is essential to attach some weights to the indicators. Any attempt to attach weights is bound to be riddled with subjectively and value judgment unless the weights are scientifically derived. There are various ways to assign weights. Some of them are explained below.

An important study using weighted indicators is by Wilfred Beckerman and Robert Bacon. [21] They re-estimate the national accounts measure of per capita consumption, using non-monetary indicators. The procedure was to start with 'corrected' measures of consumption per head. These were then correlated with a large number of non-monetary indicators for the selected countries. By a process of trial and error a particular form of equation was found which combined a group of these indicators in such a way that they were closely correlated with the corrected values of per capita consumption. The final stage was to use the coefficient of these indicators to re-estimate the real level of per capita consumption of as many countries as have data on these non-monetary indicators.

Another important study in the direction of constructing a weighted index was made by Jan Drewnowski. [22] His study relates to the problem of measuring the levels of living and welfare. In this study, he has made use of the concept of sliding weights systems which consist in making the weights depending on the value of the indicator indices and on the value of component indices in the consumption of the overall index.

The formula for weights is:

$$W = \frac{100}{I}(1 < 0)$$

Where

W = weight, and

I = the value of the index (indicator index or component index) to be weighted.

D.V. McGranahan et al., later on, in their study on 'Contents and Measurement of Socio-Economic Development,' [23] tried to develop a weighted composite index of development. The weights were supposed to reflect the degree of importance that each indicator is considered to have in the measurement of the whole. The whole problem of giving weightage revolves around the concept of `importance'. Importance of an indicator is assessed on the basis of its co-efficient of correlation with other indicators. "We consider that development is an inter-related phenomenon in which the different factors change and grow together over the long run; that the degree if inter-relatedness of an indicator with the whole-its average correlation with the other indicators is the best available criterion of the weight that should be assigned to it in a general index". [24] All that is meant by the use of correlation as basis of weighting is that the more heavily weighted indicator is the one which is most closely associated with and will best predict the others. Conversely a general index constructed on such a weighting principle will best correlate with and best predict the scores on the individual indicators.

Iyengar and Sudarshan(1981) developed an index for measuring the development of districts in Karnataka, where weights $\left(w = \frac{1}{cv}\right)$ were measured to be inversely proportional to the coefficients of variation.

The above method of deriving weights from average correlation coefficients, do not completely solve the problem. Sometime a highly correlated indicator may turn out to be a very weak indicator of development. Similarly, while one indicator may be very important in one type of countries, the same may be least important in others. Thus the high average correlation may not always reflect the importance of a variable as an indicator of development and hence the weight based on this value may be subjected to criticism.

A number of studies have been carried out to identify the backward regions of India. Ashok Mitra [25] used some 35 indicators in an attempt to classify districts in India. Mr. Nanjappa [26] used an approach based on ranking of the districts of Karnataka based on 15 variables and a simple aggregation of the different ranks so obtained.

Arbitrary weights: In Karnataka, the Planning Department has been constructing a composite index of development at the district level for purposes of preparing Five-Year and Annual Plans. They have selected some 22 indicators classified into six categories viz.:

(a) Demographic factors
(b) Occupational structure
(c) Land utilization
(d) Agricultural development
(e) Industrial development and
(f) Infra-structural development.

The weights assigned to above categories are 8, 12, 15, 12, and 45 respectively. Initially, all the districts were ranked according to the degree of development with the help of 13 indicators under the Fourth Five Year Plan. The Fifth Five Year Plan used 22 indicators. They were assigned weights, which were based on the previous plan period percentage share of sectoral outlay.

A composite index of developments was estimated by pooling the weighted values together and based on the index values, the districts were ranked and compared for the two time points – 1960-61 and 1970-71. The same method was adopted during the Sixth Plan also and the districts were ranked for the years 1974-75, 1976.

The above system of giving weightage lacks objectivity and rationality. The plan outlay in the past may well be guided by the non-economic factors and may be completely uncorrelated with the indicators selected for measuring development. Thus the above method is very much riddled with subjectivity and arbitrariness.

8.5.2 Methods of Aggregation: In the regional analysis based on multiple variables for deriving a composite index or for aggregation of indicators of development the most commonly used methods are

1. Ranking method: (a) un-weighted, (b) weighted.
2. Indexing method.
3. Principal components analysis.
4. Factor analysis with several variants to generate common factors.
5. Sudarshan & Iyengar method.
6. UNDP Method.

Ranking Method: In this method ranks are assigned to each indicator and then the pooled ranks are derived. Based on the pooled ranking the units are arranged in ascending or descending order to know the levels of development. Ranking could be Unweighted or weighted.

Unweighted Ranking Method: In this each State is provided with a range (ascending or descending order of magnitude) for each indicator separately. In final index is calculated by adding all ranks pertaining to i^{th} State.

$$I_i = R_{i1} + R_{i2} + R_{i3} + \ldots + R_{im} = \sum_{j=1}^{m} R_{ij} \qquad \ldots (6)$$

m = number of variables

I_i = Index

R_{ij} = ranks pertaining to $(i)^{th}$ State on j^{R} variable .

The adding of ranks is known as Borda Rule and the rank total is known as Borda score or index.

However, the use of the ranking method where multiple indicators are employed has been criticized by many. The major criticism is that the ranking method is arbitrary and fails to take into account the actual difference in magnitude that exists between the units. For example, if the magnitudes of an indicator 'road length per square kilometer' for three regions A, B and C are 45 km., 28 km. and 25 km. respectively, the ranking method will allocate the ranks 1, 2 and 3 to them in the order. Though the difference between A and B is 17 km. and between B and C is 3 km., the difference in ranks is the same between A and B and also between B and C. This method therefore has been criticized in view of its arbitrary nature as the unit difference in ranks does not reflect the actual differences in the magnitude of the indicators used. More importantly, the ranking method does not have any mechanism for assigning relative weights to the indicators. [27]

The ranking method which comprises the assigning of rank scores to individual indicators and aggregating them at the desired level is the simplest and the most commonly used method in regional analysis.

Weighted Rank Index: A weighted index of developments with the weights given to the indicators being determined arbitrarily or according to their importance in influencing the final outcome can be derived in the following manner:

$$I_i = W_1R_{i1} + W_2R_{i2} + W_3R_{i3} + \ldots + W_mR_{im} = \sum_{j=1}^{m} W_jR_{ij} \quad \ldots (7)$$

Usually, the weights used are value indent based.

Indexing Method: In order to derive indices, the indicators are made scale free by dividing the values of the indicators (Yi) by their averages ($\overline{Y}$) i.e. $\sum_{i=1}^{n} \frac{Yi}{n}$ or by national average or by predominant values (maximum or minimum). Then the scale free values for each unit or region are added to arrive at a final index. Sometimes, the indicators may also be converted into percentage form or to have a common base as 100 so that they can be combined. Chakravarthy Committee (1981) had opted for this as a second alternative method. The Committee constructed a composite index of development by taking a simple average of its indices corresponding to several indicators and those Districts were grouped as backward whose index values were less than 100.

The indicator for each region is either expressed as:

- a proportion of the sample average of the indicator or

- a number which ranges between 0 and 1 where these limits are determined by the minimum and maximum values, respectively of the indicator.

In both cases, the inverse of the standard deviations of each (normalized) indicator can be used as the weight of the concerned indicator. The second method implied that the resulting index is sensitive to extreme (especially maximum) values in the series. The HPC (2000) of Karnataka, [28] therefore, used the first method, which was the more robust of the two, where each indicator was expressed as a proportion of the state average. Thus, if the resulting aggregate indicator for a given taluk is less than unity, it can be assumed that the concerned taluk is below the state average in terms of relative development, and be referred to as backward.

The Ranking method and the Indexing method are good for providing a priori ground for further analysis. "These two methods give equal weights to all indicators unless the researcher allocates some weights according to his subjective preferences."

If individual preferences are considered subjective elements enter. Therefore, it is preferable to derive some sort of statistical weights while constructing a composite index.

Use of Statistical Weights: It is normally observed that most of the variables applied in socio-economic development analysis are inter-related. Kendall (1939) developed a composite index formula for simultaneously inter-dependent variables. In this method weights are based on the strength of correlation between the combined index and its constituent's variables. In this method the aggregate correlation that is accounted by the time only combined index with its constituent variables is the maximum and this makes the index optimal.

There is a lot of similarities between Kendall's method and the First Principal Component Analysis used by Hostelling (1933).

Iyengar and Sudarshan(1981) used weights $\left(w = \frac{1}{cv}\right)$ which were measured to be inversely proportional to the coefficients of variation.

Iyengar and Sudarshan (1982) also proposed a simple method for measuring the level or stage of regional development. The technique was: [29]

X_{ij} is the value of ith variable for j^{th} region (State). Then to define a new variable Y_{ij} such that:

$$Y_{ij} = \frac{X_{ij} - Min\ (X_{ij})}{Max_j(X_{ij}) - Min_j(X_{ij})} \quad \text{......... (8)}$$

Where, max and min are the maximum and minimum values for each ith variable. However, if xi is negatively associated with development, then:

$$Y_{ij} = \frac{Max_j(X_{ij} - X_{ij})}{Max_j(X_{ij}) - Min_j(X_{ij})} \quad \text{......... (9)}$$

Obviously the scaled variables Yij varies from zero to one. Then the scores are to be calculated as:

$$\bar{y}_j = w_1Y_{1j} + w_2Y_{2j} + \ldots + w_mY_{mj}$$

$$= \sum_{i=1}^{m} wiY_{ij}$$

wi's (0<wi<1) and $\sum_{i=1}^{m} wi = 1$ .... (10)

wi's are arbitrary weights.

The calculation of weights was suggested as

$$w_i = \frac{K}{\sqrt{Var\ (Y_i)}} \quad \text{......... (11)}$$

Where

$$K = \sum_{j=1}^{m}\left[\frac{1}{\sqrt{Var\ (Y_i)}}\right]^{-1} \quad \text{......... (12)}$$

The development index $\left(\overline{Y_j}\right)$ also varied from zero to one.

If Y_1, Y_2,---------------Y_m are independent then:

$$V(\overline{Y}_j) = \sum_{j=1}^{m} w_i^2 Var(y_i) \qquad \text{.........(13)}$$

Which is constant, equal to mk^2 for all the regions? For simple classificatory purposes, ranking of the regional indices ($\overline{Yj}$) serves the purpose. However, Iyengar & Sudarshan suggested that a more meaningful characterization of development would be served in terms of suitable fractile classification from an assumed distribution of ($\overline{Yj}$) assuming that ($\overline{Yj}$) has a beta distribution in the range (0,1)

UNDP Method: Human Development Index prepared by UNDP has gained lot of importance since 1990. UNDP uses mainly three indicators viz., life expectancy, educational attainment and per capita GDP. For the construction of this index three steps are involved.

Step 1: Define the average deprivation indicator for the jth country with respect to the ith variable and this is defined as:

$$I_{ij} = \frac{\left(Max_j X_{ij} - X_{ij}\right)}{\left(Max_j X_{ij} - Min_j X_{ij}\right)} \qquad \text{.........(14)}$$

Step 2: Define the average deprivation indicator (Ii) by taking a simple average of three indicators such as:

$$\text{Ii} = \frac{1}{3}\sum_{j=1}^{3} I_{ij} \qquad \text{.........(15)}$$

Step 3: Measure the HDI as one minimum the average deprivation index:

$$(HDI)_j = (1 - I_i) \qquad \text{.........(16)}$$

UNDP also constructed a modified HDI in 1991 so that HDI can be made comparable overtime. For deriving MDHI, the ith indicator for jth country was defined as:

$$Z_{ijt} = \frac{(X_{ijt} - Min_{jt} X_{ijt})}{(Max_{jt} X_{ijt} - Min_{jt} X_{ijt})} \qquad \text{.........(17)}$$

In the UNDP report till 1993 the minimum values for all the

three values was set at the level of the poorest performing country and the maximum at that of the best performing country. Hence, the values changed every year. This precluded meaningful comparisons over time. In 1994 normative values were fixed. The normative values thus fixed were the most extreme values observed or expected over a long period (UNDP, 1994, PP 91-92)

The UNDP method is just a variant of the Indexing Method. This method is sensitive to the extreme values in the series HDI gives equal weight to all the three variables.

8.5.3 Multivariate Statistical Techniques: The above list is only indicative of the number of techniques that are used in regional analysis and does not claim to be comprehensive. In the absence of any consensus in the literature regarding the appropriateness of the techniques to be adopted, researchers are constantly engaged in deriving newer methods, which overcome some of the perceived limitations of the methods derived thus far. A brief description of the various techniques used for examining multivariate data in regional analysis is discussed below.

A. Principal Component Analysis: The principal component analysis (PCA) is used to transform an original set of variables to a new set of uncorrelated variables called principal components. These new variables are linear combinations of the original variables and are derived in decreasing order of importance. The usual objective of the analysis is to see if the first few components account for most of the variation in the original data. When this is accomplished, it is argued that the effective dimensionality of the problem is less than the number of original variables and that the first few components alone could be used in subsequent analysis so that one can operate with a smaller number of variables. The lacuna of the absence of weights for the variables in the ranking method is sought to be corrected by this method, wherein the component loadings are treated as weights.

In PCA, the most common approach for constructing social development indices is to work out the first few principal components that would explain an adequate percentage of total variation. If the first component only is to be used, then the explanation provided by it should generally be so high as to not warrant the inclusion of any other component.

In most of the analyses, researchers have used only the first principal component scores as a measure of development indices. If the first component fails to explain more than 50 per cent of total variation, then the first and second components would be considered for calculation of component scores. This could be done to capture the different dimensions of development, which are reflected by these components.

There are different opinions about the selection of loadings whether the loadings should be constant for all time points or should they be variable? If constant, the next question is whether they should be taken for the base period or end period or a pooled estimate of these?

The credit for developing a composite index with the help of `Principal Component Analysis', which is a method of factor analysis, goes to Hagood, who employed this technique in regional analysis to delineate major regions or relatively greater homogeneity. By classifying some 104 variables in 14 groups, Hagood applied Principal Component Analysis to derive implicit weights (factor loading) and subsequently worked out a combined index for each group. At the next step the combined indices of each group were pooled together with their respective implicit weights and a composite index of development was thus constructed. [30]

Subsequently, Berry, [31] in a comprehensive study covering 95 countries each characterized by 43 proposed indices, however, employed a Direct Factor Analysis, where the first and the second factors are derived to identify less developed regions. There are many other studies like by Irma Adelman and S. Morris Taft, where Full Fledged Factor analysis technique is used for the regionalization purposes.

Rao (1974) developed a composite index of development, first time in India, to use the same as a criterion in the scheme of federal fiscal transfers and to measure relative fiscal need of the states. She pooled, 3 times point data relating to 24 indicators, of development pertaining to 14 major states. First sectoral indices were derived by using the principal Component Analysis, and subsequently all the sectoral indices were aggregate, by assigning weights in terms of factor loadings to arrive at the composite index of development. [32]

Later on, Rao applied the same method to measure inter-district disparities also. In 1984, the method was applied at the taluk level.

In the study on "Regional Disparities and Development" Principal Component Analysis method was employed by Rao. [33] The study covered 175 taluks of Karnataka and following sectoral indices were constructed:

1. Agriculture
2. Industry
3. Education
4. Health
5. Banking
6. Co-operation
7. Power
8. Communication and
9. Transport

The sectoral indices in turn were treated as indicators for the final construction of the composite index of development.

B. Factor Analysis: Factor analysis, somewhat similar to principal component analysis, is a statistical technique used to identify a relatively small number of factors that can be used to represent relationships among a large number of inter-related variables. In factor analysis, the idea is to derive new variables called factors, which give a better understanding of the data. The factor analysis technique permits data reduction into a fewer sets of meaningful factors without losing any sustentative information contained in the original data.

Some different types of solutions for deriving factors in factor analysis are discussed briefly as follows:

Principal Factor Solution of Principal Axis Factoring: The principal factor solution follows essentially the same procedure of principal component analysis but operates on the reduced correlation matrix (i.e. with estimates of communalities in the diagonal) employing the model. The distinction between principal components and principal factors is that the components are immediately expressible in terms of the observed variables while factor measurements can only be arrived at indirectly.

Centroid Solution: The centroid method is intended to approximate the results that obtained with the principal factor method, but with considerable savings in labour. However, the centroid solution is not unique for a given set of variables nor does it have the interesting mathematical properties of the principal factor solution.

Maximum Likelihood Solution: This solution is based on fundamental statistical considerations. It considers explicitly the differences between correlations among the observed variables and the hypothetical values in the universe from which they are sampled. The method is used in order to estimate the universe values of the factor loadings from given empirical data. Associated with the method is a loss of significance to determine the adequacy of the hypothesis regarding the number of common factors. Furthermore, convergence of the process cannot always be assured, although there is strong indication that it will do so for most practical needs. A maximum likelihood solution only determines the common factor space uniquely, but it does not have the property of principal factor solution of accounting for a maximum amount of variance for a specified number of factors.

Alpha Factoring: A method of initial factoring in which the variables included in the analysis are considered samples from a universe of variables.

Image Factoring: A method of obtaining initial factor sin which the observed variation is decomposed into (partial) images and anti-images, instead of into common parts and unique parts.

Least Squares Solution: In general, a solution that minimizes the squared deviations between the observed values and predicted values.

Besides, there are several other solutions like triangular decomposition, miners solution, multiple-group solution, multiple factor solutions, simple factor models, etc.

Section 3

8.6 Methods Used for Delineation of Homogeneous Regions

In a federal country many times the states which are similar in terms of their levels of development, economic structure or in terms of sectoral pattern of backwardness are required to be grouped together. The grouping of federating states based on their homogeneity helps formulating policies to assist such states uniformly. Grouping of states can be done in several ways like above average states or below average states. When there are several indicators, grouping is done with multivariate statistical techniques. Apart from Principle Component Analysis or Factor Analysis, there are several other method used for delineation of homogeneous regions. Some of these are discussed below:

8.6.1 Distance Analysis: This method is used for measuring similarity among the States. [34] The smaller the distance the closer the States. Generally, the Euclidean distance (d) is calculated from the variables s given below:

If $X_1 = (X_{11}, X_{12} \ldots X_{1p})$ and $X_2 = (X_{21}, X_{22} \ldots\ldots X_{2p})$ are the two standardized vector and then (d) is

$D^2 = (X_{11} - X_{21})^2 + (X_{12}-X_{22})^2 + \ldots\ldots (X_{1p}-Xp)^2$ and distance matrix is

$$D = ((d)) \qquad \ldots\ldots\ldots (19)$$

Distance analysis is not a commonly used method. The distance matrix is used in mainly open multivariate techniques as inputs, such as discriminate analysis, cluster analysis and so on. Identification of backward regions depends upon the measures of development. This is explained below:

8.6.2 Cluster Analysis: The main objective of cluster analysis is to classify the units/individuals into specific clusters/ groups according to some chosen criteria. "More formally, cluster analysis aims to allocate a set of mutually exclusive and exhaustive groups such that individuals within a group are similar to one another while individuals in different groups are dissimilar". It is, however, to be understood that there is no completely satisfactory way of defining a `cluster', although we usually have an intuitive idea as to what is meant by the word cluster'. Actually, in cluster analysis, one has to divide the individuals into smaller sets or alternatively, group them into larger sets, so that one eventually ends up with complete hierarchical structure of the given set of individuals called `hierarchical tree'. That is, in the hierarchical approach, classification starts from an elementary (or starting) point and division, sub-divisions continue at each stage. The basic aim of cluster analysis is to find the `natural groupings', if any, of a set of individuals (or objects or points). This set of individuals may form a complete population or be a sample from a larger population.

Most of the cluster analysis techniques are based on matrix of covariance or correlations between variables (sometimes called R technique by non-statisticians) and on the matrix of `distances' between individuals (known sometimes as Q technique). Generally, cluster analysis is based on both correlation matrix and distance matrix, which are commonly known as similarity and dissimilarity matrices, respectively. Standardized Euclidean distance is one of the most common measures of dissimilarity. But there are various ways of clustering based on dissimilarity between every pair of units or similarity between every pair of variables. The noted methods are single-link, complete-link or furthest-neighbor, centroid, group average, binary splitting, mode analysis (or Wishart method), etc.

An immediate difficulty in cluster analysis is that there is no completely satisfactory way of defining a `cluster'. Users of clustering methods may initially be surprised to find that different methods applied to the same set of data a will often produce structures which are substantially different. This is because the choice of a clustering method implicitly imposes a structure on the population and is often tantamount to defining a cluster. If a classification does exist, a further problem is that the data may admit more than one different but meaningful classification depending on the purpose of the investigation.

8.6.3 Discriminant Analysis: Discriminant analysis is a statistical technique, which allows the researcher to study the differences between two or more groups of objects with respect to several variables simultaneously. In the social sciences, there are a wide variety of situations in which this technique may be useful. The area in which this technique has been profitably employed include personnel placement testing, roll call analyses of legislatures, psychological testing of children, the effects of medical treatments, *economic differences between geographic regions*, predicting voting behaviour, and many more. The basic prerequisites are that two or more groups exist which we presume differ on several variables and that those variables can be measured at interval or ratio level. Discriminant analysis will then help us analyze the differences between the groups and/or provide us with a means to assign (classify) any case into the group which it most closely resembles.

First of all, the *data cases* should be members of two or more mutually exclusive *groups*. Data cases are the basic units of analysis---the elemental things being studied. These may be people, animals, countries, *the economy at different points of time*, or whatever. The groups must be defined so that each case belongs to one, and only one, group. In some research settings, we may also have some cases, which are not identified as belonging to any of the groups under analysis. This would include some number of cases whose group membership cannot be identified. Or, perhaps we are withholding them from the analysis for some reason. These are cases, which will be classified into a group *later* on the basis of mathematical equations derived from an analysis of the cases with "known" memberships. Thus future incidents can be considered as "ungrouped" or "unclassified" cases.

"Discriminant analysis" is a broad term, which refers to several closely related statistical activities. In a given research situation, the analyst may not use all of them. A researcher is engaged in *interpretation* when studying the ways in which groups differ--- that is, is one able to "discriminate" between the groups on the basis of some set of characteristics, how well do they discriminate, and which characteristics are the most powerful discriminators? The other application is to derive one or more mathematical equations for the purpose of *classification*. These equations, called "discriminant functions", combine the group characteristics in a way that will allow one to identify the group, which a case most closely resembles. Frequently, of course, researchers use discriminant analysis for both interpretation and classification. Thus Discriminant analysis is essentially conducted in three steps:

- distribution of cases into groups on the basis of a priori knowledge about them,
- finding of classification functions which best characterize the difference among these groups, and
- classification of new or unknown cases.

8.6.4 Correspondence Analysis: Researchers often face the task of detecting and interpreting relationships among the variables in a rectangular data matrix. Quite frequently, a joint graphical representation of the rows and columns of the data matrix facilitates this process. This approach to data analysis has a long history. Multidimensional scaling and unfolding, discriminant analysis, canonical correlation analysis, factor analysis and principal components analysis have all been employed to the rows and/or columns of a multivariate data matrix.

The following presents Correspondence analysis, a multivariate descriptive statistical method that represents graphically the rows and columns of a particularly data matrix in the same two-dimensional space. In correspondence analysis, numerical scores are assigned to the rows and columns of a data matrix so as to maximize their interrelationship. The scores are in corresponding units, allowing all the variables to be plotted in the same space for ease of interpretation. This representation then can be used to reveal the structure and patterns inherent in the data. In this sense, correspondence analysis belongs to that class of methods known as "Exploratory Data Analysis".

Although the theoretical origins of the technique can be traced back over 50 years, the real impetus to the modern application of Correspondence analysis was given by the French linguist and data analyst, Jean-Paul Benzécri, and his colleagues and students working initially at the University of Rennes in the early 1960s and subsequently at the Jussieu campus of the University of Paris.

Correspondence analysis as a geometric approach (rather than the usual classical inferential statistics) to multivariate descriptive data analysis first originated here.

Denote the data matrix by $\mathbf{X}_{np}$, with elements x_{ij}, where i=1...n and j=1...p. For example, xij is the indicator of banking development variable `j' in the State `i'.

The idea behind Correspondence analysis is that each row **X** represents a profile in a p-dimensional space and each column represents a profile in n-dimensional space. The problem is to find a low-rank approximation to the original data matrix that optimally represents both these row and column profiles in k-dimensional subspaces, where `k' is much smaller than either `n' or `p'. These k-dimensional subspaces have a geometric correspondence, which allows us to represent both in one joint display.

Both Principal Component analysis and Factor Analysis are also commonly used for the delineation of homogeneous regions. These are illustrated in the next chapter.

Section 4

8.7 Measures of Disparities

Several techniques have been used in regional studies to measure the magnitude of regional disparities in economic development. The measurement of disparity may be based on single or multiple indicators depending on the purpose of the study and the nature of the data to be analyzed. When one is interested in the development of material output, an indicator like aggregate output in the form of gross material product or gross domestic product becomes an adequate indicator for regional analysis. Normally, economists are concerned with the growth and development of the economy. While growth indicators are generally macro-economic parameters, development indicators take into account social aspects also and are broader in concept. The methodologies for measuring disparities based on a single indicator, `per capita income', have been discussed below. Thereafter, analyses based on multiple indicators have been discussed.

In order to measure regional disparities, Williamson (1965) used three different measures viz., 'V_{uw}' an unweighted coefficients of variation, 'V_w' a weighted coefficient of variation and M_w a measurement based on weighted absolute mean deviation. [35]

V_{uw} was defined as:

$$V_{uw} = \frac{\sqrt{\sum_{i=1}^{n} (Y_i - \bar{Y}) \Big/ n}}{\bar{Y}} \qquad \text{......... (1)}$$

V_{uw} = Standard deviation divided by mean (or average of the variable). This is the usual measure of coefficient of variation (cv) thus

V_{uw} = C.V.

Y_i = income per capita of the ith region

$\bar{Y}$ = national income per capita

n = number of States/Regions

In the case of weighted dispersion, each regional deviation was weighted by its share in the national population. More precisely:

$$V_w = \sqrt{\frac{\sum_{i=1}^{n} (Y_i - \bar{Y})^2}{\bar{Y}} \times \frac{P_i}{P}} \qquad \rightarrow (2)$$

Where:

P_i = population of the ith region

P = total national population

Similarly the alternative disparity measure Mw, used along with coefficients of variations (CV) was defined as:-

$$M_w = \frac{\sum_{j=1}^{n} \left[\left| Y_i - \bar{Y} \right| \frac{P_i}{P} \right]}{\bar{Y}} \qquad \text{......... (3)}$$

The higher the value of the coefficients, the larger the degree of regional inequality. It is possible that the coefficient might decrease over time while the relative differences between the highest and the lowest value might increase and vice-versa.

The disadvantage of CV is that the Y (Vuw and Vw) are based on squared differences between the value of the variable for each individual region and the notional value as a result of which the coefficients might be pulled upward when a few extreme deviation could be considered superior because it gives weightage to the region according to the size of population.

Apart from coefficient of variations many times Inter-State disparities are analysed with the help of ranks and State relatives. In the rank method States are ranked in terms of a variable (say per-capita income) for different time points and a matrix of rank correlation is calculated. If the ranks are stable that means the disparities have remained unchanged.

The State relative (Ry) is defined as,

$$Ry = (Y^s/Y^n) * 100 \qquad \rightarrow (4)$$

Where

Y^s = Per capita SDP for State

Y^n = Per capita NDP for Nation

The States are then arranged in ascending order of Ry and grouped there after.

In some studies coefficient of concentration is used where average is taken as 100. Taking this as the base individual values are calculated.

$$\frac{Ryi}{Yn = 100} x100 \qquad \rightarrow (5)$$

The above methods are commonly used to measure disparities in terms of single variable.

End Notes and References

1. Drewnowski. J. (1966) Social and Economic Factors in Development, *UNRISD Report No.3.* Geneva, February.

2. Government of India (1952), The Planning Commission, Five Year Plan, 1951-56.

3. U.N.O. "Measures for the Economic Development of underdeveloped countries", New York, 1951.

4. V. McGranaham et al. UNRISD, 'Contents and Measurement of Socio Economic Development: An empirical enquiry. Report No.70. 10.

Geneva 1970.

5. McGranahan, D. McGranahan,D.(1972), Development Indicators and development Models", Journal of Development Studies,vol6, No.3, pp. 91-102.

6. Op. cit.,

7. Boudhayan Chattopadhya and Moonis Raza, " Regional Development: Analytical Framework and Indicators." Indian Journal of Regional Science, Vol. VII, No.1, 1975, pp. 11-34.

8. M.L. Patel, 'dilemma of Balanced Regional Development in India, Chapter 8, pp. 68-78, Bhopal, 1975.

9. Ibid, p. 77.

10. Government of Gujarat, Report of the Backward Area Study Team Ahmedabad, 1969, also see the same by Government of Karnataka.

11. Ibid.

12. Dasgupta, B.(1071)" Socio- economic classification of istricta" Economic and Political Weekly, vol.6, No.33, August 14, Pp 1963-74.

13. McGranahan, D (1972), Development Indicators and Development Models", Journal of Development Studies,vol 6, No.3, pp 91-102.

14. Adelman and Cynthia Morris Taft, Economic Growth and Social Equity in Developing Countries" Stanford University Press, California.

15. Gothoskar, S.P.(1988) "Measurement of Real Development", The journal of Income and Wealth, vol10,No.1January, pp.84-100

16. McGranahan,D.(1972) op.cit.

17. N.S. Iyengar and P. Sudarsan, "On a Method of Classifying Regions from Multivariate Data", Paper presented at Symposium on Economic Theory and Planning, ISI, Bangalore, December 1981.

18. Rao, Hemlata (184), Regional Disparities and Development in India, Ashish publications , New Delhi.

19. Bennet, International Disparities in Consumption Levels, A.E.R., Sept. 1951 pp. 639-49.

20. Planning Commission, Report of the Working Group on Identification of Backward Regions, 1969.

21. W. Beckerman and R. Bacon, International Comparisons of Income Levels: A suggested New Measure, Economic Journal, 1966, pp. 519-536.

22. Drewnowski, Jan, Studies in the Measurement of Levels of Living and Welfare, Report No. 703, UNRISD, 1970.

23. McGranahan et al. 'Contents and Measurement of Socio-Economic Development' UNRISD, Report 70,10, Geneva 1970, p.138.

24. McGrahana, (1970) op cit.

25. Ashok Mitra, Levels of Regional Development in India: Census of India 1961, Para IA (1).

26. M.B. Nanjappa. Backward Areas in Mysore State: A study in Development.

27. The Dandekar Committee (1984) adopted this method. See Report of the Fact Finding Committee on Regional Imbalances in Maharashatra (Chairman: V.M. Dandekar), Planning Department, Govt. of Maharashatra, Mumbai.

28. Government of Karnataka, High Power Committee on Redressal of Regional Disparities in Karnataka, 2000.

29. Primal Sarkar, op.cit. P.102

30. M.J. Hagood, "Statistical Methods for the purposes of Delineation of Regions Applied to data on Agriculture and Population", Social Force, Vol.21 (1943), pp. 287-297.

31. Brian. J. Berry, "An Inductive Approach to Regionalisation of Economic Development", Essays on Geography and Economic Development, ed. Ginsburg, University of Chicago, 1960, pp.78-107.

32. Rao, Hemlata (1974) Centre State Financial Relations... Ph.D. thesis Chapter 4. Delhi School of Economics. A paper based on the chapter was presented in a National Seminar on Regional Disparities at IIPA, New Delhi on 2nd & 3rd March 1972.

33. Rao Hemlata (1984), Regional Disparities and Development in India", Ashish Publications, New Delhi.

34. Also one can refer Mahalnobis D^2 distance.

35. See for detailed discussion, Parimal Chandra Sankar. Regional Disparities in India: Issues & measurements, Ph.D thesis, Bombay University 1995, P 80-82.

9

MULTIVARIATE TECHNIQUES USED IN REGIONAL ANALYSIS

9.1 Introduction

In the previous chapter various multivariate techniques used for measuring the levels of development and for the delineation of homogeneous regions are outlined. In this section al some of the important techniques are illustrated with the help of actual data. Just for demonstration Indian banking sector data pertaining to: bank offices, bank deposits, bank credits, credit deposit ratios during the years 1972, 1981 and 1991 taken from the Reserve Bank of India's publication entitled Banking Statistics. It should be remembered that the use of data is only for illustration and not for analyzing the banking development and disparities in India.

Seven banking indicators are chosen for analysis. The indicators were scaled suitably by dividing the variables by population, geographical area, and number of branches, total deposits or credits of the particular State as the case may be. The indicators selected are:

- NOPN - number of bank offices per 10,000 population.
- NOAR - number of bank offices per 100 square kilometers of area.
- DEPN - deposit (in Rs. crores) per 10,000 population.
- DEOF - deposit (in Rs. crores) per bank office.
- CRPN - credit (in Rs. crores) per 10,000 population.
- CROF - credit (in Rs. crores) per bank office, and
- CDRA - credit (in Rs. crores) - deposit (in Rs. crores) ratio.

Only fifteen major States have been chosen for the study due to non-availability of complete data for other states. The study covers three different points of time, namely, 1972, 1981 and 1991 respectively, which approximately covers a span of 20 years.

In order to illustrate the various multivariate methods discussed earlier the above set of data is used.

9.1.1 Ranking Method: Analysis of Data:

In the ranking method, Maharashtra with a total rank of 19 in 1972 was in the first position. Even though its value increased to 25 in 1981 and 1991 respectively, it maintained its position as number one. The reason for increase in the pooled value was due to Maharashtra losing its relative position with respect to a few indicators. The second position was that of West Bengal in 1972, Punjab in 1981 and Kerala in 1991. The third position went to Tamil Nadu in 1972 and 1981 respectively and Punjab in 1991. The rank total of banking indicators is given in Table 9.1.

Table 9.1: Ranking of States According to Pooled Ranking 1972, 1981, 1991

State	1972		1981		1991	
	Total	Rank	Total	Rank	Total	Rank
Andhra Pradesh	58	9	52	9	55	9
Assam	78	12	91	14	94	15
Bihar	76	11	88	13	90	14
Gujarat	35	4	40	6	40	5
Haryana	55	8	44	7	45	8
Karnataka	39	5	45	8	44	7
Kerala	52	7	40	5	38	4
Madhya Pradesh	81	13	83	12	76	11
Maharashtra	19	1	25	1	25	1
Orissa	97	15	91	15	85	13
Punjab	42	6	30	2	27	3
Rajasthan	83	14	76	11	80	12
Tamil Nadu	31	3	31	3	26	2
Uttar Pradesh	68	10	68	10	73	10
West Bengal	26	2	36	4	42	6

The ranking position though lists the states according the pooled rank values; it fails to bring out the actual distance between the two states with two different values. For example in 1972, Maharashtra got first rank and West Bengal got the second. The difference in the poled value was 7. Whereas in 1991 Maharashtra got first rank with pooled value of 25 and Tamil Nadu got second rank with pooled value of 26. The difference was only one. Thus the ranking method fails to say how much is the actual gap in the levels of development of different states. Even over a period of time also, the ranks do not show the trend whether the states have improved or their conditions have deteriorated. More over the ranking method does not bring out the relative importance of various indicators of development and all the variables are given equal importance.

The lacuna of the absence of weights for the variables in the ranking method are sought to be corrected by various multivariate techniques like the Principal Component Analysis or factor analysis etc. Some of these methods are illustrated in the flowing:

9.1.2 Coefficient of Correlation Method: Table 9.2 shows the correlation matrix for the 7 banking sector variables relating to 15 Indian States for the years, 1972,1981 and 1991.There are many correlations that are quite high in all the three bench mark years. In general, technically superior indicators appear to have higher correlations than inferior ones. The level of correlation may thus reflect to a considerable degree, the quality and the nature of the indicators involved as well as the role of the components they represent. Low correlation between two indicators of banking development may reflect not lack of relationship between the components, but inadequacy of the indicators. We see that in some exceptional cases the indicators of per capita is correlated fairly well with the indicators with respect to number of offices. These results are a pointer to the fact that the above correlation matrices may be subjected for further analysis through techniques like the principal component analysis or factor analysis.

9.1.3 Principal Component/Factor Analysis: These are the methods, wherein the component loadings are treated as weights.

Table 9.2 Pearson Correlations for Banking Indicators - 1972, 1981, 1991 (Based on Pooled data)

1972	**CDRA 72**	**CROF 72**	**CRPN 72**	**DEOF 72**	**DEPN 72**	**NOAR 72**	**NOPN 72**
CDRA 72	1	0.468	0.305	0.089	0.272	0.302	0.321
CROF 72	0.468	1	0.623	0.910	0.616	0.098	0.565
CRPN 72	0.305	0.623	1	0.520	0.999	-0.023	0.989
DEOF 72	0.089	0.910	0.520	1	0.528	0.016	0.450
DEPN 72	0.272	0.616	0.999	0.528	1	-0.014	0.991
NOAR 72	0.302	0.098	-0.023	0.016	-0.014	1	0.061
NOPN 72	0.321	0.565	0.989	0.450	0.991	0.061	1
1981	**CDRA 81**	**CROF 81**	**CRPN 81**	**DEOF 81**	**DEPN 81**	**NOAR 81**	**NOPN 81**
CDRA 81	1	0.352	0.398	-0.102	-0.003	0.100	0.259
CROF 81	0.352	1	0.882	0.881	0.724	0.107	0.180
CRPN 81	0.398	0.882	1	0.752	0.888	0.373	0.605
DEOF 81	-0.102	0.881	0.752	1	0.810	0.129	0.132
DEPN 81	-0.003	0.724	0.888	0.810	1	0.401	0.652
NOAR 81	0.100	0.107	0.373	0.129	0.401	1	0.699
NOPN 81	0.259	0.180	0.605	0.132	0.652	0.699	1

Contd...

1991	CDRA 91	CROF 91	CRPN 91	DEOF 91	DEPN 91	NOAR 91	NOPN 91
CDRA 91	1	0.469	0.460	0.048	0.052	-0.169	0.206
CROF 91	0.469	1	0.952	0.891	0.790	0.124	0.258
CRPN 91	0.460	0.952	1	0.871	0.889	0.247	0.532
DEOF 91	0.048	0.891	0.871	1	0.922	0.272	0.289
DEPN 91	0.052	0.790	0.889	0.922	1	0.390	0.614
NOAR 91	-0.169	0.124	0.247	0.272	0.390	1	0.485
NOPN 91	0.206	0.258	0.532	0.289	0.614	0.485	1

The usual objective of the analysis is to see if the first few components account for most of the variation in the original data.

Application of the principal component analysis using the correlation matrix given in Table 9.3 shows that the first principal component alone explained about 61 per cent of the total variation for the pooled time series as shown in Table 9.4. As the pattern of development changes, the importance of the indicator as reflected by the loadings also changes over the years. For example, the value of the loading for variable number of offices per 10,000 of population was 0.458 in 1972. But the value has dramatically shown a downward trend and was 0.295 in 1991.

The indices for development or `scores' for banking development are presented in Table 9.3 for the 15 selected states. [1] As in the ranking method, Maharashtra was on the top in terms of banking development in the entire benchmark years. However its score dropped to 100.74 in 1981 from 103.88 in 1972 and went up to 106.69 in 1991. The coefficient of variation, used to measure the extent of disparity among States was 1.46 per cent in 1972, dropped to .75 per cent in 1981 and again rose to 1.89 per cent in 1991.

9.1.4 Principal Component Analysis (using Covariance Matrix): In principal component analysis using covariance matrix, the first principal component alone explained about 65 to 81 per cent of the total variation for the cross-section analysis and about 72 per cent of the total variation for the pooled time series data as shown in Table 9.4.

The indices for development or `scores' for banking development based on covariance method are presented in Table.9.5 for the pooled series. As in the ranking method, Maharashtra was on the top in terms of banking development during the years 1972 with a score of 102.14. Its score declined to 100.52,in 1981 and t increased to 106.18 in 1981. However its relative position changed during the period under study. In 1972 it occupied 1st position and also in 1991. However in 1981, Kerala got the first place with a score of 100.66 followed by Maharashtra. The coefficient of variation, used to measure the extent of disparity

Table 9.3: First Principal Component Scores for Banking Sector (Correlation Matrix and Covariance Matrix): Pooled Series

	Based on Correlation Matrix			Based on covariance Matrix		
State	1972	1981	1991	1972	1981	1991
Andhra Pradesh	98.28	99.14	101.50	98.19	98.99	101.23
Assam	97.93	98.37	99.82	98.10	98.54	99.95
Bihar	97.93	98.52	99.96	98.22	98.78	100.35
Gujarat	98.50	99.51	102.45	98.51	99.50	102.31
Haryana	98.20	99.40	102.25	98.32	99.39	102.26
Karnataka	98.57	99.36	102.06	98.40	99.22	101.72
Kerala	98.67	100.29	103.05	98.84	100.66	103.56
Madhya Pradesh	97.95	98.52	100.21	98.05	98.51	100.07
Maharashtra	103.88	100.74	106.69	102.14	100.52	106.18
Orissa	97.83	98.48	99.86	97.99	98.45	99.75
Punjab	98.47	100.16	104.50	98.72	100.38	104.69
Rajasthan	97.95	98.66	100.14	98.04	98.55	100.04
Tamil Nadu	98.82	99.85	103.58	98.61	99.69	103.17

Contd...

Uttar Pradesh	98.00	98.79	100.64	98.24	99.00	100.95
West Bengal	99.20	100.10	103.21	99.22	100.35	103.63
Average	98.68	99.33	102.00	98.64	99.37	101.99
Standard Dev.	1.44	0.74	1.93	0.99	0.76	1.87
C.O.V (%)	1.46	0.75	1.89	1.01	0.77	1.84

among States was 1.01 per cent in 1972, dropped to .77 per cent in 1981, and again rose to 1.84 per cent in 1991.

Table 9.4: First Principal Component Loadings for Banking Sector (Correlation Matrix) 1972, 1981, 1991

Variable	Pooled Correlation Matrix	Pooled Covariance matrix
NOPN	0.292	0.103
NOAR	0.279	0.478
DEPN	0.470	0.501
DEOF	0.437	0.538
CRPN	0.467	0.318
CROF	0.440	0.346
CDRA	0.114	0.009
Variance (%)	61.05	71.78

9.2 Comparison between Correlation Matrix and Covariance Matrix in Finding Principal Components

A major argument for using correlation matrices, rather than covariance matrices, to define principal components is that the results of analyses for different sets of random variables are more directly comparable than for analyses based on covariance matrices. The big drawback of principal component analysis based on covariance matrices is the sensitivity of the principal components to the units of measurement used for each element of the indicators (or variables). If there are large differences between the variances of the elements of indicators, then those indicators whose variances are largest will tend to dominate the first few principal components. This may be entirely appropriate if all the elements of indicators are measured in the same units, for example, if all the elements of the indicators of development on a particular sector of the economy are recorded in per capita terms. Even in such examples, arguments can be presented for the use of correlation matrices.

The above arguments can also be observed in our data. Here we have combination of banking development indicators, which are

Table 9.5: First Principal Component Scores for Banking Sector (Correlation Matrix and Covariance Matrix): Pooled Series

	Based on Correlation Matrix			Based on covariance Matrix		
State	1972	1981	1991	1972	1981	1991
Andhra Pradesh	98.28	99.14	101.50	98.19	98.99	101.23
Assam	97.93	98.37	99.82	98.10	98.54	99.95
Bihar	97.93	98.52	99.96	98.22	98.78	100.35
Gujarat	98.50	99.51	102.45	98.51	99.50	102.31
Haryana	98.20	99.40	102.25	98.32	99.39	102.26
Karnataka	98.57	99.36	102.06	98.40	99.22	101.72
Kerala	98.67	100.29	103.05	98.84	100.66	103.56
Madhya Pradesh	97.95	98.52	100.21	98.05	98.51	100.07
Maharashtra	103.88	100.74	106.69	102.14	100.52	106.18
Orissa	97.83	98.48	99.86	97.99	98.45	99.75
Punjab	98.47	100.16	104.50	98.72	100.38	104.69
Rajasthan	97.95	98.66	100.14	98.04	98.55	100.04

Contd...

Tamil Nadu	98.82	99.85	103.58	98.61	99.69	103.17
Uttar Pradesh	98.00	98.79	100.64	98.24	99.00	100.95
West Bengal	99.20	100.10	103.21	99.22	100.35	103.63
Average	98.68	99.33	102.00	98.64	99.37	101.99
Standard Dev.	1.44	0.74	1.93	0.99	0.76	1.87
C.O.V (%)	1.46	0.75	1.89	1.01	0.77	1.84

measured per capita, per unit of geographical area and by ratio. The correlation matrices give equal distribution of principal component loadings. But it is quite opposite in covariance matrices, where a particular indicator(s) are highly loaded for further details, please refer Joliffe (1986). [2]

Therefore, it is unwise to use principal components on a covariance matrix when the indicators consist of measurements of different types, unless there is strong conviction that the units of measurement chosen for each element of indicators are the only ones, which make sense. Even if this condition holds, using the covariance matrix will not provide very informative principal components if the indicators have widely differing variances.

The use of covariance matrices does have one general advantage over correlation matrices, and one advantage that occur in a special case. The general advantage is that statistical inference regarding population principal components, based on sample principal components is easier for covariance matrices. This is an important advantage, if statistical inference is thought to play a crucial rôle in principal component analysis. However, in practice, it is more common to use principal component analysis as a descriptive, rather than inferential tool, so that the advantage becomes less critical.

The second advantage of covariance matrices holds in the special case when all the elements of indicators are measured in the same units. It can then be argued that standardizing the elements of indicators to give correlations is equivalent to making an arbitrary choice of measurement units. This argument of arbitrariness can also be applied more generally to use of correlation matrices, but when the elements of indicators are measurements of different types, the choice of measurement units leading to a covariance matrix is even more arbitrary, so that the correlation matrix is preferred.

9.2.1 Factor Analysis: As discussed in an earlier chapter, this method, somewhat similar to principal component analysis, is a statistical technique used to identify a relatively small number of factors that can be used to represent relationships among a large number of inter-related variables. The factor analysis technique permits data reduction into a fewer sets of meaningful factors without losing any sustentative information contained in the original data.

Some different types of solutions for deriving factors exist in factor analysis literature. However we have utilized Principal Axis Factoring, Maximum Likelihood, Alpha Factoring, Image Factoring, and Un-weighted Least Squares. The analysis was performed for two kinds, namely, cross-section and pooled time series data. We start with explaining the results for Image Factoring below.

9.2.2 Image Factor Analysis: The viewpoint of the alpha factor analysis explained below, in which the variables are conceived of as a sample of population of variables, also holds for image factor analysis. The `image' of a variable is the part that this variable has in common with the other variables. The anti-image is the unique part, which is not associated with other variables.

It is argued that the common score of the variables is what can be predicted by multiple regression of all the other variables on to each variable. Thus the multiple regressions between variable 1 and all others is computed followed by the multiple regression of variable 2 with all others and so on throughout the matrix, resulting in a set of predicted variables. The predicted part is equal to the image, and the error term to the anti-image. From these predicted variable an image covariance matrix, rather than an image correlation matrix, is computed. This covariance matrix is then subjected to analysis.

In Image factoring, the first factor explained about 52 to 57 per cent of the total variation for the cross-section analysis (Banking Data) and 59 per cent of the total variation for the pooled time series analysis as shown in Table 9.6 under the image method and ULS method.

The row of *common variance,* which appears in the table, is an integral part of factor interpretation, which elucidates that part of variance among all the indicators that is accounted for by this factor. The common variance ranges between 58 to 77 per cent for cross section analysis and 82 per cent for pooled time series analysis.

Table 9.6: First Varimax Rotated Image Factor Analysis Pooled Loadings for Banking Sector (1972, 1981, 1991)

Variable	Pooled loadings (Image)	Pooled (ULS)
NOPN	0.116	0.172
NOAR	0.454	0.463
DEPN	0.794	0.847
DEOF	0.973	0.999
CRPN	0.752	0.783
CROF	0.967	0.927
CDRA	0.086	0.066
Variance (%)	59.10	59.60
Common Var.(%)	81.77	82.07

In general we can name the new factors as `deposit mobilization and development of credit' dimension, as these are highly loaded which can be seen in the table above. However there is an exception for the year 1972.

The indices for development or `scores' based on the pooled series are displayed in table 9.7. [3] As can be seen, Maharashtra was on the top in terms of this dimension in the entire benchmark years. However its score dropped to 102.59 in 1981 from 103.49 in 1972 and again went up marginally to 102.81 in 1991. The coefficient of variation, used to measure the extent of disparity among States show very low level of disparity under this method.

In ULS factoring, the first factor explained about 55 to 58 per cent of the total variation for the cross-section analysis and 60 per cent of the total variation for the pooled time series analysis as displayed in Table 9.7. The row of *common variance* which appears in the table is an integral part of factor interpretation, which elucidates that part of variance among all the indicators that is accounted for by this factor. The common variance ranges between 61 to 82 per cent for cross section analysis and 82 per cent for pooled time series analysis.

Table 9.7: First Image and First ULS Factor Analysis Scores for Banking Sector-Pooled Series

	Image Pooled			ULS Pooled		
State	**1972**	**1981**	**1991**	**1972**	**1981**	**1991**
Andhra Pradesh	99.25	99.61	100.87	100.07	99.40	100.10
Assam	99.31	99.51	100.17	99.73	99.88	100.46
Bihar	99.39	99.44	100.14	100.37	99.44	101.10
Gujarat	99.32	99.78	101.26	98.79	99.10	101.51
Haryana	99.24	99.60	101.15	98.99	99.12	101.35
Karnataka	99.20	99.49	100.61	99.74	98.93	100.84
Kerala	99.17	99.40	100.70	99.29	98.92	100.70
Madhya Pradesh	99.21	99.40	100.25	99.35	99.13	99.78
Maharashtra	98.89	100.70	104.14	100.11	99.65	103.85
Orissa	99.21	99.36	99.95	99.42	99.37	99.41
Punjab	99.27	99.72	101.65	98.12	98.03	101.51
Rajasthan	99.16	99.40	100.19	98.94	99.20	99.77
Tamil Nadu	99.32	99.74	101.68	100.61	99.75	100.89
Uttar Pradesh	99.33	99.62	100.50	99.64	99.83	101.43
West Bengal	100.25	100.46	101.99	99.42	101.02	103.95
Average	99.30	99.68	101.02	99.51	99.38	101.11
Standard Dev.	0.28	0.38	1.03	0.63	0.62	1.27
C.O.V (%)	0.28	0.38	1.02	0.63	0.63	1.26

9.2.3 Alpha Factor Analysis: In alpha factor analysis we are dealing with another viewpoint. The roles of variables and cases of the data matrix are now interchanged. In the classical viewpoint a sample was always a set of `cases' sampled from a population of `cases' and the number of variables was fixed. We now reverse the argument. We consider the number of cases as fixed and the set of `variables' is now conceived of as a sample from a population of `variables'.

In Alpha factoring, the first factor explained about 58 per cent of the total variation for the cross-section analysis and 57 per cent of the total variation for the pooled time series analysis as shown in

Table 9.8. Note that the solution is obtained only for the year 1991 in cross-sectional analysis.

Table 9.8: First Varimax Rotated Alpha Factor Analysis Loadings for Banking Sector (1972, 1981, 91)

Variable	Pooled
NOPN	0.191
NOAR	-0.095
DEPN	0.592
DEOF	0.689
CRPN	0.887
CROF	0.979
CDRA	0.478
Variance (%)	57.20
Common Var.(%)	84.84

Note: N.S. implies No Solution.

The indices for development or `scores' under the Alpha method are given for the pooled series in Table 9.9.

The indices for development or `scores' for the dimension are mentioned in Table 9.9 for the pooled time series analysis As can be seen, West Bengal was on the top in terms of this dimension during 1981 and 1991 with scores of 102.56 and 108.48 respectively. Tamil Nadu was on the top during 1972 with a score of 103.36. Maharashtra did not figure in the first place in any of the benchmark years. The coefficient of variation, used for measuring the extent of disparity among States was 1.94 per cent in 1972 and 1.59 % in1981 and rose to 2.57% in 1991.

This method brings out that Bihar and UP were more developed than Maharashtra, or any other state except West Bengal. It is rather difficult to logically accept such results.

However the method can be visualized as, that there exists more banking development indicators in the population of indicators and only a sample of them is subjected for analysis. It follows from this viewpoint that two factor analyses can be considered, one on the sample of variables and one on the population of variables. In alpha factor analysis the factors of sample variables are determined in such a way that the squared correlation with the corresponding factors of the population variables is as high as possible. This (squared) correlation between the sample and population is called Cronbach's `coefficient alpha (α), whence the name alpha factor analysis. For more technical details refer Tacq (1997). [4]

Table 9.9: First Alpha Factor Analysis Scores for Banking Sector-Pooled Series

State	1972	1981	1991
Andhra Pradesh	101.61	99.21	98.51
Assam	100.07	100.48	101.51
Bihar	101.80	99.30	103.47
Gujarat	97.81	98.10	102.19
Haryana	98.27	98.34	101.85
Karnataka	101.00	98.14	100.66
Kerala	99.36	97.90	100.03
Madhya Pradesh	99.20	98.67	99.18
Maharashtra	102.32	97.86	102.76
Orissa	99.25	99.42	98.58
Punjab	95.80	95.10	101.34
Rajasthan	98.10	98.96	99.38
Tamil Nadu	103.36	99.88	98.04
Uttar Pradesh	99.79	100.27	103.82
West Bengal	98.28	102.56	108.48
Average	99.73	98.95	101.32
Standard Dev.	1.93	1.58	2.61
C.O.V (%)	1.94	1.59	2.57

The row of *common variance* which appears above in the table is an integral part of factor interpretation, which elucidates that part of variance among all the indicators that is accounted for by this factor. The common variance for the year 1991 is 80 per cent for and 85 per cent for pooled time series analysis.

9.3 Comparison of Different Factor Extraction Procedures

The following comparison of extraction procedures is presented in Dillon & Goldstein (1984). [5] It states, in general, different extraction methods will yield different factor solutions. The disparity between factor analysis solutions derived from the use of different extraction methods will depend on such data considerations as the sample size available, the number of variables, the magnitude of the communalities, and the variation among the variables in terms of their communalities. Two generally accepted conclusions are that (1) with communalities in the neighborhood of one, all extraction methods, produce nearly identical results; and (2) with increasing numbers of variables, communality estimates and the choice of a factor analysis procedure assume less importance. The few studies that have used Monte Carlo techniques or real data sets to investigate the relative performance of alternative factoring methods generally conclude that all of the factoring techniques will yield similar results in situations of large number of observations and variables. Gorsuch (1974), [6] after examining the available evidence, concluded that if the number of variables is large (greater than 30) and no variables have low communalities (less than 0.40), then all factor extraction methods will yield roughly the same interpretation. Some evidence does suggest, however, that the Maximum Likelihood Method will yield more accurate estimates of factor loadings with extremely large sample sizes (greater than 1500).

However, in "problematic" data situations (i.e., small number of observations and/or variables), the results are less clear. A note about a study in Dillon & Goldstein (1984) [7] suggested that the alpha and image factor analysis methods are superior in recovering known factor loadings and variance-covariance structures. This is quite evident even in our study where we could recover loadings with a small data set and indicators for the cross-sectional analysis. Even the pooled time series analysis failed to recover factor loadings in the other procedures rather than the three methods where we have results.

Since we could recover loadings in the alpha factor analysis, where the goal is to yield factor scores of the highest possible reliability. Reliability refers to the consistency over time of variables and their internal consistency. However, α factor analysis yields results little different from those of other methods and it is a matter of dispute whether the gains in the reliability of factor scores are of substantive value (Cattell, 1978) [8] as mentioned in Kline (1994). [9]

The question of factor loadings in image analysis is a subject of debate. Clearly they are not correlations with the variables. The image analysis factor loadings are covariance of the image variables with a linear combination of the image variables. This is not easy to understand and makes interpretation tricky, although Nunnally (1978) [10] suggests that they may be interpreted as if they were ordinary factor loadings as mentioned in Kline (1994). [11]

In order to make a comparison of the ranks obtained by 15 states under various methods we have used Spearmen's Rho method. The following matrices give the Rho matrix for cross section and the pooled data on Banking development.

9.4 Hierarchical Ranking Analysis

The hierarchical positions of States in banking development according to various methods are assessed below. As usual the comparison is different for results obtained from cross-sectional and pooled time series analysis respectively. Here we should remember that factor or component scores is used for ranking purposes and rank total is used for ranking in the ordinary rank method.

Spearman's rank correlation coefficient or spearman's rho is used to assess the fit between hierarchical positions of two methods. Here below we present tables pertaining to spearman's rho only. In all, the coefficient assesses whether two methods give ranking positions. The labels in the tables pertain to the following methods, namely, FAALP - Alpha Factoring, FAIMG - Image Factoring, FAULS - Unweighted Least Squares Factoring, PCCOR - Principal Components by Correlation Matrix, PCCOV - Principal Components through Covariance Matrix and RANK - Ordinary Ranking of Rank Totals.

In 1972 (Table 9.10), cross-sectional analysis, PCCOR was highly correlated with PCCOV and RANK. The same is the case of PCCOV with RANK and RANK with PCCOR and PCCOV.

In 1981 (Table 10.11), we see improvement in the results such that, leaving one or two coefficients all the ranking positions are significant.

In 1991 (Tables 9.12 and 9.13), we see significant improvement in the correlation of FAIMG with PCCOR and PCCOV in comparison to 1981. So the ranking position of FAIMG with PCCOR and PCCOV is near to similar. The ranking positions are not at all similar of PCCOR and FAULS as compared to the position to 1981, where it was nearing similarity.

9.5 Delineation of Homogeneous Regions

9.5.1 Cluster Analysis: The main objective of cluster analysis is to classify the units/individuals into homogeneous clusters/groups according to some chosen criteria. The matrix of raw data is transformed into a matrix of (dis) similarity measures, alternatively, distance measures. The most commonly used and most familiar distance measure is Euclidean or in general Squared Euclidean (Everitt, 1993). [12] The other popular measure is the city block metric. After the choice of an appropriate distance measure, the next step is to select a particular type of clustering scheme. We are interested in the agglomerative methods of the hierarchical clustering scheme, which are far more widely used. Amongst this type, empirical studies point to ward's method, group average and complete linkage as the most useful in practice, although the results are not clear cut, and a large `method x type of data structure' interaction seems to exist (Everitt, 1993). [13] So our analysis also goes in the same direction.

Table 9.10: Rank Correlation Coefficients, 1972

		FAIMG	FAULS	PCCOR	PCCOV	RANK
Spearman's Rho	FAIMG	1	0.450	0.218	0.318	0.236
	FAULS	0.450	1	0.021	0.011*	0.011
	PCCOR	0.218	0.021	1	0.971	0.993*
	PCCOV	0.318	0.011	0.971*	1	0.979*
	RANK	0.236	0.011	0.993*	0.979*	1

Table 9.11: Rank Correlation Coefficients, 1981

		FAIMG	FAULS	PCCOR	PCCOV	RANK
Spearman's Rho	FAIMG	1	0.775	0.796	0.661	0.832
	FAULS	0.775	1	0.729	0.529	0.721
	CCOR	0.796	0.729	1	0.893	0.982
	PCCOV	0.661	0.529	0.893	1	0.879
	RANK	0.832	0.721	0.982	0.879	1

Table 9.12: Rank Correlation Coefficients, 1991

		FAIMG	FAULS	PCCOR	PCCOV	RANK
Spearman's Rho	FAIMG	1	0.104	0.907	0.854	0.907
	FAULS	0.104	1	0.121	0.029	0.168
	PCCOR	0.907	0.121	1	0.954	0.993
	PCCOV	0.854	0.029	0.954	1	0.932
	RANK	0.907	0.168	0.993	0.932	1

Table 9.13: Rank Correlation Coefficients, 1991 (Pooled Series)

		FAALP	FAIMG	FAULS	PCCOR	PCCOV
Spearman's Rho	FAALP	1	0.196	0.764	0.139	0.289
	FAIMG	0.196	1	0.739	0.946	0.921
	FAULS	0.764	0.739	1	0.696	0.775
	PCCOR	0.139	0.946	0.696	1	0.975
	PCCOV	0.289	0.921	0.775	0.975	1

It is often the case, when hierarchical clustering techniques are used in practice, while the investigator is not interested in the complete hierarchy but only in one or two partitions obtained from it. In hierarchical clustering, partitions are achieved by `cutting' a dendogram or selecting one of the solutions in the nested sequence of clustering that comprise the hierarchy. In particular applications it will be of interest to try and determine which of all possible partitions produce the best fit to the data; essentially this means deciding on the appropriate number of clusters for the data. One informal method, which is often used for this purpose, is to examine the differences between fusion levels in the dendogram. Large changes are taken to indicate a particular number of clusters. Various researchers have suggested different procedures to ascertain fusion levels in the dendogram. [14]

The results for the squared Euclidean and city block distance measures are given in Table 9.14. The table is self-explanatory.

For the identification of the level of banking development, the States are usually grouped into different levels. However, it is not necessary that the States within each group be similar in nature of development. Within the same group there may be wide differences between two States in the pattern of development. The identification of level of development only reflects the hierarchical positions and offers no clue as to the pattern of development. To study the pattern of development, cluster analysis, which enables an analyst to form groups based on their similarity pattern was used. As explained earlier, a large number of methods are available for clustering units.

Based on the above for assessing clustering solution, it is observed for 1972 that there exist two clusters for all the methods with squared Euclidean measure. Maharashtra formed one group and all the other fourteen States were grouped in the other. The same is the case of Euclidean and block measures. For the Chebychev measure it was a mix of two and three groups, whilst, for the cosine measure there did not exist any solution for all the methods.

During 1981 it is observed that there exist two clusters for all the methods with squared Euclidean and Euclidean measure. Kerala formed one group and all the other fourteen States were grouped in

Table 9.14: Cluster Analysis by Various Methods using Squared Euclidean Distance

Year	Method	Groups	Description About Groups
	Average Linkage	2	MH in group 2 and the rest 14
	(Within Group)		States in group 1.
1972	Average Linkage	2	MH in group 2 and the rest 14
	(Between Groups)		States in group 1.
	Complete Linkage	2	MH in group 2 and the rest 14
			States in group 1.
	Ward	2	MH in group 2 and the rest 14
			States in group 1.
	Average Linkage	2	KE in group 2 and the rest 14
	(Within Group)		States in group 1.
1981	Average Linkage	2	KE in group 2 and the rest 14
	(Between Groups)		States in group 1.
	Complete Linkage	2	KE in group 2 and the rest 14

Contd...

			States in group 1.
	Ward	2	KE in group 2 and the rest 14
			States in group 1.
	Average Linkage	3	MH in group 3, KE in group 2
	(Within Group)		& the rest 13 States in group 1.
1991	Average Linkage	3	MH in group 3, KE,PJ & WB in group
	(Between Groups)		2 & the rest 11 States in group 1.
	Complete Linkage	3	MH in group 3, KE,PJ,TN & WB in
			grp. 2 & rest 10 States in group 1.
	Ward	2	KE,MH,PJ,TN & WB in group 2 and
			The rest 10 States in group 1.

the other. But for the Ward method in Euclidean measure three groups was formed, viz., Kerala; Maharashtra, Punjab, Tamil Nadu, West Bengal; and the remaining other States. For the block and Chebychev measure it was a mix of two and three groups, whilst, for the cosine measure there did not exist any solution for all the methods except for Ward method which produced three groups.

In 1991 for all the methods with squared Euclidean, Euclidean, block and Chebychev measures, two and three cluster groups were formed and the latter dominated in all the measures. Like in 1972 and 1981, cosine measure showed no solution for most of the methods, except for one three cluster solution and single linkage showed a peculiar fifteen different groups solution.

9.5.2 Discriminant Analysis: The application of discriminant analysis is in fact not allowed if the within-groups covariance matrices are significantly different (Tacq, 1997). [15] It means to say that we need not go further if the above condition is not satisfied. However the *Box's M* test, which is used for testing the significance could not be performed. This is so because we are dealing with a small data set of 15 observations (States) and these again divided into three different classes, namely, developed, average and backward.

Discriminant analysis is performed to estimate the cumulative effect of the above 7 ratio-level indicators of banking development upon the single dependent nominal variable of time point level (Table 9.15).

Table 9.15: Data Description for Discriminant Analysis

Sl. No.	Number of Cases	Group
1	15 states	YEAR 1972
2	15 states	YEAR 1981
3	15 states	YEAR 1991

Two discriminant functions is the solution developed by the program, with the first one explaining most of the variation in the data (82 percent) as shown in Table 9.16.

Table 9.16: Canonical Discriminant Functions

Fcn.	Eigen value	Pct. of Variance	Cum. Pct.	Canonical Corr.
1	1.7353	82.21	82.21	0.7965
2	0.3754	17.79	100	0.5224

The standardized coefficients indicate the direction and intensity of contribution of each variable to the discriminant process; thus, credits per bank office contributes the most on function no. 1 followed by number of offices per 10,000 population (Table 9.17).

Table 9.17: Standardized Canonical Discriminant Function Coefficients

	FUNC 1	FUNC 2
NOPN	1.03136	3.41728
NOAR	0.25369	0.12156
DEPN	0.28542	4.21139
DEOF	0.73773	-4.40998
CRPN	-1.93861	-9.44183
CROF	1.21533	7.61346
CDRA	-0.08541	-0.64423

The contribution of deposits per bank office cannot be ignored. Credits per 10,000 population contribute very significantly, too, but in a negative way. Finally, number of offices per 100 square kms. of area, deposits per 10,000 population and credit-deposit ratio contribute little. The less significant function no. 2 is mostly contributed negatively by CRPN and DEOF and positively by CROF, DEPN and NOPN; these contributions are, to a certain extent, contradictory but one should remember that they account for only a minimal residual variation of 18 percent.

Overall, the contributions to the vital function no. 1 are as expected, in the sense that the higher the number of banks offices served per 10,000 population (NOPN) and the better its deposit mobilization per office (DEOF) vis-à-vis its credit deployment per office (CROF). The fact that the credit deployment per 10,000 population also contributes more to this function, points with great intensity to the primary objectives of bank nationalization, viz., to ensure that no viable productive (populist) endeavour should be stalled merely for lack of credit support.

Discriminant analysis was applied to a selected number of States with the most reliable data. Seven variables covering major aspects of banking development were selected for this analysis. An original classification in three groups was made on the basis of time points, namely, 1972, 1981 and 1991 and the classification results as given in Table 9.18 were obtained from the analysis. We observe that around 73% of the cases were correctly classified and the rest 17% were re-classified into different groups.

The effectiveness of prior group allocation can be evaluated by the re-classification of the 15 States in the 3 time points on the basis of their discriminant scores.

Table 9.18: Classification Results

Actual Group and Year	No. of Cases	Predicted Group Membership		
		1	2	3
Group 1 – 1972	15	12	3	0
		80.00%	20.00%	0.00%
Group 2 – 1981	15	4	10	1
		26.70%	66.70%	6.70%
Group 3 – 1991	15	0	4	11
		0.00%	26.70%	73.30%

The effectiveness of prior group allocation can be evaluated by the re-classification of the 15 states in the 3 time points: 1 = 1972, 2 = 1981 and 3 = 1991 on the basis of their discriminant scores, Table 9.19 displays reclassification of states. The Cols D and E show discriminant scores, Col A displays original classification of the states according to time points (1, 2, 3). Col B shows reclassification according to discriminant score based on Fcn.1 and Col C shows classification based on Fcn.2. (it is not considered here for analysis).

Table 9.19: Reclassification of States Based on Discriminant Scores

Case Label	Original Class.	Reclassi-fication based on Fcn.1	Reclassi-fication based on Fcn.2	Discriminant Scores	
				Fcn. 1	Fcn. 2
	A	B	C	D	E
1972					
AP72	1	1	2	-1.8297	-1.0579
AS72	1	1	2	-1.8346	-1.5234
BI72	1	1	2	-1.5712	-2.004
GJ72	1 **	2	1	-1.0864	0.6024
HY72	1	1	2	-1.493	-0.2355
KA72	1	1	2	-1.4573	-0.0311
KE72	1	1	2	-1.1776	0.2449
MP72	1	1	2	-1.9327	-1.1498
MH72	1	1	2	-1.0064	-1.6541
OR72	1	1	2	-2.0845	-1.5744
PJ72	1 **	2	1	-0.7814	1.1461
RJ72	1	1	2	-1.8739	-0.7031
TN72	1	1	2	-1.4505	-0.5695
UP72	1	1	2	-1.5959	-1.2622
WB72	1 **	2	3	0.3072	1.8055
1981					
AP81	2	2	1	-0.7063	0.7664
AS81	2 **	1	2	-1.0423	-0.6365
BI81	2 **	1	2	-0.8623	-0.1153

Contd...

GJ81	2	2	1	0.0182	1.1645
HY81	2	2	1	-0.3313	1.1626
KA81	2	2	1	-0.4929	1.3659
KE81	2	2	3	0.4539	2.2899
MP81	2 **	1	2	-1.1071	0.2938
MH81	2	2	3	0.9493	1.5202
OR81	2 **	1	2	-1.2958	-0.0177
PJ81	2	2	3	0.771	2.4785
RJ81	2	2	1	-1.0955	0.4607
TN81	2	2	1	-0.3566	0.9347
UP81	2	2	1	-0.507	0.0109
WB81	2 **	3	2	1.2057	0.7101
1991					
AP91	3	3	2	1.0273	0.6674
AS91	3 **	2	3	0.6614	0.4386
BI91	3	3	2	1.0484	0.0639
GJ91	3	3	2	1.893	-1.0154
HY91	3	3	2	1.9856	-0.3414
KA91	3	3	1	0.3983	-1.294
KE91	3	3	2	2.1028	-0.1818
MP91	3 **	2	3	0.4616	0.8276
MH91	3	3	2	4.9776	-2.0258
OR91	3 **	2	3	0.0549	1.0365
PJ91	3	3	2	3.109	-2.1307
RJ91	3 **	2	3	0.5103	0.7469
TN91	3	3	2	1.4044	-0.7273
UP91	3	3	2	1.583	0.1098
WB91	3	3	2	4.0494	-0.5968

** The states which were reclassified.

A = original class; B = Reclassification based on Discriminant Score

C= Based on Fcn.2

We note that out of 15 states, 12 states were remained in group 1 (1971) and 3 were reclassified to different time points. However this may not be a case of mis-classification but instead may be interpreted along the following lines. Gujarat, Punjab and West Bengal are re-classified in group 2, i.e., 1981, when they should have been in 1972 (group 1). This illustrates the fact that they were far ahead of times as against the other 12 States.. Their banking development resembles akin to 1981 rather than 1972. In the case of group 2 (1981), we notice that the States of Assam, Bihar, Madhya Pradesh and Orissa were backward in the sense that their overall banking development resembled those States in 1972 rather than 1981, i.e., they were reclassified to remain in group 1.

Further, West Bengal's banking development resembles the 1991 picture rather than its group 2 position. Similarly, the re-classification of the States of Assam, Madhya Pradesh, Orissa and Rajasthan from group 3 to group 2 show that these states were not in tune with the time. Andhra Pradesh banking sector which was re-classified to group 1 from group 2 has shown a lot of improvement and joined group 3 (1991). Rajasthan, which was in its own group during 1972 and 1981, did not improve during 1991 and showed backwardness in 1991. Astonishingly, a State like Bihar where backwardness was expected showed that it is consistent in performance for its time, but for a case during 1981 when it was re-classified to 1972. Amazingly, it caught up with its time during 1991 and was in its own group.

9.5.3 Correspondence Analysis: Correspondence analysis has better features than traditional multivariate analysis. It examines the relations not only among row or column variables but also between row and column variables. It provides a larger degree of insight into the information about the pattern of closeness among the individuals or among the variables and helps to identify the specific relationship between individuals (here, States) and variables which can not be attempted in principal component analysis or factor analysis.

9.6 Conclusions

A wide variety of techniques have been used in regional studies. The choice of the most appropriate method depends on the type of data, the nature of the problem and the objectives of analysis. The simplest techniques used are descriptive, ranking and coefficient of correlation methods, whereas in case of standard multivariate analysis, the most frequently used techniques are principal component analysis and factor analysis. The ranking method gives a preliminary idea about the relative positions of regions. Coefficient of correlation method gives an idea on how indicators are related to each other. Principal component analysis and factor analysis methods are superior to both of them as they not only to both of them as they not only take into account, the magnitude of the variables but also allocate weights to the variables for arriving at the index of development. Since principal component analysis does not involve any statistical assumptions about the distribution pattern of indicators, it may be preferred to factor analysis for use in regional analysis. Also the use of cluster analysis, discriminant analysis and correspondence analysis in regional analysis cannot be ruled out. However their usage in development of composite index of development is not possible.

However, they have their own appropriate uses. Correspondence analysis enabled the identification of particular indicators that were closely associated with the level of development of individual States. Cluster analysis is a multivariate procedure for detecting natural groupings in data. Cluster analysis classification is based upon the placing of objects into more or less homogeneous groups, in a manner such that the relationship between groups is revealed. Cluster analysis lacks an underlying body of statistical theory and is heuristic in nature. Cluster analysis requires decisions to be made by the user relating to the calculation of clusters, decisions that have a strong influence on the results of the classification. Cluster analysis is useful to classify groups or objects and is more objective than subjective. Clustering methods may be top down and employ logical division, or bottom up and undertake aggregation. Aggregation procedures, which are based upon combining cases through assessment of similarities, are the most common and popular. Care should be taken that groups (classes) are meaningful in some fashion and are not arbitrary or artificial. To do so the clustering techniques attempt to have more in common with own group than with other groups, through minimization of internal variation while maximizing variation between groups. Homogeneous and distinct groups are delineated based upon assessment of distances. Though we could not proceed further in discriminant analysis due to the small set of data, it helps in identifying those indicators that influenced the prior grouping of regions (States).

Appendix Table A9.2.3: Hierarchical Positions of States According to Different Methods in Banking Development

State	1991					
	Rank	PC (Cor)	PC (Cov)	FA (Alp)	FA (Img)	FA (Uls)
Andhra Pradesh	9	9	9	6	6	4
Assam	15	15	14	3	14	10
Bihar	14	14	11	5	15	12
Gujarat	5	6	6	13	5	7
Haryana	8	8	7	12	8	6
Karnataka	7	7	8	14	7	14
Kerala	4	4	4	8	9	2
Madhya Pradesh	11	11	12	11	10	5
Maharashtra	1	1	1	10	1	1
Orissa	13	13	15	4	13	9
Punjab	3	2	2	1	4	13
Rajasthan	12	12	13	15	11	3
Tamil Nadu	2	3	5	2	2	8
Uttar Pradesh	10	10	10	9	12	11
West Bengal	6	5	3	7	3	15

Appendix Table A9.3.3: Hierarchical Positions of States According to Different Methods in Banking Development (pooled time series)

State	1991				
	PC (Cor)	PC (Cov)	FA (Alp)	FA (Img)	FA (Uls)
Andhra Pradesh	9	9	14	7	12
Assam	15	14	7	13	11
Bihar	13	11	3	14	7
Gujarat	6	6	5	5	3
Haryana	7	7	6	6	6
Karnataka	8	8	9	9	9
Kerala	5	4	10	8	10
Madhya Pradesh	11	12	12	11	13
Maharashtra	1	1	4	1	2
Orissa	14	15	13	15	15
Punjab	2	2	8	4	4
Rajasthan	12	13	11	12	14
Tamil Nadu	3	5	15	3	8
Uttar Pradesh	10	10	2	10	5
West Bengal	4	3	1	2	1

End Notes and References

1. Note that the original scores were added with a constant of '100' for interpretability reasons.

2. Jolliffe, I.T. (1986). Principal Component Analysis, Springer-Verlag, New York.

3. See end note 2.

4. Tacq, J. (1997). Multivariate Analysis Techniques in Social Science Research: From Problem to Analysis. Sage Publications, London.

5. Dillon, W.R. & M. Goldstein (1984). Multivariate Analysis: Methods and Applications, John Wiley, New York.

6. Gorsuch, R.L. (1974). Factor Analysis, Saunders Publishing House, Philadelphia.

7. Ibid.

8. Cattell, R.B. (1978). The Scientific Use of Factor Analysis. Plenum, New York.

9. Kline, P. (1994). An Easy Guide to Factor Analysis. Routledge, London.

10. Nunnally, J. (1978). Psychometric Theory. McGraw-Hill, New York.

11. Ibid.

12. Everitt, B.S. (1993). Cluster Analysis (3/e), Edward Arnold, London.

13. Ibid.

14. Mojena, R. (1977). Hierarchical grouping methods and stopping rules: an evaluation. Computer Journal, 20, 13-24. Milligan, G.W. and Cooper, M.C. (1985). An examination of procedures for determining the number of clusters in a data set. Psychometrika, 50, 159-179.

15. Ibid.

10

TECHNIQUES OF REVENUE FORECAST

10.1 Need for Revenue Forecasts

Forecast of revenue is an integral part of the federal Fiscal Transfer Policies in any federation. This is so for more than one reason. Apart from the annual budgetary exercises to estimate the current deficit or surplus and also the overall budgetary deficit taking into account capital receipts and estimated outlays on development expenditure, projection of tax revenue is necessary also to work out the long term prospects of buoyancy and growth in revenue which form a corner stone of future fiscal action by government. In India, the Finance Commission has to resort to forecasting of tax yield, as it is the task of the Finance Commission to identify states, which are to be provided with grants-in-aid and also to recommend the quantum of grants-in-aid to states adjudged to be in need of revenue. In a federation, the federating units also need to forecast their revenue in order to make a case for getting financial assistance from the federal government. Similarly, analysis of the past trends in growth of tax-revenue and estimation of elasticity and buoyancy coefficients for different Taxes enable the Union and the state governments to form value judgments on the effect of the past taxation policies as well as its future trend with a view to optimizing the revenue from certain sources without unduly causing hardship to the tax payers or restraining demand more than necessary. Such analysis also gives an insight into the trend in which the state tax revenue and the central tax revenues are moving. Planning future resource allocation also requires forecasting of governments fiscal parameters.

Forecasting Tax Yield of different states is one of the important tasks before a federal government. Often, the forecasting exercise is riddled with complexities as several unknown factors influence the future performance. In a country like India, forecasting becomes more complicated as uncertainty is more significant due to excessive dependency of our agriculture on monsoon, which results in cyclical changes in agricultural operations, variations in industrial output. Whenever a country goes for structural changes forecasting becomes much more complex. During structural adjustment, sectoral performance owing to liberalization, new industrial and trade policies, fiscal and monetary reforms, are bound to vary from state to state owing to different socio-politico-economic situation. Changing prices and political scenarios also influence future tax performance of the states. The Tax-Policies existing as well as future measures are important determinants of tax yield, which depend upon political decisions and also on the administrative efficiency. During the forecast horizon in a democratic country if elections are expected, this may further complicate forecasting. With each election, new political dimensions are expected to crop up. With all these uncertain but important tax determinants, to make forecasts is a difficult task. As these factors are highly volatile in nature and difficult to perceive fully, the actual budgetary figures are always different from the budget or revised estimates. Nevertheless, forecasts are essential.

10.2 Techniques of Revenue Forecasts

The importance and usefulness of the forecasts depend upon the method and accuracy of predictions. A brief description of these techniques is given below.

10.2.1 Qualitative Method: Under this method forecasts are made on the basis of past experience, future expectations, feelings and value judgments. These estimates are unscientific as they are not amenable to systematic verification.

10.2.2 Quantitative Forecasts:- These forecasts are based on actual availability of adequate quantitative information and on the condition that there is rationale to accept the relationship indicated by past. In other words, it requires the condition of constancy.

The quantitative methods, generally used are put into three

broad groups namely

- Univariate time series technique,
- An Econometric method based on multiple variables
- A combined technique.

All these alternative methods are based on the premises that if a set of values of `y' i.e. dependent variables have to be predicted, the problem can simply be equated with the question of identifying a method that facilitates predicting for 'y' at a future time say, Tnk given `n' observation..... y1, y2...yn Alternatively, `value' of 'y' at a future time can also be predicted, if observations on certain other relevant variables such as x1, x2, x3 etc, are available for `m' number of years, and whose values can be predicted for future years. The time interval 1 to n is called a sample period and the positive time interval say `K' number of years is called the forecast horizon. Thus, all quantitative measures depend upon data pertaining to sample period and then generate data for the forecast horizon and based on these information, future values of `dependent' variable is predicted.

10.2.3 Time Series Analysis: Most commonly used forecasting method relates to univariate time series method, where dependent variable is regressed on `time' which is taken as an independent or explanatory variable. Thus, future movements of dependent variable are inferred based on its own past movements. This method is simple in application, gives quick results, and also provides reasonably acceptable predictions for limited use. There are three methods under the category of `time series' which are generally employed for forecasting of revenue or expenditure. They are:

- Compound Growth method (C G method)
- The Exponential Smoothing, (including Holt-Winter method)
- The Auto Regressive Integrated Moving Average (ARIMA) method.

A. Compound Growth method (CG Method): The assumption of (CG) method is that variable grows more or less in proportion to its base values. The linear CG function is of the form:-

$Y_t = Y_0 + (1+r)^t + e^{ut}$ →(1)

Where the variable Y_t is assumed to grow overtime at an annual compound rate `r' from a base `Y_0'. The parameters `Y_0' and (1+r) are usually estimated by the ordinary least square. e^{ut} is the error term.

The same may be expressed in log linear form also,

$\ln(Y_t) = \ln(Y_0) + t\ln(1+r) + u_t$ → (2)

Let $\ln(Y_0) = \alpha$; $\ln(1+r) = \beta$

$\ln(Y_t) = \alpha + \beta t + u_t$

ut' the stochastic error term.

Annual Compound Growth Rate (ACG) = $(e^{\beta} - 1) \times 100$ i.e the Anti log of the value.

Compound growth rate is very commonly used for population projection. This method makes use of the values at the starting and end period and in between values are predicted.

B. Exponential Smoothing Techniques: These are popular in making short-term predictions of future sales, costs etc pertaining to some business they are not used for long-term projections.

Basically, `ES' method treats a time series variable as being made up of the actual values, and previous periods predictable level. The `E S' function can be explained as below: Let P_t denote prediction of the variable x_t in period `t'. Then the forecast for next period (t+1) could be written as:

$P_t + 1\ A\ x_t + (1+A)\ P_t$ → 5

The equation is used to obtain a method for the period (t+1) as a weighted average of the actual xt and the forecast `pt' of the previous period. There are different versions of this method, most popular one being the single Exponential Moving Average. Other methods are Holt Winter Type model, the conventional moving average model, adaptive expectations model and so on.

These models, however, are useful only for making very short term forecasts say for a few weeks, or months.

C. ARIMA Model: The Auto Regressive Integrated Moving Average (ARIMA) model, also known as Box-Jenkins (BJ) model refer to a wide range of models that seem to represent the real world time series variables closely. There are three types of transformations of pure random variables (white noise) which leads to the systematic movement of a variable. The first is known as the auto-regressive (AR) process where the current value of the variable is taken to be finite weighted sum of its past values. The second is termed as the Moving average (MA) process where current values of the residuals are viewed as weighted sum of the past residual. The third, is known as `integration' process, where in a stationary series is transformed into a non-stationary series.

`ARIMA' method requires large number of observations, at least 35 to 40 observations or time points to make short term projections say for maximum 2 or 3 years. In spite of all complications, what we get is a tool for very short term forecasting.

The univariate projections thus are made on the average annual growth of dependent variables for a selected period of past years. Projections are made on the assumption that the growth is unaffected by any other factor, or if it is affected by other factors, these factors (the independent variables) also grow at same rate as in the past.

10.3 Multivariate Technique

The Econometric method views the movement of a variable as caused by a set of exogenous factors, in accordance with a definite causation process. This approach translates theory on a hypothesis regarding a causal relationship into an algebraic equation or system of equations whose parameters are estimated by econometric methods. As in the case with trend extrapolation method, the adoption of modeling approach too necessitates a priori specification of the explanatory variables and the type of the functional relationship to be employed.

Some of the econometric models for forecasting of tax-yield are in the form of tax-income response model, namely the buoyancy and elasticity models, and the multi-determinants model, which seeks to explain the movement of tax yield in terms of its determining factors. These methods are briefly sketched below:-

10.4 Elasticity and Buoyancy Method

The growth of a tax is usually judged in relation to certain quantifiable economic variables such as national income, since an absolute increase in the yield of any tax may not by itself have much significance. A straight forward way of obtaining a measure of the relative growth of tax-revenue is to compute the percentage change in revenue that has taken place for a 1% change in national income.

In order to measure buoyancy of a tax, total tax yield is regressed upon SDP and a double log function is fitted. Buoyancy measures, changes which one is due to both built-in-flexibility and due to discretionary changes. Elasticity, on the other hand measure changes in tax-yield owing to automatic growth, leaving out the changes due to discretionary action. There are various ways to make adjustments for discretionary changes. One very popular method is known as `Prest method'. In this method, first step is to adjust the historical tax receipts for discretionary changes by subtracting from each year's actual tax revenues the estimated revenue effect of that years' discretionary actions. Second, to further adjust the so obtained tax-revenues of each year to the cumulative effect of the discretionary changes tried till that year. The Prest method is

T1 = Ti-1 + (T1-Ti-1) (Ti-1/Ti-1)

Ti = Tax collection in the ith year adjusted to the statutory rates of year 1.

Ti-1 = Tax collections in the ith year adjusted to rates in year (t-1)

Ti = Actual tax collections in the `i'th year

The basic objective of this methodology is to accommodate both rate and base changes. However, in the absence of such detailed data the Prest method suggests the derivation of the adjusted data from the raw data as follows.

Let,

T1, T2.... Tt ....Tn...... be the actual tax yield series of years;

Di, D2.....Dt....Dn..... be the estimates of the revenue effect of discretionary changes tried over the corresponding years and,

Tij represent the ith years's actual tax yield adjusted to the tax-structure that existed in the year (i)

Then if i = 1 is taken as the reference year the series T11.. Ti2......Tit.......Tin.......represent what the tax-receipts would have been if the tax structure had remained as in the year 1, with all discretionary changes removed from the following 1. And these could be developed as:

T11 = T1

T12 = T2 - D2

T13 = T23 (T12/T2)

T14 = T3u (T23/t2) (T12/T2)

\- - - - - - -

\- - - - - - -

Tij = Tj-1 -1 T2-2j-1/tj-1)...(T23/T3) (T12 t12)

This means adjusting the tax yield of any year to the simulated yield for that year, if a base year tax had prevailed, the actual tax yield is to be multiplied by a sequence of multiplicative factors. This, is how one cleans up the tax-series and removes the discretionary effects. When such cleaned tax series is regressed upon SDP, by using double log function, elasticity coefficients are obtained.

By using the buoyancy or elasticity coefficients and relating them with projected SDP, one can forecast future tax-yield. Or alternatively by multiplying growth rate of SDP with elasticity coefficient one can get growth rate of tax Yield, applying this to the selected base year compute Tax yield for future years, To put it in a simple manner.

Thus for purposes of making projections the elasticity coefficient say (0.75) would be applied to the growth of income (say 4% per annum) and the rate of growth of tax-revenue would be computed as follows:

$\Delta T/T = a * bT$

Where T is Tax revenue, `a' is growth rate of income and `b' is elasticity coefficient i.e.

Growth rate of Tax revenue $\Delta T/T = 4 * .75 = 3\%$ per annum.

Using this growth rate, tax yield in a given year can be estimated thus, if in a base year if `X' tax yield is Rs 100, in year X1 it would be 100 + 3% = 103, in the year X2 it would be 103 + 3% = 106.09, in the year X3 = 106.09 + 3% = 109.27 and so on.

Alternatively, based on the historical trend state domestic product of individual states is projected and this projected value is replaced in the tax-buoyancy or elasticity coefficient to get the estimated values of tax yield:

Tax yield = $\alpha + \beta X_{i+1}$

$X_i + 1$ = Future values of SDP

β = elasticity coefficient and

α = Constant term

In the first, growth rate of SDP is an assumed rate based on national norms or plan targets etc. In the latter, growth is estimated based on historical trend.

This method of forecasting tax-yield gives normative estimates compared to the estimates based on historical growth. However, in this method, it is assumed that tax-yield is dependent only on state domestic product, whereas, as we have described at another place, tax-yield is influenced by many other factors. Further, the estimates of tax-yield varies from one method of estimating elasticity/buoyancy to the other method e.g. if tax yield is regressed upon net national (state) product at current prices, we get one coefficient and when it is regressed upon gross state domestic product we get another. Similarly, when tax is regressed upon prices and real income, elasticity coefficient obtained would be different. Thus, this method faces the problem of getting a right definition of income which is to be used as independent variable. Should one take GDP or NDP, as explanatory variable, whether the national income should be in current or constant prices, should national income be taken along with a price index, and so on form crucial issues in this regard. If we advocate for including a price index in the list of independent variable the problem arises, which price index to be taken, an implicit index or wholesale price index or consumer price index and so on and even if this is resolved, next problem arises as to whether such information is available for all the states.

The use of buoyancy coefficient has a different role to play than the elasticity coefficient the elasticity coefficient gives us an idea of the inherent responsiveness of the tax yield to SDP (national income), the buoyancy coefficient simply indicates how the actual growth of revenue compares with the growth in income, since actual collections are influenced by discretionary changes in the tax-rates or legal bases, introduced by the government from time to time, such collections may bear systematic relationship to national income particularly the impact of such measures has been significant. It may thus be even conceptually illegitimate to try to correlate actual or historical revenue yield with national income. If one uses only elasticity coefficient for forecasting of tax-yield, the estimated values only speak of the expected yield due to a given built in elasticity factor, whereas the trends in discretionary measures, which influence the tax yield are completely left out.

In spite of these limitations, elasticity/buoyancy coefficients are used, for forecasting purposes. It has got its own merits and demerits. Depending upon the availability of data and its quality, one can use the method for forecasting tax-yield. However, forecast based on just elasticity or buoyancy coefficients, only gives the projections based on the rates prevailing in the base year. In order to get projections at current rates, if data on future ARM are available such as period targets, they may be added to the estimated future tax yield.

10.5 Multivariate Determinants Model

This method is similar to the method of forecasting based on elasticity/buoyancy coefficients. However, the major difference lies in the explanatory determinants. In the multivariate determinant model, tax yield is taken to be influenced by several factors apart from state domestic product, such as, level of consumption expenditure, distribution of income, sectoral composition of income, urbanization and so on which influence the taxable capacity and in turn the tax-yield of a state. The determinants function should ideally also include a suitable proxy representing the changes in tax rate structure, as tax yield is affected by such changes. But the difficulties of finding such proxy are well known. However, as suggested in the case of elasticity/buoyancy measures, if some future estimates of additional resource mobilization as planned by the states are available, one can add those values to the estimated tax-yield to get a more realistic forecast of tax yield.

10.6 Combination Techniques

In this approach, historical or time series and economic approaches are combined together. The forecasts obtained by selected time series methods or by econometric methods is used as weighted average. This method incorporates the lagged effects of determining factors.

Thus, various methods of forecasts are available. However, while adopting a method, care should be taken to see that the forecasts are not unrealistic. Forecasts should be able to adjust to the changes in the economy. The model should be simple.

There are a few tests, available for testing the validity of a method such as, working out the Average Absolute Percent Error (APE) and the Thiel U-coefficient, which can be employed to assess the forecasts based on different methods. Whichever method gives the least variation between the actual and the forecast values that can be selected for forecasting tax-yield in future. These various methods e.g. may be employed for a period between 1970-71 and 1980-81. Using these co-efficient and the estimated explanatory variables for the next period i.e. 1981-82 to 1989-90, tax yield may be estimated, these estimated yield figures should then be compared with the actual figures for the same period. Later on by using the Theil `U' coefficient, or APE method, the best model can be selected. Alternatively, a model can be selected on theoretical and conceptual basis.

The various methods of forecast described above are illustrated with the help of data relating to Indian States, Commodity wise Sales tax in Karnataka, and major four taxes viz., Sales tax, State excise, Motor vehicle taxes and Stamp and Registration Duties in Karnataka.

10.7 Methodology for Forecasting Tax Yield of Indian States

The forecasting techniques are illustrated by taking the data relating to Indian States. [1] The present author for the Tenth Finance commission did the study. In this study, tax-yield forecasts are made on the basis of multivariate determinants model and historical time trend method. The former method is adopted for the 15 major states for which time series data on explanatory variables were available for the past twenty years. A semi log time trend method was adopted for minor states for which tax-yield data was available at least for a period of 10 years. For other states like Goa, Arunachal Pradesh and Mizoram etc for whom tax-yield data was not available for more than 5 years. Holt-winter exponential Smoothing method was adopted to predict future tax yield. The projected figures based on the determinants model, in fact gives tax yield at 1990-91-tax structure.

In order to derive estimates of tax-yield at current tax rates, one should add the revenue effect of discretionary measure actually undertaken during 1991-92 to 1993-94 and the ARM as promised by the states during the rest of the 8th plan period. However, information on the yield of discretionary or targeted additional resource mobilization data was not available. Information on ARM was available only for 12 states. Hence, ARM figures could not be added to the forecast figures of tax-yield, the Tax yield projections thus derived are at 1990-91 tax rates.

The forecasting of tax yield based on `Determinant Model' involved the following steps:

1. Building up of structural equations, whose coefficients are used for making forecasts. This was done by using 8 years

panel data from 1983-84 to 1990-91

2. Prediction of explanatory variables over the forecast horizon based on their past historical trend (1970-71 to 1990-91 information).
3. Estimation of tax-yield for the forecasting period by replacing the predicted values of explanatory variables in the structural equation.
4. Addition of Additional Resource mobilization figures as promised by the states during the Eight five year Plan, to estimate tax-yield during the Forecast period. This can be done only if information on ARM is available.

The determinant model for forecasting was:

$$Pt_{ij} = \beta 1\, X1_{ij} + \beta 2\, X\, 2_{ij} + \beta 3\, X\, 3_{ij} + \beta 4\, X\, 4_{ij} + \beta\, X\, 5_{ij} + D1 + D2 \rightarrow (1)$$

i = 1, 2 ...... 15 states

j = 1991 to 20001 years

Pt = Per capita Tax, i^{th} state j^{th} period.

X1 = Adjusted income i^{th} state j^{th} period.

X2 = PACE i^{th} state j^{th} period.

X3 = % share of non agricultural income

X4 = urbanization

X5 = Inequality index

D1 = Dummy representing High income states

D2 = Dummy representing Medium income states

In the case of states where time trend method was used, tax-yield data of individual states for a period of past 15 years and based on this trend - future tax yield were estimated. The equation used was of the following form:

$$\text{Log } Pt = \alpha + \beta t + u_t \rightarrow (2)$$

And this was corrected for auto-correlation by search method and based on this forecasts of tax-yield for the selected special category states were made.

In the case of some states like Goa, Mizoram, and Arunachal Pradesh, for whom actual tax-data was available for less than 5 years period, we used Holt Winter method for forecasting tax-yield:

For a given State, let

X_t denote tax realization for period 't'.

Exponential smoothing is the basis for Holt's two-parameter method.

The smoothed series $\widetilde{X}_t$ is found from two recursive equations and depends on two smoothing parameters, α and γ,

$0 < \alpha < 1$

$0 < \gamma < 1$

$$\widetilde{X}_t = \alpha \widetilde{X}_t + (1-\alpha)(\widetilde{X}_{t-1} + r_{t-1})$$

$$r_t = r(\widetilde{X}_t - \widetilde{X}_{t-1}) + (1-r)r_{t-1}$$

Where r_t is a smoothed series representing the trend i.e., the average rate of increase in the smoothed series $\widetilde{X}_t$.

Then an l - period forecast can be generated as

$$\hat{X}_{T+l} = lr_t \qquad \rightarrow (3)$$

Thus based on the above three methods forecasts of tax-yield for 15 major states, 6 minor states, 4 minor states were made separately.

The four methods compared are (1) Multivariate Determinant Model; (2) Time Trend Method; (3) Buoyancy Method; and (4) Elasticity Method. It may be observed from the table that forecasts based on elasticity equation gives very depressed projections; the implicit growth rate is very low in this case. The four projections based on multivariate models are more or less similar for all the states, with marginal differences. Trend projection shows an increase by 3 to 3.5 times during the forecast period for all the states. Even the implicit growth rates are comparable with marginal difference for all the states. Buoyancy based estimates, depresses the figures for states with low capacity and low efforts and exaggerates the figures for high capacity and high effort states. Thus, e.g. for a states like Gujarat, Haryana, etc, the forecasts appear to be rather over optimistic, and this over optimism increases over the time. On the other hand, the projections are rather depressed for states like Bihar, M.P, Orissa, Rajasthan, U.P, etc. The trend thus based on buoyancy either overstates or understates the forecasts. The elasticity based projections give very unrealistic implicit growth for states like Bihar and Orissa and also the projections are unbelievably very low.

Thus based on merits finally equation 1 was chosen for making forecast of tax yield of the 15 major states.

10.8 Forecasts of Tax Yield of Indian States

Forecasts made on the basis of multivariate determinant model, are presented in Table 10.1.

Table 10.1: Forecasts of Per Capita Tax Yield 1991-92 to 2000-2001 (in Rs.)

State	Year			Implicit Growth (Regression Trend)
	1991-92	1995-96	2000-2001	
Andhra Pradesh	400.36	594.21	939.76	9.928
Assam	302.69	512.08	911.81	12.973
Bihar	188.17	320.33	555.67	12.695
Gujarat	592.85	849.81	1322.07	9.317
Haryana	595.88	888.57	1420.85	10.121
Karnataka	479.63	704.59	1118.03	9.849
Kerala	453.89	673.65	1072.04	10.278
Madhya Pradesh	288.32	447.27	726.25	10.77
Maharashtra	704.01	1024.58	1648.47	9.915
Orissa	239.97	411.35	722.12	12.936
Punjab	754.64	1122.39	1822.6	10.286
Rajasthan	335.49	509.77	819.36	9.986
Tamil Nadu	880.42	1240.5	1879.79	8.786
Uttar Pradesh	313.95	491.42	810.7	11.077
West Bengal	664.13	933.69	1407.12	8.692

Table 10.1 presents forecasts of per capita tax yield. It may be stated here that the forecasts do not include the possible additional resource mobilisation estimates. The equation used for the projection is:

X1i = .07123121 * X2i +.1207136 * X 3i + 2.716128* X4i + 4.66470 * X 5i - 112.0704 * X6i - 272.0932 * D1 -267.9945 * D2 - 282.5579

i = 1991-92, 1992-93 - - - - - - - - - 1999-2000 - - - - 2000 - 2001.

X1 = Per capita Tax yield in (i)th year

X2 = Adjusted income (per capita income – per capita consumption expenditure) in (i)th year

X3 = Pace (Per capita annual consumption expenditure) in (i)th year

X4 = Non-Primary Sectoral income share in the year (i)

X5 = Urban % in (i) the year

X6 = Index of inequality in (i) the year

D1, D2 = dummies for HIG, MIG

Taking the above coefficients and multiplying by the determinant values the forecasts figures were obtained and the same are exhibited in Table 10.1.

Tax-forecast for 7 out of the 10 special category states are given in Table 10.2 by using the Time trend method. Data on tax yield per capita of the states like Nagaland, Manipur, Tripura, Meghalaya, Sikkim, J & K and Himachal Pradesh were obtained for past 15 years i.e. from 1975-76 to 1990-91 and a semi log time trend was fitted. Based on this O.L.S equation future values of expected Tax-yield were derived. The data relating to other determinants such as per capita consumption, development index etc. were not available for these states hence we had to rely only on forecasts based on time trend method.

It may be seen from the Table 10.2 that during the period between 1991-92 and 2000-2001, tax yield is likely to go up by 2.75 to 4.5 times in various states. The Tax-Yield is expected to grow more rapidly in states like Meghalaya and Tripura, while, states like Nagaland, J&K and Manipur & H.P are likely to have increase in Tax yield only by 3 times.

Table 10.2: Forecast of Tax Yield Per Capita for Seven Minor States 1991-2001

State	Year			Implicit Growth (Regression Trend)
	1991-92	1995-96	2000-2001	
Himachal Pradesh	357.01	613.51	1207.11	14.495
Jammu & Kashmir	276.59	455.09	848.02	13.257
Nagaland	196.99	309.13	542.94	11.924
Meghalaya	252.35	493	1138.68	18.225
Manipur	95.62	156.77	290.87	13.158
Tripura	110.65	205.78	446.93	16.779
Sikkim	369.07	613.51	1157.98	13.547

For the remaining 3 states viz, Arunachal Pradesh, Goa and Mizoram, we did not have tax-yield data for the years prior to 1985-86. Hence with Five year data for Arunachal Pradesh and Goa and six year data for Mizoram, we have to forecast their future tax yield. For this purpose, we followed the method of exponential smoothing (Holt - winter type) method. Though this is not a satisfactory method for making such forecasts we have used it as this was the best method available for estimating based on such few observation. The forecast of Tax yield for these three states are presented in Table 10.3 of additional resource mobilization as promised by these states during the Eight Five Year Plan and added to these estimates that would give us a rough estimate of future total tax yield of these three minor states.

10.9 Forecasts of Sales Tax, State Excise and Motor Vehicle Tax

In order to ascertain the growth of tax-yield by its major components, Rao [2] had made the forecast of sales tax, State excise and MV tax for the period between 1991-92 and 2000-

2001 AD by using the following two methods:

1. Time-Trend method
2. Determinant model (modified-RTS method)

The forecasts are given in Table 10.4 the last row gives the implicit growth rate of individual tax yield under various methods.

Table 10.3: Forecast of Tax Yield of 3 Special Category States

State	Year			Implicit Growth (Regression Trend)
	1991-92	1995-96	2000-2001	
Arunachal Pradesh	34.1452	43.2156	54.5537	5.344
Goa	623.648	769.274	951.306	4.803
Mizoram	52.9906	71.3726	94.3502	6.62

Table 10.4: Forecast of Tax Yield by Type of Tax 1991-92, 1995-96, 2000-2001 (Projection Based on RTS Equations)

State and Year	Sales Tax	State Excise	Motor Vehicle
Andhra Pradesh			
1991-92	1198.45	517.67	127.24
1995-96	1841.09	1004.52	182.9
2000-2001	3091.05	1960.52	287.29
Growth Rate	11.102	15.947	9.471
Assam			
1991-92	294.8	202.92	42.94
1995-96	634.57	478.59	73.3
2000-2001	1317.72	1004.7	131.79
Growth Rate	18.102	19.451	13.269
Bihar			

Contd...

1991-92	717.17	400.72	86.94
1995-96	1235.41	790.85	135.62
2000-2001	2233.69	1536.87	226.86
Growth Rate	13.455	16.109	11.245
Gujarat			
1991-92	1389.25	404.9	145.48
1995-96	1982.88	789.06	195.5
2000-2001	3156.63	1525.97	290.94
Growth Rate	9.548	15.884	8.005
Haryana			
1991-92	619.15	242.36	74.3
1995-96	1026.71	531.79	111.16
2000-2001	1761.4	1069.24	174.92
Growth Rate	12.319	17.93	9.98
MYSORE			
1991-92	1193.24	366.63	127.14
1995-96	1806.73	742.69	179.49
2000-2001	3023.83	1473.27	279.11
Growth Rate	10.884	16.713	9.13
Kerala			
1991-92	811.93	247.46	98.43
1995-96	1137.64	544.8	129.96
2000-2001	1744.34	1099.5	187.59
Growth Rate	8.868	18.023	7.428
Madhya Pradesh			
1991-92	803.09	432.94	93.14
1995-96	1307.98	835.59	139.49
2000-2001	2250.36	1599.5	223.36

Contd...

Growth Rate	12.13	15.628	10.206
Maharashtra			
1991-92	2577.28	747.03	243.34
1995-96	3798.83	1353.94	339.15
2000-2001	6410.84	2584.48	539.45
Growth Rate	10.655	14.787	9.249
Orissa			
1991-92	334.88	200.02	47.31
1995-96	678.37	466.78	79.19
2000-2001	1299.06	958.1	134.88
Growth Rate	16.256	19.013	12.345
Punjab			
1991-92	719.37	272.94	80,34
1995-96	1135.05	563.83	115.55
2000-2001	1934.25	1102.86	181.06
Growth Rate	11.617	16.784	9.448
Rajasthan			
1991-92	496.14	296.87	65.13
1995-96	871.99	634.32	100.5
2000-2001	1612.63	1277.18	168.35
Growth Rate	13.994	17.601	11.129
Tamil Nadu			
1991-92	1724.97	389.27	182.16
1995-96	2398.77	769.94	240.79
2000-2001	3719.66	1506.67	351.48
Growth Rate	8.913	16.227	7.576
Uttar Pradesh			

Contd...

1991-92	1779.77	705.16	184.46
1995-96	2848.13	1287.07	279.59
2000-2001	5007.53	2445.83	466.16
Growth Rate	12.181	14.819	10.85
West Bengal			
1991-92	1344.99	460.88	140.96
1995-96	1923.69	865.73	190.73
2000-2001	3053.46	1630.42	285.8
Growth Rate	9.538	15.072	8.17

The above exercise only supports the theoretical possibilities of adopting RTS method both for measuring Taxable Capacity and efforts and for making forecast of tax-wise tax-yield. However, due to severe data bottleneck, non-availability of information for item-wise tax-yield, tax rates and also, for tax base, the estimates are not recommended for policy use. The estimates based on the aggregate regression approach using panel data model and the forecast of aggregate tax yield based on the determinant or structural model is suitable for policy purposes.

Rao tried Modified RTS method in her another study making Forecast of Karnataka's Revenue. In this study forecasts were made for individual taxes based on their tax base or proxy bases. This is illustrated in the following section.

10.10 Methodology Adopted by the Tenth Finance Commission [3]

There are several methods of making forecast of tax revenue. The Tenth Finance Commission had adopted the Buoyancy Model. The buoyancy coefficient indicates how the actual growth of revenue compares with the growth in nominal income. In the log form the equation used by the Commission was:

$$\text{Log } R = \log \alpha + \beta \log Y + \log U$$

R = Tax Revenue

Y = NSDP

U = Random Terms

By using the buoyancy coefficients and relating these with the assumed rate of growth of NSDP future tax yield were derived. For making projections the buoyancy coefficient was applied to the rate of growth of income and the rate of growth of tax revenue was estimated. Yield in a given year (future) was projected by applying the estimated rate of growth of tax revenue to the base year figure.

$R' = R + (y \times \beta)$

R′ = Forecast

R = Base Tax Yield

The base year, 1994-95, figures were arrived at by using a semi log trend The estimated buoyancy coefficients were moderated by the T F C. by assuming upper and lower limits of buoyancy coefficients.

The method adopted by TFC suffers from several shortcomings:

First, the time series data was not adequate to make a meaningful projection.

Second, the forecast of tax yield based on the independent variables that were projected by using trend data without modification tend to over/under estimate figures for the future.

Thirdly, TFC had arbitrarily moderated the Buoyancy Coefficient.

Fourth the forecasts made by TFC and the actual data when compared differ considerably. There is a wide gap between the forecast and the actual for the same period.

It may be seen from Table 10.5 that there was overestimation of tax yield from sales tax, State Excise Duties for Karnataka. The figures for Stamp and Registration and Motor Vehicle Tax were underestimated.

However, as the bulk of tax revenue i.e. more than 75% comes from Sales Tax and State Excise Duty, Karnataka suffered under the TFC recommendations mainly because of defective method of forecast of revenue for the State.

Table 10.5: Forecast by Tenth FC for Karnataka

	Sales Tax		Motor Vehicle Tax		Stamps & Regn.	
Year	Forecast	Actual	Forecast	Actual	Forecast	Actual
1995-96	302,958	255,721	82,993	45,603	39,133	53,653
1996-97	348,402	323,728	93,460	32,936	45,238	49,362
1997-98	400,662	402,300	105,447	448,93	52,295	61,698

10.11 Forecasting of Sales Tax Yield for Karnataka, 1996-97

In another study Rao [4] made forecast of sales tax revenue for Karnataka State for the period 1995 to 1997. The study selected top 17 items, which contributed the maximum to the total sales tax revenue. The list is given below:

1. Diesel and petrol (Combined)
2. Liquor and beer
3. Petroleum products
4. Cement
5. Automobile and spare parts
6. Electrical goods
7. Medicines And Pharmaceutical
8. Iron & Steel
9. Machinery
10. Sugarcane purchase
11. Tyres & Tubes
12. Areca nut
13. Machinery parts
14. Fertilizer
15. Coffee seeds
16. Electronics goods
17. Paints

Forecasting of tax yield from a specific commodity involves the following steps:

1. Collection of data on tax yield for a period of about 15 years;
2. Identification and Selection of general determinants of tax yield like per capita state domestic product (sdp), Whole Sale Price index , per capita consumption, percentage of sectoral income, percentage of urban population and so on;
3. Identification and selection of specific determinants of tax yield of the specific commodity such as sale or production of liquor, or motor spirit, in the case of liquor and motor spirit, Number of motor vehicles in the case of Tyre and tube etc. Thus the following determinants were considered for estimating the tax function of the selected 17 commodities in this study:

- sale of the product
- production
- commodity price or price index
- tax rate
- consumption
- number of vehicles

1. weighted
2. total unweigthed

- crushing capacity of sugar factories in the state.

Since taxes are paid out of the current income there is every reason to believe that per capita income is a good determinant of tax yield. Taxes especially when they are ad volerem are deeply influenced by the price of the commodity and also by the general price level. Per capita consumption expenditure shows the extent of consumption of goods which in turn yield tax. The variables such as urbanisation and sectoral composition of income indirectly explain the movement of the tax yield.

While the above list of variables are theoretically justified as proxy determinants of tax yield, however all of them cannot be included in one tax function. Quite often these independent determinants are highly correlated among themselves and hence while fitting a regression equation the problem of multi colinearity arises. Therefore, in the final equation determinants are included, based on their relative economic and statistical significance after screening them statistically.

Statistical screening of the determinants so as to exclude the variables which pull down the explanatory power of the model is done in the following way:

- First regress dependent variable on each determinant separately;
- Make combinations and derive the equation and test the significance of the coefficients, explanatory power and the goodness of the fit;
- Drop the variables which bring down the explanatory power of the model and the variables;
- Select the final functional form.

Data selection is based not only on the statistical consideration but also on the practical consideration namely the availability of reliable, consistent and continuous time series data pertaining to various general and specific determinants as well to KST figures. Since the tax model is entirely based on the data, availability of data is the most important factor.

Selection of the model for making forecast is very crucial. The model varies from commodity to commodity depending upon the behaviour of and the availability of tax data and the economic and statistical significance of the selected determinants. Based on the nature of the dependent variable the statistical equation like linear, log lincar, quadratic or exponential smoothing, structural deterministic model etc. are chosen.

Once the model is derived the next task is to make the projection of the future values of the determinants which are replaced in the basic tax function while making forecast of tax yield. For this purpose first a structural equation using dependent variable and the selected determinants are specified and the α and β coefficients are derived. And subsequently the projected values of the independent variables are replaced in the structural equation to make forecast of the dependent variable i.e. tax yield. For this purpose, following method are used for forecast of tax yield:

1. In most of the cases a multivariate deterministic model, where tax yield of the specific commodity is regressed upon one or more independent variables, is adopted. The tax function of the following type is developed:

KSTy = *f*(general determinants and specific determinants)

Where KSTy = sales tax yield of 'y' commodity.

Thus to put in equation form

$$KSTy_t = \alpha + \beta_1 x1_t + \beta_2 x2_t + ... + \beta_n \ xn_t + u_t \qquad \rightarrow (1)$$

2. Second for all the selected taxes and aggregate sales tax Income buoyancy based tax function is derived in the following manner:

Log KSTy = *f*(log SDP)

Where SDP = state domestic product at current price.

log $KSTy_t = \alpha + \beta \log SDP_t + u_t$ → (2)

3. For purpose of making a comparison we have also fitted a time trend of the following three types based on the nature of the data:

linear trend

$KSTy_t = \alpha + \beta t + u_t$

log linear trend

log $KSTy_t = \alpha + \beta t + u_t$

quadratic trend

$KSTyt = \alpha + \beta_t + r_t^2 + u_t$

4. For the commodity where long time data is not available, Holt's exponential smoothing is used.

This form of trend is fitted in the case of those commodities for which time series data on the tax yield was available for less than eight years and hence no other model could be adopted.

10.11.1 Exponential Smoothing Model: In the cases of those commodities for which KST data were not available on continuous basis for a period of more than 8 years, we could neither fit a linear, loglinear time trend or a multivariate equation. Hence we have used the technique of exponential smoothing which is a tool generally used for making short term forecasts based on very few observations (years). We have used this method in the case of the following commodities: petroleum products and electronic goods (Table 10.6).

Table 10.6: Forecast of Tax Yield

Year	Electronic Goods	Petroleum Product
1995-96	2090	12187
1996-97	2307	18120
1997-98	2525	26942
1998-99	2743	40060
1999-2000	2961	59564

In the cases of multivariate, buoyancy, and trend models the time series data was corrected for auto correlation. Selection of the final equation for a specific commodity was based on the following considerations:

1. The determinants included should be justifiable on economic basis,
2. The model should be statistically significant as reflected by R^2, $\overline{R}^2$, F value and individual β coefficients.

Selection of independent determinants was guided by their explanatory power. The variables with strong multicollinearity were excluded from the equations

3. The third consideration was the forecast value in relation to the base year value. The condition for the selection was that the forecast value should be greater than the base year value.

Based on the above statistical and logical ground forecasts are made. In this exercise an attempt is made to discuss the future course of major taxes and to make the forecast of yield from these taxes and from total State's own taxes.

Yet another study made by Rao, projected revenue from important taxes in Karnataka. In this exercise of making forecast of revenue from major taxes and from total state's own taxes an attempt is made to establish relationship between tax yield and the specific tax base. Following steps were taken for this purpose:

- Data For Forecast:
- Data for 4 Major Taxes were collected from 1980-81 to 1997-98
- Tax Base: Following variables were taken as individual tax base: N S D P, Registered Documents, Liquor Consumption, number of registered Motor vehicles. Data for these variables were collected from1980-81 to 1997-98.

10.11.2 Projection of Independent Variables: Forecast of independent and dependent variables is made by taking 1998-99 as the base year for which future values were projected by applying various method explained in the next section. And future values are projected from 1998-99 to 2004-2005.

The following steps were involved in projecting the values of independent variables:

First projection of independent variable was made on the basis of linear trend, and later by applying Semi - log/ compound growth method.

Second, the values of independent variables were projected for the year 1998-99.

Third, 1998-99 is taken as the base year. Next, on the basis of certain economic assumptions, like the recessionary trend in the economy, power constraint, lower profile of the primary and secondary sectors and speculative forces which were active in the past and which faded away and so on the growth rates were assumed and based on the expected growth rates over the base year 1998-99, independent variables were projected.

In order to make forecast of yield from selected taxes two methods were tried. These are explained below:

10.11.3 Buoyancy Coefficient Method: Under this method tax yield is regressed upon NSDP by replacing the future values of NSDP (based on trend and its modified values, and in another equation based on compound growth and the modified growth rates) the Forecast is made. A double log function gave the buoyancy coefficient. The modified projected independent variables were replaced in the buoyancy equation and taking 1998-99 as the base year forecast for tax yield from selected taxes were made.

$$\text{Log } T j = \alpha + \beta \log X + \beta u \qquad \rightarrow(1)$$

Where: T j = Specific Tax yield

α = Contant trm(Intercept)

= Regression coefficient, here called buoyancy coefficient.

U = error term

Structural/Deterministic Model: Here tax yield is taken as depending upon one or more number of actual tax base, e.g. for Motor Vehicle Tax - number of vehicles, for Stamps and Registration - number of registered documents and for State Excise Duties - consumption of liquor.

The projected values of independent variables are derived in the same way as explained above. By replacing the projected independent variables in the equation forecast of tax yield is made and here again 1998-99 is taken as the base year.

10.11.4 Growth Rate: Growth rates of various taxes are worked out using the past trend (compound growth) till 1998-99. And taking 1998-99, as the base year, future growth rates are assumed and final forecast of tax yield is made. The assumptions and the economic rationale of such assumptions are given in the next section.

The model:

$T j = \alpha + \beta \log X1 + \beta X2 + \beta U$ →(2)

X1 and X2 are independent variables representing actual tax base.

Total Tax Revenue:

Here again we have used two methods:

First, The buoyancy method;

Second aggregation of tax yield from major taxes and deriving the total tax yield on the assumption that the four major taxes contribute 90% to total state's own tax.

Total Tax Yield is arrived at by adding up the forecast values of the 4 major taxes (Σ FTi) and then taking this as 90% of total tax revenue, forecast of Total Tax Revenue is made.

$\Sigma FTi = 90\%$ Total Tax (TT)

$TT = \Sigma F Ti \times 100. /90$

This is calculated for years from 1998-99 to 2004-2005

Following models are adopted in this exercise to forecast the yield from various taxes in Karnataka:

1. Sales Tax: Buoyancy Coefficient method
   $\log KST = \alpha + \beta \log NSDP + \beta u$
   (Double log function)
2. Motor Vehicle Tax: (Deterministic model)
   $MVT = \alpha + \beta MVN + \beta u$
3. State Excise Duties
   $Stx = \alpha + \beta$ liquor consumption $+ \beta u$ and
4. Stamps and Registration
   $SR = \alpha + \beta DOC + \beta u$

Apart from the above buoyancy equations were also used and

a comparison of the forecasts based on these two methods were made for the final selection of the model.

While making projections of the independent variables and the forecasts for various taxes, the projected or estimated values were compared with the actual data for the year 1997-98. For this purpose equations were worked out after leaving the year 1997-98. After data validation, a new set of equations inclusive of actual data of 1997-98 were derived and the forecasts were made on the basis of equations which gave estimated tax yield comparable with actual figures for 1997-98. Final adoption of the model was also guided by the statistical significance of the fit.

Thus, several methods of forecasts are developed to project revenue figures from taxes at the aggregate level and also projection of tax yield by industrial taxes. Though lots of literature is available on forecasting and projection of revenue, there is hardly any satisfactory method of forecast, which can make realistic projection. There is always a huge gap between the actual future values and the projected values. Nevertheless forecasting method is an important policy tool and one can opt for a method, which gives relatively better forecasts, which are nearer to the reality. For this purpose one can even try with the method using the past data relating to independent variables and project the values of the dependent variable (Backward projection) and then the results may be compared with the actual. Even here some differences are bound to remain because the quantitative method used for forecasts cannot capture policy changes or other qualitative changes.

End Notes and References

1. Rao, Hemlata,(1993), Taxable Capacity, Tax Efforts and Forecast of Tax yield, ISEC, mimeograph,1993, A study sponsored by the Tenth Finance Commission.

2. Rao, Hemlata (1993) op.cit.

3. Government of India, The Tenth Finance Commission Report.

4. Rao, Karnataka (1996), forecasting Of Tax Yield from Karnataka Sales Taxes and Rationale of Exemptions. ISEC mimeograph, study sponsored by Government of Karnataka, Commercial Tax department.

11

CONCLUSIONS

For the most part in this study, the focus is on major issues raised in all federations – whether developed or developing, typical federal system or *quasi*-federal system. The issues pertaining to Vertical Fiscal Imbalances basically addressing at the distribution of powers and responsibilities – leading to mismatch between resources and responsibilities at various levels of government, the fiscal adjustment mechanism – types of tax-sharing, grants and grants-in-aid are typical to any federation. In fact, the fiscal adjustment mechanism often leads to the issue of centralization of resources and also of responsibilities. While too much of centralization is not welcomed, decentralization is advocated in the recent years to improve efficiency in the delivery of goods and services and to encourage local participation in development and planning at the local level.

A parallel issue to Vertical Fiscal Imbalances' is Horizontal Fiscal Imbalances arising out of diversity and socio-economic disparities among the federating units. The size of the federating units, their population, natural resource endowment, etc. are not uniform across the states. Disparities are often attributed to historical, political, cultural and economic factors. This leads to differences in the resource raising capacity and in fiscal need. Resource raising capacity is closely linked with variation in the taxable capacity as measured by per capita income or by any other method. Fiscal need varies according to revenue capacity, population, area, local needs and aspirations and already realized levels of development and so on.

The above issues can be tackled meaningfully when they are quantified. This necessitates developing and applying quantitative techniques. If the levels of development are not assessed properly, one may place an actually backward state into the category of developed states. Similarly, taxable capacity and tax-efforts if measured arbitrarily, the goal of fiscal adjustment may be defeated.

Keeping these in mind in this study various quantitative techniques are examined and they are applied on actual data.

The quantitative techniques discussed and illustrated are not exhaustive. There are many more techniques used in federal finance. One can mention techniques like cost-benefit analysis, input-output techniques, Autoregressive Distributed Lag Estimates, co-integration error model and so on which are widely used in the analysis of federal state issues. Even the issues are not exhaustive, e.g., in a federal country – issue pertaining to state's public debt is equally important. There may be other issues relating to fiscal performance of the federating states, deficits, other problems like natural calamities affecting state finances. However, in this study, these issues are not discussed. Even issues relating to natural resources, revenue arising from these sources and non-tax resources are not discussed.

The basic purpose of the study is to discuss various quantitative techniques used in the field of federal finance and to illustrate the techniques with the real situation. The study also brings out how the results vary when different techniques or definitions are adopted and the study cautions about the selection of the right data and right technique of analysis for formulating effective policies.

BIBLIOGRAPHY

BIBLIOGRAPHY

A Breton, (1965), 'A Theory of Government Grants', Journal of Economics and Political Science, Vol. XXI, No.2, May, pp. 175-87.

A. Scott, (1964), 'The Economic Goals of Federal Finance', in Public Finance, Vol. XIX, No.3, p.254.

A.D. Scott, (1950) 'A Note on Grants in Federal Countries', Economica, Vol.17, p.416-22.

ACIR (1984) Representative Tax System Method for Estimating the Fiscal Capacity of the 50 State – Local Systems', an ACIR Paper presented to the Tax Policy Round Table, Cambridge, Massachusetts, November 2.

Adarkar, B.P., (1933), Principles and Problems of Federal Finance, P S King and Son Ltd., London, Ch, XII, p. 215.

Adebayo Adedji, (1969), Nigerian Federal Finance: Its Development Problems and Prospects, Hutchinson Educational Ltd., London, pp. 14-15.

Adelman and Cynthia Morris Taft 'Economic Growth and Social Equity in Developing Countries', Stanford University Press, California.

Adelman and Cynthia Morris Taft, (1967), Society Politics& Economic Development: a Quantitative Approach. The Johns Hopkins Press, Baltimore

Aggarwal, P.P. (1959),'The System of Grants in Aid in India', IIPA, New Delhi, 1959.

Ahmad, E., Craig, J and Mihaljek, D. (1995) Implementing and Managing Grants - Institutional and Data Requirements. In Ahmad, E., Quiang, G. And Tanzi, V. (1995) Reforming China's Public Finances, International Monetary Fund

Ahmad, Ehtisham (1997), Decentralizing Expenditures, Edward Elgar, Brookfield.

Ajam, T (1995) The Use of Alternate Deficit Measures in Assessing Fiscal Stance, Discussion Paper No 4, The Budget Project, University of Cape Town

Akin, (1973), 'Fiscal Capacity and the Estimating Methods of the ACIR,' National Tax Journal, Vol.26, June, pp 275-92

Alan T. Peacock and Jack Wiseman, (1967) 'The Growth of Public Expenditure in the United Kingdom', 2nd ed., George Allen and Unwin, London, p.29-30

Albert Breton and Anthony Scott, (1978), 'The Economic Constitution of Federal States', Toronto, University of Toronto Press, p.15.

Albert Breton and Anthony Scott, (1978), 'The Economic Constitution of Federal States', University of Toronto Press, Chapter 3, p.22-30.

Andrews Title X, Finance, (1963), Constitutions and Constitutionalism, 2nd ed., New York, 133-140

Anthony Scott, (1964), 'The Economic Goals of Federal Finance', Public Finance, No.3, p.241-88.

Anwar Shah, (1990) Inter-governmental Fiscal Relations in Sri Lanka, mimeographed, August.

Arnold J. Heidenheimer, Hugh Heclo, and Carolyn Teich Adams, (1975), Comparative Public Policy, ST. Martin's Press, New York, 1975

Arrow, Kenneth J. (1970), 'Political and Economic Evaluation of Social Effects and Externalities', in Julius Margolis, ed., The Analysis of Public Output, (New York: Columbia University Press, NBER), 1-23.

Asher, William and Dennis, A. Rondinelli (1999), 'Restructuring the Administration of Service Delivery in Vietnam: Decentralisation as Institution Building', in Jennie I. Litvack and Dennis A. Rondinelli (Eds.) Market Reform in Vietnam, Quorum Books, Westport, pp.133-151.

Ashok Chanda, (1965), 'Federalism in India', Allen and Unwin, London,

Ashok Mitra, (1961), 'Levels of Regional Development in India: Census of India', Para IA (1).

B.S. Grewal, (1974), 'Fiscal Federalism in India', Centre for Research and Federal Finance Relations, The ANU, Canberra.

Bahl, Roy W (1999), Implementation Rules for Fiscal Decentralisation, Working Paper No.10, School of Policy Studies, Georgia State University.

Bahl, Roy W and Christine, Wallich (1992), Inter-governmental Fiscal Relations in China, Policy Research Working Paper No.863, World Bank, Washington D.C.

Bahl, Roy W. and Johannes F. Linn. (1992), Urban Public Finance in Developing Countries. Oxford: Oxford Univ. Press.

Bator, Francis M. (1958), 'The Anatomy of Market Failure', Quarterly Journal of Economics, Vol. 72, No. 3, August 351-379.

Beckerman W., and R. Bacon, (1966), 'International Comparisons of Income Levels: A suggested New Measure', Economic Journal, pp. 519-536.

Bennet, (1951), 'International Disparities in Consumption Levels', American Economic Review, Sept., pp.639-49.

Besley Timothy and Anne Case (1995), 'Incumbent Behaviour: Vote-Seeking, Tax- Setting, and Yardstick Competition', American Economic Review (AER), Vol. 85, No. 1, March 25-45.

Bhargava, R.N. (1953), 'The Theory of Federal Finance', The Economic Journal, Vol. IXIII, 1953, pp. 841-97.

Bhargava, R.N. (1954), 'The Theory of Federal Finance: A Rejoinder', The Economic Journal, pp. 407-408.

Bhargava, R.N. (1971), 'The Theory and Working of Union Finance in India', 3rd edition, Chaitanya Publishing House, Allahabad, Chapter 8, p.109.

Biehl, D. (1994) Lessons form a Federal Case: Germany, In Gupta, S., Knight, P., Waxman, R., and Yin-Kann Wen (eds) Intergovernmental Fiscal Relations and Macroeconomic Management in Large Countries, World Bank, Washington DC

Bird, Richard (1983) Threading the Fiscal Labyrinth: Some issues in Fiscal Decentralisation, National Tax Journal, volume XLVI, no 2

Bird, Richard and Christine, Wallich (1993), Fiscal Decentralisation and Inter-governmental Relations in Transition Economies, Policy Research Working Papers, WPS, 1122, The World Bank.

Bird, Richard and Francois, Vaillancourt, (Eds.) (1998), Fiscal Decentralisation in Developing Countries, Cambridge University Press, Cambridge.

Bird, Richard M Tax Separation (1986), Federal Finance in Comparative Perspective, Canadian Tax Foundation, Toronto, p.231-239 (Section on Fiscal Imbalance).

Bird, Richard M, (1974), 'Vertical Inter-governmental Financial Imbalance', A Framework for Evaluation, No.32, Finanzarchive, No.3, pp.481-92.

Bird, Richard M, (1986) Federal Finance in Comparative Perspective, Canadian Tax Foundation.

Bird, Richard M, Robert D. Ebel and Christine I. Wallich, (Eds.) (1995), Decentralisation of the Socialist State, World Bank Washington D.C.

Bird, Richard M. (1986), 'On Measuring Fiscal Centralization and Fiscal Balance in Federal States,' Gov. Pol., 4, pp. 384–404.

Bird, Richard M. (1992), Tax Policy and Economic Development, Baltimore: Johns Hopkins Press.

Bird, Richard M. (1993), 'Threading the Fiscal Labyrinth: Some Issues in Fiscal Decentralization', National Tax Journal, Vol. 46, No. 2, June 207-227.

Bird, Richard M. (2000), 'Fiscal Decentralization and Competitive Governments', in Gianluigi Galeotti, Pierre Salmon, and Ronald Wintrobe, Eds. Competition and Structure. The Political Economy of Collective Decisions: Essays in Honour of Albert Breton, (New York: Cambridge University Press), 129-149.

Bird, Richard M., (1979), 'Central-Local Fiscal Relations and the Provision of Urban Pubic Services', Canberra, Australian National University, Centre for Research on Federal Financial Relations, p.21.

Bird, Richard M., (1986), Federal Finance in Comparative Perspective, Canadian Tax Foundation, Toronto, p.13-21

Bird, Richard M., (1989), 'Central-Local Fiscal Relations and the Provision of Urban Public Services,' Research Monograph No.30, Australian National University, Centre for Research on Federal Financial Relations, Canberra, 5-9.

Boadway, Robin (1996), 'Review of 'The Uneasy Case for Equalization Payments' by Dan Usher,' National Tax Journal, 49:4, pp. 677–86.

Boadway, Robin and Frank Flatters (1982), Equalization in a Federal State: An Economic Analysis, Economic Council of Canada, Ottawa.

Boadway, Robin and Frank R. Flatters (1982), 'Efficiency and Equalization Payments in a Federal System of Government: A Synthesis and Extension of Recent Results,' Canadian Journal of Economics, 15:4, pp. 613–33.

Bös Dieter (1983), 'Commentary on Roger Gordon's 'An Optimal Taxation Approach to Fiscal Federalism' ', in Charles E. McLure Jr., ed., Tax Assignment in Federal Countries, (Canberra: Centre for Research on Federal Financial Relations, Australian National University), 43-47.

Boudhayan Chattopadhya and Moonis Raza, (1975), 'Regional Development: Analytical Framework and Indicators.' Indian Journal of Regional Science, Vol.VII, No.1, 1975, pp. 11-34.

Bradford, David F. and Wallace E. Oates, (1971b), 'The Analysis of Revenue Sharing in a New Approach to Collective Fiscal Decisions,' Quarterly Journal of Economics, 85:3, pp. 416–39.

Bradford, David F. and Wallace E. Oates. (1971a) 'Towards a Predictive Theory of Intergovernmental Grants,' Amer. Econ. Rev., 61:2, pp. 440–48.

Break, George F. (1967), Intergovernmental Fiscal Relations in the United States, (Washington DC: Brookings Institution).

Brennan, G and Buchanan, J.M. (1980), The Power to Tax: Analytical Foundations of a Fiscal Constitution, Cambridge University Press, New York

Brennan, G. and Pincus, J (1996) A Minimalist Model of Federal Grants and Flypaper Effects, Journal of Public Economics, Vol. 61, 229-246

Breton Albert and Anthony Scott (1978), The Economic Constitution of Federal States, (Toronto: University of Toronto Press).

Breton, A and Fraschini, A. (1992), "Free-Riding and Intergovernmental Grants", Kyklos, vol 45, no3, 347-362

Breton, Albert (1996), Competitive Governments. An Economic Theory of Politics and Public Finance, (New York: Cambridge University Press).

Breton, Albert, Alberto Cassone, and Angela Fraschini (1998), "Decentralization and Subsidiary: Toward a Theoretical Reconciliation", University of Pennsylvania, Journal of International Economic Law, Vol. 19, No. 1, Spring, 21-51.

Brian. J. Berry, (1960), 'An Inductive Approach to Regionalization of Economic Development', Essays on Geography and Economic Development, ed. Ginsburg, University of Chicago, pp.78-107.

Brown, Charles C. and Wallace E. Oates (1987), 'Assistance to the Poor in a Federal System,' Journal of Public Economics. 32, pp. 307–30.

Bruce, N (1995), A Fiscal Federalism Analysis of Debt Policies by Sovereign Regional Governments, Canadian Journal of Economics, vol XXVIII, s196-s206

Buchanan J.M., and Richard E. Wagner, (1971), 'An Efficiency Basis for Fiscal Equalisation', in Julius Margolis (ed.), An Analysis of Public Output, NBER, p.139-58.

Buchanan, J.M. (1949), 'The Pure Theory of Government Finance: A Suggested Approach', Journal of Political Economy, Vol. L, VII, Dec. pp. 96-505, and

Buchanan, J.M. (1952), 'Federal Grants and Resource Allocation', Journal of Political Economy, Vol.XX, P. 209.

Buchanan, J.M., (1950), 'Federalism and Fiscal Equity', American Economic Review, Vol. XI, Sept. pp. 583-99.

Calvert, Randall L. (1986), Models of Imperfect Information in Politics, (Chur, Switzerland: Harwood Academic Publishers).

Campos, E and Pradhan, S (1996), The Impact of Budgetary Institutions on Expenditure Outcomes: Binding Governments to Fiscal Performance, World Bank, Washington

Carey, William L. (1974), 'Federalism and Corporate Law: Reflections Upon Delaware', Yale Law Journal, Vol. 83, No. 4, March 663-705.

Cattell, R.B. (1978), The Scientific Use of Factor Analysis, Plenum, New York.

Chanda, Ashok (1965), Federalism in India, George Allen and Unwin Ltd. 1965

Charles, Tiebout, (1956), 'A Pure Theory of Local Expenditure', Journal of Political Economy, October, pp.416-24.

Chelliah, Raja (1991) 'Towards a Decentralized Polity', (L. K. Jha Memorial Lecture), Fiscal Research Foundation, New Delhi.

Coase, Ronald H. (1960), 'The Problem of Social Cost', Journal of Law and Economics, Vol. 3, October 1-44.

Crémer Jacques, Antonio Estache, and Paul Seabright (1995), 'The Decentralization of Public Services: Lessons from the Theory of the Firm', in Antonio Estache, ed., Decentralizing Infrastructure: Advantages and Limitations, Discussion Paper No. 290, (Washington: World Bank).

Dasgupta, B., (1971), 'Socio-economic Classification of District' Economic and Political Weekly, Vol.6, No.33, August 14, Pp 1963-74.

David, Kwavnick, ed., (1973), The Tremblay Report, Toronto, McClelland and Stewart, p.215.

Davies, D.G. (1976), International Comparisons of Tax Structures in Federal and Unitary Countries, Australian National University, Centre for Research on Federal Financial Relations, Canberra.

Davoodi, Hamid and Heng-fu Zou. (1998), 'Fiscal Decentralization and Economic Growth', Journal of Urban Economics, 43, pp. 244–57.

Dillinger, W. (1994), Decentralization and Its implications for Urban Service Delivery, Urban Management Program Discussion Paper, World Bank, Transport, Water and Urban Development Department, Urban Development Division, Washington DC

Dillon, W.R. & M. Goldstein (1984), Multivariate Analysis: Methods and Applications, John Wiley, New York.

Drewnowski, Jan, (1970), 'Studies in the Measurement of Levels of Living and Welfare', Report No.703, UNRISD.

Drewnowski. J. (1966), 'Social and Economic Factors in Development', UNRISD Report No.3. Geneva, February.

Eichenberger, R. (1994), The Benefits of Federalism, Kyklos, vol 47, no 3, 403-420

Elazar, D. (1994), Can American Federalism Help South Africa? In Licht, R and De Villiers, B. (eds) South Africa's Crisis of Constitutional Democracy, Can the US Constitution Help? Juta, Johannesburg

Elazar, D. (1994), Can American Federalism Help South Africa? In Licht, R and De Villiers, B. (eds) South Africa's Crisis of Constitutional Democracy, Can the US Constitution Help? Juta, Johannesburg

Everitt, B.S. (1993), 'Cluster Analysis', Edward Arnold, London.

Fastrup, (1986), 'Local Governments: Targeting General Fiscal Assistance Reduces Fiscal Disparities', GAO/HRD, 86-113, July.

Federal Provincial Division, Ottawa, The Fiscal Equalization Program, October 1990.

Feldstein, Martin S. (1975), 'Wealth Neutrality and Local Choice in Public Education,' American Economic Review, 65:1, pp. 75–89.

Ferris, J. and Winkler, D. (1991), Agency Theory and Intergovernmental Relations. In Prudhomme, R (ed) Public Finance with Several Levels of Government, Foundation Journal of Public Finance, The Hague

Fisher, Ronald C. (1982) 'Income and Grant Effects on Local Expenditure: The Flypaper Effect and Other Difficulties,' Journal of Urban Economics, 12, pp. 324–45.

Flatters, Frank, Vernon Henderson, and Peter Mi-eszkowski. (1974), 'Public Goods, Efficiency, and Regional Fiscal Equalization,' Journal of Public Economics, 3, pp. 99–112.

Forest, La G.V., (1981), 'The Allocation of Taxing Power Under the Canadian Constitution, Second Edition,' Canadian Tax Paper, No.65, May.

Frederic, L. Pryor, (1968), Public Expenditures in Communist and Capitalist Nations, George Allen and Unwin Ltd., London, p.70-79.

Friedrick J. Grasberger, (1980), Principal Investigator (Developing and Applying Analytical Tools to evaluate the distributional effects of Federal Grant-in-aid formulas and to improve formula performance, Jan.1980.

Gamkhar, Shama and Wallace Oates (1966) 'Asymmetries in the Response to Increases and Decreases in Intergovernmental Grants: Some Empirical Findings,' National Tax Journal, 49, pp. 501–12.

Geoffrey Brennau and James M. Buchanan, (1980), The Power to Tax, Cambridge, Massachusetts, Cambridge University Press, p.184-85.

Gordon, Roger. (1983), 'An Optimal Tax Approach to Fiscal Federalism,' Quarterly Journal of Economics, 97, pp. 567–86.

Gorsuch, R.L. (1974), Factor Analysis, Saunders Publishing House, Philadelphia.

Gothoskar, S.P., (1988), 'Measurement of Real Development', The Journal of Income and Wealth, vol10, No.1, January, pp.84-100

Government of Gujarat, (1969), Report of the Backward Area Study Team, Ahmedabad.

Government of India (1952), The Planning Commission, Five-Year Plan, 1951-56.

Government of Karnataka, (2000), High Power Committee on Redressal of Regional Disparities in Karnataka.

Graham, J.F. (1963), Fiscal Adjustment and Economic Development: A Case Study of Nova Scotia, University of Toronto Press, 1963, p.178

Gramlich, E (1983), A Policymaker's Guide to Fiscal Decentralisation, National Tax Journal, volume XLVI, no 2

Gramlich, Edward M. (1977) 'Intergovernmental Grants: A Review of the Empirical Literature,' in The Political Economy of Fiscal Federalism. Wallace Oates, ed. Lexington, MA: Heath-Lexington, pp. 219–39.

Groenwegen, P (1990), Taxation and Decentralisation, In Bennet, R.J (ed) Decentralisation, Local Governments and Markets, Clarendon Press, Oxford

Hagood, M.J. (1943), 'Statistical Methods for the purposes of Delineation of Regions Applied to data on Agriculture and Population', Social Force, Vol.21, pp.287-297.

Hamlin, Alan P. (1991), 'Decentralization, Competition and the Efficiency of Federalism', The Economic Record, Vol. 67, No. 196, September 193-204.

Haq, Mahboob Ul, (1993), The Strategy of Economic Planning: A Case study of Pakistan, Oxford University Press, Karachi, and p. 130.

Harold L. Wilensky, (1975), The Welfare State and Equality, University of California Press, Berkeley, p.52.

Heynes, J. V.d.S. (1995), Equity and Redistribution in South Africa: Some Fiscal Federal Perspectives, South African Journal of Economics, Vol.63, No.2, 150-173

Hines, James R. Jr., and Richard H. Thaler (1995), 'The Flypaper Effect,' Journal of Economic Perspective, 9, pp. 217–26.

Hommes, R. (1996), Conflicts and Dilemmas of Decentralisation, In Bruno, M and Pleskovic, B. (Eds). Annual World Bank Conference on Development Economics 1995, World Bank, Washington DC

Horst Zimmerman, (1981) 'Popitz' Law' 'Finanz – und Steuerbelastungs – Vergleiche, Internationale,' in Handworterbuch der Wirt-schaftswissenschaft (Stuttgart: Gustav Fischer, 1980), 119 and 'Studies in Comparative

Federalism: West Germany,' Advisory Commission on Intergovernmental Relations, p.62 (The original reference is to a 1927 article by J. Popitz).

Hunter, J.S.H., (1973-74), 'Vertical Intergovernmental Financial Imbalances ; a frame work for evaluation,' Finanzarchive (FINANZARCHIVE), Vol. 32, 1974, PP 481 – 492

Hunter, J.S.H., (1977), Federalism and Fiscal Balance, Canberra: Australian National University, Centre for Research on Federal Financial Relations, p.21.

Huther, Jeff and Anwar Shah (1996), 'A Simple Measure of Good Governance and Its Application to the Debate on the Appropriate Level of Fiscal Decentralization.' Washington, DC: World Bank.

India, (1978), Report of the Committee on Panchayat Raj Institutions, Ministry of Agriculture and Irrigation, New Delhi.

Inman, Robert and Daniel Rubinfled (1992), 'Rethinking Federalism', Journal of Economic Perspectives, Vol. 11, No. 4 Pp. 43-64.

Inman. Forthcoming. 'On Designing Intergovernmental Transfers With an Application in the New South Africa,' in Environmental and Public Economics. Arvind Panagariya, Paul Portney, and Robert Schwab, eds. Cheltenham, UK: Edward Elgar.

James A. Maxwell (1946), 'The Fiscal Impact of Federalism in the United States' Harvard University Press, Massachusetts, Chapter 1.

James A. Maxwell (1962), 'Tax Credits and Inter Governmental Relations', Brookings Institution.

Jennie Litvack, Junaid Ahmad, Richard Bird, Rethinking Decentralisation in Developing Countries, Sector Studies Series, The World Bank, Washington D.C., pp. 4-9

Jolliffe, I.T. (1986), Principal Component Analysis, Springer-Verlag, New York.

Jose Sebastian, (19920, 'Sales Tax-Efforts of States', Artha Vijnan, Sept, V.34. No.3 pp.302-3.

Keohane, Robert O. (1984), After Hegemony. Cooperation and Discord in the World Political Economy, Princeton: Princeton University Press.

Kindleberger, Charles P. (1986), The World in Depression, 1929-1939, Revised and Enlarged Edition, Berkeley: University of California Press.

Kirchgässner, Gebhard (2000), 'Probabilistic Voting and Equilibrium: An Impossibility Result', Public Choice, Vol. 103, Nos. 1&2, April 35-48.

Klevorick, Alvin K. (1996), 'Reflections on the Race to the Bottom', in Jagdish Bhagwati and Robert E. Hudec, eds. Fair Trade and Harmonization. Prerequisite for Free Trade? Volume 1, Economic Analysis, (Cambridge MA: The MIT Press), 459- 467.

Kline, P. (1994), 'An Easy Guide to Factor Analysis', Routledge, London.

Kotze, D (1996), The Provinces and Local Government, Politeia, Vol.15, No.2, 71-73

Labuschagne, G. (1996), Finance, Politeia, Vol.15, No.2, 92-93

Lahiri, Ashok, Sub national Public Finance in India, Economic and Political Weekly, April, 29.

Lawrence H.Hunter, (1986), 'The Desirability and Feasibility of Fiscal equalization in a federal system of Governments,' Federal State Local Fiscal Relations Technical Paper, Vol.1, office of State and Local Finance, Department of Treasury, Sept., P.25 (17-39)

Lawrence, H. Hunter, (1986), 'The Desirability and Feasibility of Fiscal Equalisation in a Federal System of Government' in Federal State – Local Fiscal Relations, Vol.1, 1986, Office of the State and Local Finance, Department of the Treasuries.

Lazear, Edward P. and Sherwin Rosen (1981), 'Rank-Order Tournaments as Optimum Labor Contracts', Journal of Political Economy, Vol. 89, No. 5, October, 841-864.

Leslie, P.M. (1988), National Citizenship and Provincial Communities: A Review of Canadian Fiscal Federalism,

Research Paper 23, Institute of Intergovernmental Relations, Queen's University, Kingston, Ontario

Levaggi, R. (1991), Fiscal Federalism and Grants in Aid, Avebury, Aldershot

Levaggi, R. (1994), On the Intergovernmental Fiscal Game, Public Finance, vol 49, no 1, 72-86

Levmore, Saul (1993), 'Commissions and Conflicts in Agency Arrangements: Lawyers, Real Estate Brokers, Underwriters, and Other Agents' Rewards' Journal of Law and Economics, Vol. 36. No. 1, Pt 2, April 503-539.

Litvack, Jenny, Junaid Ahmad and Richard Bird (1998), 'Rethinking Decentralization at the World Bank'. Sector Studies Series, The World Bank.

Louis Lefeber, (1962), 'Regional Allocation of Resources in India', Pricing and Fiscal Policy: A Study in Method(ed), P. N Rosenstein Rodan, London, George Allen & Unwin Ltd., p. 22.

Ma Jun (1995), 'The Reform of Inter-governmental Fiscal Relations in China', Asian Economic Journal, Vol.9, No.3. Pp.205-231.

Malme, J. H and Joan M. Youngman (Eds.) (2001), The Development of Property Taxation in Economies in Transition. The World Bank.

Mancur Olson, (1983),'The Political Economy of Comparative Growth', in Dennis C. Muller ed. The Political Economy of Growth, New Heaven, Yale University Press.

May, P.J. and Burby, R.J (1996), Coercive versus Cooperative Policies: Comparing Intergovernmental Mandate Performance, Journal of Policy Analysis and Management, vol 15, no 2, 171-201

May, R.J., (1969), 'Federalism and Fiscal Adjustment', Oxford University Press, London,

McGranahan V., et al. UNRISD, (1970), 'Contents and Measurement of Socio Economic Development: An Empirical Enquiry. Report No.70. 10. Geneva.

McGranahan et al. (1970), 'Contents and Measurement of Socio-Economic Development', UNRISD, Report 70, 10, Geneva, p.138.

McGranahan, D., (1972), 'Development Indicators and development Models', Journal of Development Studies, Vol6, No.3, pp91-102.

McGranahan, D. (1972), 'Development Indicators and Development Models', Journal of Development Studies, Vol.6, No.3, pp91-102.

McGuire, Therese J. (1997), 'Intergovernmental Fiscal Relations and Social Welfare Policy,' in Intergovernmental Fiscal Relations. Ronald C. Fisher, ed. Boston: Kluwer, pp. 173–98.

McLure Jr., Charles E. Jr. (1995), 'Comment on 'The Dangers of Decentralization' by Prud'homme', World Bank Research Observer, Vol. 10, No. 2, August, 221-226.

McLure, C (1994), Intergovernmental Fiscal Relations in South Africa: The Assignment of Expenditure Functions and Revenue Sources and the Design of Intergovernmental Grants and Transfers, World Bank, Washington D.C.

McLure, Charles E., Jr. ed. (1983), Tax Assignment in Federal Countries. Canberra: Australian National University.

Milligan, G.W. and Cooper, M.C. (1985), 'An Examination of Procedures for Determining the Number of Clusters in a Data Set', Psychometrika, 50, 159-179.

Mintz, Jack and Henry Tulkens (1986), 'Commodity Tax Competition Between Member States of a Federation: Equilibrium and Efficiency', Journal of Public Economics, Vol. 29, No. 2, March 133-172.

Mojena, R. (1977), 'Hierarchical Grouping Methods and Stopping Rules: An Evaluation', Computer Journal, 20, 13-24.

Morris Beck, (1981), 'Government Spending,' Praeger, New York, 60-68.

Musgrave, R.A., (1959), The Theory of Public Finance, Mc. Graw Hill, 1959, Chap. VIII, p.160.

Musgrave, R.A., (1961), 'Approaches to Fiscal Theory of Political Federalism', Public Finance: Need, Sources and Utilisation, A

Report of the National Bureau of Economic Research (Princeton University Press), pp.97-122; comments pp.122-33, p.98.

Musgrave, Richard M (1978), 'The Changing Structure of Intergovernmental Fiscal Relations,' in Secular Trends of the Public Sector. H. Recktenwald, ed. Paris: Editions Cujas, pp. 151–60.

Musgrave, Richard M. (1959), The Theory of Public Finance. New York: McGraw-Hill.

Musgrave, Richard M. (1985), 'Searching for Leviathan: An Empirical Study,' American Economic Review, 75, pp. 748–57.

Musgrave, Richard M. (1989) 'Searching for Leviathan: A Reply and Some Further Reflections,' American Economic Review, 79, pp. 578–83.

N.S. Iyengar and P. Sudarsan, (1981), 'On a Method of Classifying Regions from Multivariate Data', Paper presented at Symposium on Economic Theory and Planning, ISI, Bangalore, December.

Nanjappa, M.B. Backward Areas in Mysore State: A study in Development.

Nathan, R and Balmaceda, M. (1990), Comparing Federal Systems of Government, In Bennet, R.J (ed) Decentralisation, Local Governments and Markets, Clarendon Press, Oxford

Oates, W. E. (1972), Fiscal Federalism, Harcourt, Brace, Jovanovich, New York

Oates, W.E. (1968), The theory of Public Finance in Federal Systems, Canadian Journal of Economics, vol 1, 37-54

Oates, W.E. (1983), Fiscal Decentralisation And Economic Development, National Tax Journal, vol XLVI, no 2, 237-243

Oates, W.E. (1989), Searching for Leviathan: A reply and Some Further Reflections, American Economic Review, vol 79, 578-83

Oates, Wallace E. (1972), Fiscal Federalism. NY: Harcourt Brace Jovanovich.

Oates, Wallace E. (1978), 'The Changing Structure of Intergovernmental Fiscal Relations,' in Secular Trends of the Public Sector. H. Recktenwald, ed. Paris: Editions Cujas, pp. 151–60.

Oates, Wallace E. (1998), 'Environmental Policy in the European Community: Harmonization or National Standards?' Empirica, Vol. 25, 1-13.

Oates, Wallace E. (1998), 'On the Welfare Gains from Fiscal Decentralization,' University of Maryland, Economic Department, WP 98–05.

Oates, Wallace E. (1999), 'An Essay on Fiscal Federalism', Journal of Economic Literature, Vol. No. XXXVII. No. 3. Pp. 1120-1149.

Oates, Wallace E. and Robert M. Schwab (1988), 'Economic Competition Among Jurisdictions: Efficiency-Enhancing or Distortion-Inducing?' Journal of Public Economics, Vol. 35, No. 3, April 333-354.

Parimal Chandra Sankar, (1995), 'Regional Disparities in India: Issues & Measurements, Ph.D thesis, Bombay University, p.80-82

Patel, M.L., (1975), 'Dilemma of Balanced Regional Development in India', Chapter 8, pp. 68-78, Bhopal, 1975.

Planning Commission, (1969), 'Report of the Working Group on Identification of Backward Regions'.

Preston King, (1982), Federalism and federation, (Baltimore, Johns Hopkins University Press, 11.

Prud'homme, Rémy (1995), 'The Dangers of Decentralization', World Bank Research Observer, Vol. 10, No. 2, August 201-220.

Rao, Govinda M (2001), Challenges of Fiscal Decentralisation in Transitional Economies - Asian Perspective, Public Finance in Developing and Transition Countries: A Conference in Honour of Richard Bird', April 5-6, 2001. Andrew Young School of Policy Studies, Georgia State University, Ever Green Hotel and Resort, Stone Mountain, Georgia.

Rao, Govinda M., (1998), 'Intergovernmental Fiscal relations in a Planned Economy: The case of India' in Richard Bird and Francois Vaillancourt (Eds), Fiscal Decentralization in Developing Countries, Cambridge University Press. Pp. 78-114

Rao, Govinda M., (2000), Fiscal Decentralisation in Indian Federalism, ISEC, Bangalore, Mimeograph.

Rao, Govinda M., (2001), Invisible Transfers in Indian Federation, Public Finance/Finances Publiques, Vol.52, No.3, pp.299-316.

Rao, Govinda M., and Raja J. Chelliah (1995), A Survey of research in Fiscal Federalism in India, Indian Council of Social Science Research, New Delhi.

Rao, Govinda M., and Tapas K. Sen (1996), Fiscal Federalism in India – Theory and Practice, Macmillan India, New Delhi.

Rao, Govinda M., Richard M. Bird and Jennie I. Litvack (1998), 'Fiscal Decentralisation and Poverty Alleviation in a Transitional Economy', Asian Economic Journal, Vol.12, No.4, pp.353-378.

Rao, Govinda M., Richard Shand and K. P. Kalirajan (1998), 'Convergence of Incomes in Indian States: A Divergent View', Paper presented at the IIPF Conference in Cordoba, Argentina in (August)).

Rao Govinda M., B. Kamaiah, Allen Roy, 'Measuring Expenditure Needs of the States', Study sponsored by the Eleventh Finance Commission, ISEC, Mimeograph (2000-01).

Rao, Hemlata (1972), 'Identification of Backward Regions and Trends in Regional Disparities', Seminar paper presented at 'National Seminar on Regional Development, IIPA, New Delhi, March 3-4, 1972. Also see Artha Vijnan, No.2, pp.98-117, June 1977.

Rao, Hemlata (1974), 'Centre-State Financial Relations and the Problems of Financing Regional Development in India': Ph.D. Thesis, Delhi School of Economics, and University of Delhi.

Shah, Anwar. (1994), The Reform of Intergovernmental Fiscal Relations in Developing and Emerging Market Economies. Washington, DC: World Bank.

Shannon, J. (1986), Interstate Tax Competition - The Need for a New Look, National Tax Journal, vol 39

Singer, H.W. (1953), 'The Theory of Federal Finance: A Comment', The Economic Journal, Sept. p.726.

Sobei Mogi, (1970), 'The Problem of Federalism' for details see, R.K.Sinha, 'Finance Commission in India', Economic Affair, March, Calcutta, p.97.

Stephen M Barrow, (1975), Equalization and Equity in General Revenue Sharing: An Analysis of Alternative Distribution Formulas', Part-I.

Switzerland: A Survey, (1982), The Economist, October 30, supplement, at 7.

Tacq, J. (1997), 'Multivariate Analysis Techniques in Social Science Research: From Problem to Analysis', Sage Publications, and London.

Tanzi, V. (1996), Fiscal Federalism and Decentralization: A Review of Some Efficiency and Macroeconomic Aspects, In Bruno, M and Pleskovic, B. (Eds). Annual World Bank Conference on Development Economics 1995, World Bank, Washington DC

Taylor, P (1993), State Federalism in a World System, Development and Democracy

The Dandekar Committee, (1984), 'Report of the Fact Finding Committee on Regional Imbalances in Maharashatra' (Chairman: V.M. Dandekar), Planning Department, Govt. of Maharashatra, Mumbai.

Thimmaiah, G, (1976), 'Vertical Inter-Governmental Financial Imbalance: A Restatement, Finanzarchive, Vol.33, and No.3.

Thimmaiah, G. (1981), 'Critique of the Finance Commission', Wheeler Publishing, Allahabad.

Thimmaiah, G. and Rao, Hemlata (1986), 'Finance Commission and Centre-State Financial Relations', Ashish Publishing House, New Delhi.

Thimmaiah, G., (1976), 'Vertical Intergovernmental financial imbalances: A Restatement',Finanzarchive, 34, 3, pp 497-508.

Tiebout, Charles M. (1956), 'A Pure Theory of Local Expenditure', Journal of Political Economy, Vol. 64, No. 5, October 416-424.

Tocqueville, Alexis de. (1945), Democracy in America. NY: Vintage Books Random House: first published 1838.

U.N.O. (1951), 'Measures for the Economic Development of Underdeveloped Countries', New York.

Usher, Dan (1994), 'The Significance of the Probabilistic Voting Theorem', Canadian Journal of Economics, Vol. 27, No. 2, May 433-445.

W. Douglas Morgan, (1974), 'An Alternative measure of Fiscal capacity,' NTJ, Vol.27, June, pp.361-6.

Wallace E. Oates, (1999), 'An Essay on Fiscal Federalism,' Journal of Economic Literature, Vol. XXXVII, September, pp. 1120–1149]

Walsh, Cliff (with contributions by Jeff Petchey) (1992), Fiscal Federalism. An Overview of Issues and a Discussion of their Relevance to the European Community, (Canberra: Federalism Research Centre).

Warren Nutter, (1978), 'Growth of Government in the West,' American Enterprise Institute for Public Policy Research, Washington, 1978, 90-94.

Watts, R. L (1994), Is the New Constitution Unitary or Federal? In De Villiers, B. (Ed) Birth of a Constitution, Juta, Cape Town

Watts, R. L. (1989), Executive Federalism: A Comparative Analysis, Research Paper 23, Institute of Intergovernmental Relations, Queen's University, Kingston, Ontario

Wehner, J (forthcoming) The Role of Equity in Intergovernmental Relations: An Analysis of the Relationship between Fiscal Federalism and Citizenship from a Comparative Perspective. Idasa: Budget Information Service, Cape Town

Wheare, K.C., (1963), 'Federal Government', 4th ed., Oxford University Press, London, 1963, p.93.

Wildasin, D. (1992), Relaxation of Mobility Barriers and Redistribution, Public Finance, vol 47, no 4

Wildasin, D. (1996), Comment on 'Fiscal Federalism and Decentralisation', In Bruno, M and Pleskovic, B. (Eds). Annual World Bank Conference on Development Economics 1995, World Bank, Washington DC

Wildasin, D. (1996), Fiscal Decentralization and Public Expenditures, Paper prepared for a World Bank Workshop on 'New Directions in Public Expenditure Analysis', June 13, 1996

Wildasin, David E. (1988), 'Nash Equilibria in Models of Fiscal Competition', Journal of Public Economics, Vol. 35, 229-240.

Wildasin, David E. (1998b), 'Externalities and Bailouts: Hard and Soft Budget Constraints in Intergovernmental Fiscal Relations,' World Bank Policy Research WP 1843.

Wilson, John Douglas (1996), 'Capital Mobility and Environmental Standards: Is There a Theoretical Basis for a Race to the Bottom', in Jagdish Bhagwati and Robert E. Hudec, eds. Fair Trade and Harmonization. Prerequisites for Free Trade? Volume 1, Economic Analysis, (Cambridge MA: The MIT Press), 393-427.

Winkler, D.R. (1994), The Design and Administration of Intergovernmental Transfers: Fiscal Decentralisation in Latin America, World Bank Discussion Paper 235, World Bank, Washington DC

Wittman, Donald (1995), The Myth of Democratic Failure. Why Political Institutions Are Efficient, (Chicago: University of Chicago Press).

Wolman, H. (1990), Decentralisation: What it is, In Bennet, R.J (ed) Decentralisation, Local Governments and Markets, Clarendon Press, Oxford

Wong, Christine (2000), 'Central-local Relations Revisited: the 1994 Tax Sharing Reform and Expenditure Management in China', paper presented at the International Conference on

'Central-Periphery Relations in China: Integration, Disintegration or Reshaping of an Empire?' Chinese University of Hong Kong, March 24-25.

World Bank (2000), 'China: Managing Public Expenditures for Better Results', Report No.20342-CHA.

Zhang, Tao and Heng-fu Zou. (1998), 'Fiscal Decentralization, Public Spending, and Economic Growth in China', Journal of Public Economics, 67, pp. 221–40.

INDEX

INDEX